POLISH YOUR STAR

POLISH YOUR STAR

Three-Minute Daily Lessons to Become an Extraordinary Leader

VOLUME TWO

VALERIE L. BÉRUBÉ

NEW YORK

LONDON • NASHVILLE • MELBOURNE • VANCOUVER

POLISH YOUR STAR

Three-Minute Daily Lessons to Become an Extraordinary Leader

VOLUME TWO

Published in New York, New York, by Morgan James Publishing. Morgan James is a trademark of Morgan James, LLC. www.MorganJamesPublishing.com

The Morgan James Speakers Group can bring authors to your live event. For more information or to book an event visit The Morgan James Speakers Group at www.TheMorganJamesSpeakersGroup.com.

ISBN 9781683509738 paperback
ISBN 9781683509745 eBook
Library of Congress Control Number: 2017918567

Cover & Interior Design by:
Christopher Kirk
www.GFSstudio.com

In an effort to support local communities, raise awareness and funds, Morgan James Publishing donates a percentage of all book sales for the life of each book to Habitat for Humanity Peninsula and Greater Williamsburg.

Get involved today! Visit
www.MorganJamesBuilds.com

DEDICATION

This book, and all of my work, is dedicated to everyone seeking a second chance in life; who seek to empower themselves and others as authentic leaders, no matter their background or current shortcomings; and, who understand that their true legacy isn't their fame or fortune (or lack thereof), but the lives they impacted in a positive way.

OVERVIEW

Volumes one and two contain seven series collectively: four in volume one and three in volume two. volume two builds upon the material learned in volume one. You'll want to keep the series summaries from volume one available for reference as you progress through volume two.

If you complete one lesson a day, you should finish volume two in just over three months. Since the material is easy to read, you might choose to read several lessons at once, which will certainly speed your progress. You may go as fast or slow as you need to learn and live the material.

Given the two-page, three-minute design of this book series, references are not noted in the body of the lessons. References and resources are listed in their own section at the end of both volumes one and two.

VOLUME ONE REVIEW

BRAIN RESET: Here we created your Reality Show, your unique tool to deposit more optimal programming in your automatic mind. We learned a technique for recognizing and managing our thoughts and emotions called Ground Control. We presented the three laws of the automatic mind to empower you with essential knowledge about how your mind works. With this knowledge, you can continue optimizing the programming in your automatic mind over time.

AWARENESS: Our journey to expand our awareness began with an overview of personality traits, emotional intelligence, and hot buttons. We learned how awareness of emotions and personality preferences fuels personal growth, and helps us navigate the social world. Additionally, we learned how reactive we are to certain hot buttons to better understand ourselves.

COMMUNICATION: In this series, we learned about the presence in every conversation and how to navigate it. We revealed how communication is largely a function of automatic programming, and if that programming is faulty, then we could be sabotaging ourselves, our relationships, and our dreams in life without even knowing it. We presented practical tools for communicating in healthier, more effective ways you can use immediately in your daily interactions.

NEURO-SCIENCE: In this fascinating series, we explored the physical parts of the brain and its paleo past. We then connected it all to help explain why we behave the way we do. We learned why we get upset at certain things, or behave irrationally sometimes. We gained an understanding of the driving forces in our brain, so we can gain the upper hand instead of letting these forces control us without our knowledge.

VOLUME TWO

WISDOM: This series presents eye opening, inspiring, and insightful lessons building upon the material from volume one. It provides practical wisdom to issues such as love, making decisions, and learning how to say *no*. We'll challenge common, self-sabotaging thinking traps and help you escape them with the tools of *rational thinking*. Rational thinking leads to much healthier thinking, emoting, and behaving than irrational thinking, and more importantly, to better outcomes.

LEADERSHIP: This series synthesizes learning from the last five series into a powerful leadership framework, the GEMS model. It doesn't matter what you do or where you are in life. The better your leadership abilities, the better the outcomes in every area of your life—both professional and personal. You'll learn valuable leadership truths and tools in this series to propel your journey for true personal growth and real impacts on the world.

SELF-CARE: Health and well-being are critical to looking and being your best. The health of your body impacts the health of your brain, which impacts every aspect of your life. Health doesn't happen by chance. It takes actionable knowledge and a committed decision to balance your life. In this series, you'll learn some of the latest and most interesting discoveries about nutrition, exercise, sleep, and more. While health is addressed last in this series, it is not an afterthought. Great health enhances your ability to be your best self and an inspiring leader.

TABLE OF CONTENTS

PART 2

PART 3

FOREWORD

You have been blessed with a copy of Valerie Berube's, *Polish Your Star—Volume 2*. That means, if you read it and reflect on what you read, you are going to develop into a leader that stands above those with only the title of leader.

There is no such thing as a born leader. We all have to learn. Anyone can learn how to lead. Everyone should not lead. In far too many cases, those in leadership positions fail miserably. There is a lack of a sense of self that is imperative to becoming a successful leader. Moreover, the trained leader that possesses wisdom is the leader most effective and most remembered.

Valerie's *Polish Your Star—Volume 2* is a book of Wisdom. It is a book that, although intended for the new leader, should be read and reread by all of us in leadership positions.

This Volume of work provides insight into areas that can be vexing for the best leaders, e.g. focusing on goals, not problems; asking questions; being humble; and one of my favorites—failure. These are issues every leader will face. How you handle these topics can make or break a leader. The book goes into far more than one can discuss in a Foreword.

Many people labor under the false premise that leadership is all about manipulating others to get the job done or being the most competent technocrat. Valerie's first book, *Polish Your Star—Volume 1*, provides the how-to's of leadership. This superb follow-up, *Polish Your Star—Volume 2*, provides the reader with the wisdom to lead.

I have had the honor of serving as a leader of Marines for over 30 years and as a Vice President in business. The advice Valerie offers will help you improve how you lead, and how to develop other leaders. Valerie has gifted you with the wisdom of the ages.

John Boggs,
Colonel, U.S. Marine Corps (Ret.)

INTRODUCTION:
YOU CAN EITHER PROGRESS OR REGRESS; MAKE THE BEST OF IT

My mother told me about a dream she had when she was seven years old. She dreamed she had "died and gone to heaven" except heaven wasn't what she thought it was at all. To her surprise, there were no fluffy clouds, angels playing harps, or choir music in the background.

Instead, she was on a super-highway of balls of light, shooting along in the darkness with purpose, love, and serenity. She was one of the speeding balls of light, feeling exhilarated by a boundless sense of freedom and happiness. At the same time, she also felt lonely. She sensed these balls of light were departed souls, and she longed to run into someone she once knew. The thought no sooner entered her mind when another speeding ball of light stopped in front of hers.

The two balls of light hovered silently in front of each other while all the other balls of light kept whizzing by. After a moment of this, her ball of light suddenly shot back toward the earth.

She protested, "No! I want to stay here!" A powerful voice said very simply, "You can either progress or regress; make the best of it."

In an instant she was back in her little body and she startled awake from her strange sleep. She never had the dream again, but she never forgot it.

A dream such as this can have many different meanings and interpretations.

This is the dream of a young, healthy, American child growing up in the 1950s. She was not a priest, guru, shaman, or anything like that. She wasn't "smoking" anything or on some kind of drug. She was an ordinary, white female in a middle class family that was sometimes happy, sometimes dysfunctional, and inconsistently practiced their Christian faith.

I will leave you to your own interpretations of this dream.

There is, however, one thing about this dream that is *both* a blinding flash of the obvious *and* deeply mysterious. It is the message from the voice in the dream: "You can either progress or regress; make the best of it."

The voice doesn't offer any clues on *how* to progress. Nor does it offer any idea of what it *means* to progress. We are left to our own definition of *progress* and to our own means of achieving it.

Many people earnestly want to progress, but don't know how. Many people think they're progressing, only to learn with disappointment they're *regressing*—that is, going backward from the direction they want to go. It seems we're all on our own individual discovery journey that's full of bumps, confusion, and setbacks.

Some people spend a substantial amount of time and large sums of money seeking "progress." Most common areas include relationships, health and fitness, spirituality, personal interests, and career ambitions. I was one of them.

When I learned from the wisdom and experience of others, I progressed faster. When I insisted on learning all by myself, I progressed more slowly and sometimes even *regressed*.

If this is your experience in life and you prefer to progress faster than your current abilities permit, regardless of the area of life you wish to progress, then you've come to the right place.

This book aims to facilitate your quest to progress in *any* area of your life, by giving you the tools and guidance to become a role model and leader. By becoming a role model and leader we not only progress ourselves, we also contribute to the progress of the human race.

We started by building a foundation in volume one, to reset your brain, build your awareness, improve your communication, and educate you on human behavior.

In volume two, we start construction on a framework for rational thinking, leadership, and self-care to further build your life and make an impact. Remember, growth is a life-long journey. You won't "arrive" at perfect knowledge by the end of volume two, but you will have a tremendous start with steepening your future trajectory toward your goals in life.

The end of volume two will not be the end for you, but rather the beginning of your new life.

Now, let's get started.

PART 1
THE WISDOM SERIES

EVERYONE IS WATCHING—
EVEN WHEN THEY'RE NOT

As I turned the aisle corner of a grocery store, I saw a young father holding his toddler son's hand while wearing a T-shirt reading, "Not A Role Model." I wanted tell him so badly he was *way* too late for that. His son looks up to him no matter what his T-shirt says.

Everyone, and I do mean *everyone*, is a role model for someone, for better or worse. There is no escape from this fact.

Kids, family, friends, co-workers, neighbors, even perfect strangers do judge you, every day, in an instant as to whether you're a good role model, a poor one, or just so-so.

Here's some good news.

Being a *fantastic* role model—the kind that earns you respect and inspires others to be their best selves—is easy when you *pursue* being your best self.

You don't actually have to *be* your best self, you just need to *sincerely* try.

It's ok to struggle as long as you never give up. It's ok if you're not perfect. Really.

Even children are role models. When children are well behaved, other children usually follow suit. Adults love and admire well-behaved children. What happens when children behave badly? Other kids behave badly too, and adults aren't so enamored by those kids.

As children, we look to everyone around us, even other children, as role models. We watch and analyze others well into our teenage years.

Teenagers seek positive role models to show them how to behave as adults. I think many teenagers are disappointed in what they see in adults. Indeed, many adults are disappointed in what they see in adults. The desire for role models never ends.

We seek role models well into our adult years. It's why we're so disappointed when someone we once admired derails their career or life through immorality, drugs, toxic communication, or other problem.

The formula that makes you a good role model to others is *exactly* the formula that helps bring good things into your life.

The formula is: optimistic *Vision,* positive *Energy,* unyielding *Grit,* authentic *Empathy,* sound *Morality,* good *Self-control,* and a common denominator of healthy *Communication: VEGEMS/C.* We'll talk about the role model formula in more detail in the LEADERSHIP series. For now, you just need to understand what a role model is and that it's *you.* Whether, you want it or not.

The problem is we're confused on what a "good" role model truly looks like. We don't know what "right" looks like. Or, when we see it, we're suspicious.

The more we see "wrong" the more we *think* it's right! It's no wonder we're so confused.

Striving to be a good role model will help you be your best "you;" the you that loves unconditionally, puts forth genuine effort in your work, communicates in a healthy way, perseveres through setbacks, sees challenges as opportunities to learn, and has a positive vision for yourself. By striving to be your best self, you set yourself up for a whole lot more love, happiness, and success in your life. But that's not all…

Others are watching you strive to improve yourself.

Your very act of striving is modeling behavior for others, even if you don't always get it right.

You don't just strive when people are watching, you strive when you're alone. You strive when you're adopting new habits.

You strive when you talk to yourself.

You strive when you exercise or meditate or reflect.

The outcome of this private strife *does* show in a public way at some point. People can tell if you've been striving in private or not.

The WISDOM series is designed to begin the refinement process of your development. You have learned a tremendous amount so far to give you *knowledge.* The WISDOM and LEADERSHIP series will help give you *understanding.*

If you did not have good role models growing up, don't worry. You're going to be just fine.

If you were not a good role model in the past, don't worry. You will change, you will love who you become, and you will redeem yourself.

2 SURPRISE! LOVE IS *NOT* A FEELING

It's a *decision*.

Feelings come and go very, very easily and with little provocation.

Feelings are highly fluid and largely a product of the automatic mind. If you rely on feelings to build and sustain your love for someone, that is a shaky foundation.

Decisions, on the other hand, are more enduring because they're more concious.

Sure, decisions can change, but they're much less fluid than feelings.

A *decision* to love someone is a much stronger foundation to build and sustain love than feelings.

Let's take your everyday toddler. Recall that toddlers operate heavily on their wide open automatic mind. They're notoriously narcissistic, selfish, insecure, hypersensitive, and dependent. Parents could feel totally exasperated by their toddler, point to these flaws, and simply say they don't love their toddler.

Fortunately, the vast majority of them don't. Why?

Because they made the *decision*, despite their feelings, to *love* their child.

We *choose* to be patient, enduring, and kind, while also setting and enforcing healthy boundaries, encouraging toddlers with stretch goals, and lovingly showing them what "right" looks like.

Consciously remembering all the cute, loving, wonderful things about their toddler is a powerful technique many parents use to reinforce this important decision.

Let's take marriage. I once heard a man say he never really "loved" his wife, even though she adored him, worked full time as a teacher, gave him two children, and supported his being gone half the time on work-related travel. Despite his over-controlling ways, his reactive temper, and being gone so often, she *decided* to love him anyway and stay with him.

They originally married because they were "in love" but those feelings quickly subsided as the newness of the relationship wore off. She tried desperately to communicate, but he resisted counseling. While she *decided* to love him, he never made that decision and treated her with disdain, blaming *her* for his own feelings of not loving her! After threatening to divorce her one too many times because of some minor flaw, like not losing weight or having sex on demand, she finally *decided* she did not "love" him anymore. They divorced.

Happily married couples *choose* to love each other despite each other's flaws.

They *choose* to work on their communication, to empathize and see the other side, and to openly listen.

They *choose* to compromise, to trust, and to be *vulnerable*.

They *choose* to look at the positive and reframe, to be honest with each other, and to honor each other's preferences.

They *choose* to appreciate the other's contributions, and to be nurturing and supportive.

Nobody just *feels* like doing any of these things.

Instead, we choose to do these things because we make the *decision* to love.

Of course there are limits. When you're grievously harmed through the three A's: Abuse, Addiction, & Adultery, the decision to love must be made very carefully.

How about loving yourself? Is that a decision?

You bet it is!

You could tear yourself apart over your own perceived or real flaws. That will only make things worse.

This doesn't mean you don't hold yourself accountable. It means you consciously choose to love yourself and make changes, *despite* your flaws.

Rarely will you *feel* like loving yourself.

Loving yourself is 100% *decision*.

3 ★ CLASS IS ABOUT CHARACTER, NOT YOUR BANK STATEMENT

Anna Lee grew up in poverty in the rural south during the Great Depression. She slept in the same bed with five other siblings. One of her siblings died from lack of medical care. She walked to school in cold weather with no coat. She was literally beaten with an electric cord whenever she did the slightest thing wrong. Alcoholism was a common sight. Few kids graduated high school. She had few good role models in her young life. She had every reason to grow up a complete mess of an adult.

But she did not.

Instead, she made the *choice* to present herself with *class*.

That choice helped her to earn a high school diploma, get a job at a department store, work her way up to becoming an executive secretary to a military general, and to own her own home.

Her decision to have *class* altered her entire life.

She was never fiscally wealthy, rather she was wealthy in character.

Often when we think of class, we think of money. We associate "high-class" with a large bank account, fancy possessions, and a prestigious position.

But there's another side of "high-class" that has *nothing* to do with material things.

Instead, it has every bit to do with *character*.

Indeed, you could possess a tremendous amount of financial wealth and still be quite bankrupt in character.

To have "high-class" without wealth speaks to how you present yourself, and to your morality.

First, how you present yourself.

It takes very little money to sustain good hygiene habits, to wear clean, appropriate clothes, to have good posture, to walk with your head high, and to practice good manners. It doesn't cost you a thing to refrain from bad habits like drinking, smoking, or using drugs. Saying "yes, sir" or "yes, ma'am," "please," and "thank you" and avoiding foul language tells the world you are a considerate person. Showing up on time, keeping your promises, and treating others with respect shows you're a conscientious person.

The sum of these things is your *personal brand*. These are the things people notice about you from day to day.

The second half is your morality. These are the things you do when no one is watching.

Do you lie, cheat, or steal?

Do you cause or contribute to situations bringing grievous harm to others?

Do you put in an honest day's work? Do you keep your commitments?

These traits don't show right away, but eventually they reveal themselves. At some point, people know if you possess these traits or not. It becomes part of your reputation for a very long time.

Anna Lee *chose* to find ways to keep herself clean even when there was no running water.

She *chose* to mend her clothes, keep them in good repair, and walk with good posture, despite the emotional turmoil she felt.

She *chose* to stay in school despite bullying and mean teachers.

She *chose* to exercise good manners, to avoid bad habits like drinking and foul language—despite her environment.

She *chose* to practice good morality and to surround herself with good people.

She *chose* to work hard and to respect others, no matter their lot in life.

I doubt she ever *felt* like doing any of these things! She *chose* instead.

Anna Lee was, indeed, a high-class person with the kind of character no amount of money could buy.

What was the return on investment for Anna Lee?

Good character didn't cost her a dime, yet it earned her a good job, a modest home, and many friends who loved, admired, and respected her. She was a role model to everyone who encountered her. By serving as a role model for others, she helped others to realize better for themselves.

It would have been much easier for her to succumb to the pressures of poverty. If she had made that choice, the outcome for her quality of life would have been very different.

You will never hear about Anna Lee anywhere else but here. She was never on TV, much less famous. But she, and many others like her, are role models nonetheless.

4 A GENTLE ANSWER

You've probably heard the saying, "A gentle answer turns away wrath, but a harsh word stirs up anger."

That's not just a "wise" saying, it's a law of the universe.

It's easy to speak harshly to others when you're angry, defensive, or upset. It's particularly difficult when you're the recipient of toxic communication.

The problem is that responding in kind only makes matters *worse*.

I'm not saying to take verbal abuse like a door mat, or to refrain from expressing negative emotions or disapproval. What I'm saying is to *THINK* before you respond.

THINK is an acronym to help you with healthy communication. I don't know who made it up, but it's a real gem. When you *THINK* before communicating, you ask yourself the following questions.

Is it True?

Is it Helpful?

Is it Inspiring?

Is it Necessary?

Is it Kind?

By asking these questions and answering yes to all of them, you're less likely to escalate a tense situation by attacking someone's Facts, Identity, and Feelings, thereby resulting in a negative Impact (FIFI).

To do this well when the situation is tense, it's important to do this well as often as you can. It's remarkable how our *everyday* communications can be poisoned. Your *routine* communication with everyone you encounter matters.

Email and social media is a fantastic place to practice THINK.

Why?

Because you don't actually deliver the message until you click the "send" button.

That doesn't mean you can't deliver bad news or a negative opinion over email. It just means your word choice and how you deliver your message matters.

Put yourself in the position of the recipient and ask yourself if your communication aligns with THINK.

A lot of grade-school kids are exposed to this acronym, and yet they still say some pretty awful things to each other.

Why?

Because THINK isn't practiced very well at home.

THINK is not practiced very well in social media.

THINK is not practiced very well in some television programing targeted to children, let alone adult programming.

A lot of adults don't practice THINK.

We have an epidemic of mindless communication. This is not helpful.

You don't want to contribute to the poison. Rather, you want to be the role model people admire and respect.

Agree to disagree *respectfully*.

Will people say all sorts of hurtful things to you because they disagree with you?

On social media, you can pretty much count on that. Do not respond in kind. It's better to simply distance yourself from toxic people as opposed to responding at all.

How about giving someone negative feedback?

First of all, you don't want to do that in front of other people, call them names, or kill their motivation. I realize a lot of television reality shows have exactly this sort of thing going on for entertainment.

Let me be very clear, television reality shows are *not* an example for you to follow. It's not funny or cute. It's ugly.

Instead of watching those shows, try watching shows that are inspiring and actually *teach* you something.

Try interacting with people on social media who have interesting, truthful things to say.

Try looking for good examples of healthy communication to model.

These better habits will help you to THINK much better.

5 BEING RIGHT CAN COST YOU

A perceived threat to Status or Identity will elicit a negative response from most people.

For example, if you're rejected for a date, job, or position on a team, there's a perceived threat to Status or Identity.

If you lose a championship game, retire from a job you've had for thirty years, or get arrested for the first time, there's definitely going to be a reaction to that.

Fear of challenge to Status or Identity can also cause people to *avoid* unfamiliar situations or activities.

For example, you might avoid playing golf with co-workers to avoid revealing your poor golf skills. You might avoid asking someone out on a date for fear of rejection. You might avoid applying for a higher position fearing your friend may get picked over you.

These fears are all very normal and understandable. They're also holding you back from being your best self.

There's an additional fear stemming from Status or Identity that's *worse* than any of that.

The fear of being *wrong*.

It is an unhealthy fear wreaking havoc in your relationships, your career, and your *life*.

Being wrong "drops" your Status. At least that's how the automatic mind perceives it. It's not true at all, but the automatic mind sometimes believes this ugly lie quite strongly.

Some people cannot bear a perceived drop in Status, no matter how slight.

People who are impaired by a hyper-protective sense of Status avoid apologizing. If ever they do apologize, they do it in a way that "puts you in your place" to ensure their Status remains intact. They make you pay the price for their apology. This kind of behavior is toxic.

Being "right" can come at a cost, often to your relationships.

If you've ever had to live with someone who always had to be "right," rarely if ever apologized, and insisted on dominating every situation, you know it's painful. You and others see the problem clearly, but this person is totally blind to the problem within him or herself. It can feel oppressive, and in many respects it is.

If you're in this situation now with a parent, boss, spouse, or other and can't just "walk away" from it, understand you're not going to change this person.

The best thing to do is focus on the things you *can* do as opposed to the things you can't, being grateful for anything and everything that's good, communicating in a healthy manner, and seeking to empathize.

Understand this person has crippling fears keeping him or her from being their best self. Try not to be resentful. Resentment only hurts *you* and keeps you from being *your* best self.

On the other hand, if you can keep your distance from this person, it's a good idea—especially if they're not willing or ready to change.

Now on to you. What if *you're* the one with the strong need to be "right?"

You very well could be "right" about many things. Understand they're not all worth fighting for.

Only after you've honestly listened to the other position, reflected on your contribution to the problem, and chatted with your Toddler assuring his or her Status and Identity are going to be just fine, should you consider what to do next. Understand the other person's FIFI and yours as well. Then weigh all the information and decide if your "rightness" is *really* worth fighting for. Chances are, there's a compromise available that saves face for both of you.

What if *you* are the hypersensitive type?

Don't worry or beat yourself up. Many people are like that. The very fact that you're aware of this is huge.

When you learn to apologize sincerely without a "cost" from others, you earn more respect.

Your Status will actually "rise," not drop.

6 ★ THE SPECTRUM BETWEEN CHAOS AND RIGIDITY

There's a common theme in the areas of psychology, neuro-science, management, and leadership. That theme is the spectrum between chaos and rigidity.

On the chaos side of the spectrum, there's no structure, control, or organization. Everything is random, fluid, and unpredictable. It's nearly impossible to get anything done in this environment.

On the rigidity side of the spectrum, there's no flexibility, adaptation, or change. Everything is fixed, highly certain, and highly predictable. It functions well only when the parameters fit precisely within its highly structured mechanics—when there are few to no variables. It's nearly impossible to improve or grow in this environment.

The ideal place to be is right in the middle of these two poles.

That is, you need enough structure, organization, and discipline to get things done, *and* enough flexibility, open-mindedness, and wriggle-room to adapt quickly to changes or make improvements.

Finding the ideal place on this spectrum is no easy matter. What does this spectrum look like in families, teams, and organizations?

Setting the *right* boundaries in the *right* places is a real challenge. You want to be on the ideal spot of the spectrum between chaos and rigidity.

For example, let's say a business fires anyone who is late for work just one time. That's probably not a good boundary to set. This organization may want to build in some flexibility on that one. However, firing someone who deliberately sabotages the business is an appropriate boundary.

This example is simplistic. Many families, teams, and organizations have areas within their culture that are rigid, while others have areas that lean toward chaos.

For example, a business may allow people to come and go as they please, but they better get their assignments done on time. A culture like that would likely produce better results than a business requiring people to be at work during certain hours, but is lenient on deadlines. Those are poorly set boundaries.

A chaotic business culture would be lenient on *both* work schedules and deadlines.

This is a recipe for getting little accomplished.

A rigid business culture would be inflexible on *both* work schedule and deadlines.

This is a recipe for change resistance, inability to adapt to evolving business climates, and blindness to opportunities.

What does this spectrum look like on a personal level?

Individuals can range from chaotic and emotional in their thinking, to rigid and highly logical in their thinking.

Recall the personality types of iNtuitive, and Sensors where N's think big picture and S's think step by step.

Recall the personality types of Thinkers and Feelers, where T's think logically and F's think emotionally.

Recall the personality types of Judgers and Perceivers, where J's like structure and organization, while P's like openness and "free-birding," so to speak.

(The Extrovert and Introvert dichotomy plays less of a role here.)

So a person who's an (E or I) NFP is likely to have a more chaotic looking personality than a person who's a (E or I) STJ, who will appear more rigid.

E/INFPs will do better to adopt more organization and self-discipline in their lives, otherwise they may have trouble holding a job, achieving goals, or meeting their responsibilities in life.

E/ISTJ's will do better to "let their hair down" a little more, open up their mind, and enjoy an adventure every once in a while.

You may want to give some thought about your personal spectrum. If you're happy with the results in your life, then carry on. If you're relationships are rocky, your career is less than ideal, and your happiness meter is barely registering, you may want to consider refinement of your thinking and personality within the spectrum of rigidity and chaos. Perhaps you are too far to one side or the other, or perhaps there are better personal boundaries to set.

Being too chaotic or too rigid will produce less than desirable outcomes in your life. You want to have the right mix and balance with boundaries set at the right places.

7 NAVIGATING PARADOX

Remember when we talked about the "and" technique? This is where you present two seemingly contradicting positions at the same time to give equal attention to both sides.

For example, "I don't like the guy *and* I'm still voting for him" or, "We're working hard *and* we can't seem to meet our deadlines."

The "and" technique is a great way to navigate paradox.

Your ability to navigate paradox impacts your relationships, career, and success in life. It is a worthwhile skill to have no matter where you are in life.

Let's say you have a job that's far from your first career choice. A statement to yourself like "I'm not crazy about this job, *and* I will do it well and learn from it" is a whole lot better than "I hate my job."

Let's say you're a parent grocery shopping with your kids. The kids see the candy and demand it. A statement such as "That candy is yummy *and* we'll put it on the list for your birthday" usually works better than "No, you can't have that."

Let's say your significant other has some annoying habits. Saying "I love you *and* I prefer you not tailgate like that" will go over a lot better than "For God sakes, stop doing that!"

You see, in every instance above, you acknowledge two seemingly contradictory positions. The first is that you don't like you're job, while at the same time you make the best of it. The second is you acknowledge your child's keen interest in the candy while denying the candy at the same time (at least until a future date). The third is while you're annoyed by the habit of your significant other, you still love him or her.

Too often we get stuck in absolutes. Absolutes can trap our thinking, emoting, and communicating in the land of poor empathy and limited options. When we're not empathetic, we're not connecting or influencing.

Remember, empathy does *not* mean you agree. It simply means you can put your position aside and truly see things from another point of view.

Navigating paradox gets more challenging as you rise to higher positions of leadership. In most instances, the higher the leadership position, the more political it is. The more political a position is, the more careful you must be in your outspokenness. This can present a real dilemma for people who are passionate about certain things.

For example, if you were a factory worker who over the years made it to the board of directors, your outspokenness for protecting workers could be frowned upon. This is where you want to tread carefully.

You can still be authentic in your passion for protecting workers *and* be considerate of the board's interests to generate profits. Making the case that you *can* do both—protect workers *and* make a profit—is where your skill at navigating paradox, finding the right compromise, and communicating in a healthy way will bridge the divide. This is where being an authentic leader, as opposed to being a leader in name only, can make a big difference.

Middle managers and senior leadership positions desperately need authentic leaders. True authentic leaders navigate paradox brilliantly.

They set firm expectations where it counts and are flexible in other areas.

They set stretch goals that are rigorous and challenging, yet nurture and encourage others to help them achieve those goals.

They hold themselves and their peers strictly accountable, and readily admit when they're wrong.

They take on the criticism and give credit to the people below them.

They constantly seek to understand the views of others, even if they don't agree.

Every one of these situations is a paradox. The better you are at navigating paradox, the better influencer, communicator, role model, and leader you'll become.

8 FOCUS ON GOALS, NOT PROBLEMS

Have you ever noticed how some people are so distracted by their perceived problems they struggle to achieve happiness and success? That very well could be you.

All those pesky problems like paying the bills, passing exams, losing weight, caring for a loved one, finding a job, fixing the car, or managing your health can feel like running on a hamster wheel.

There are some techniques to improve this scenario. They require some tough decisions on your part, which you're ready to do.

The first is to manage your commitments.

Before committing to anything beyond your essential responsibilities, ask yourself, "Do I *want* to do this? *Can* I do this? Do I have the *will* to do this?"

If any of those answers are no, politely but firmly turn down the commitment.

The more you commit to things, the more likely problems will crop up to distract you from your real goals in life.

When it comes to additional activities in your life, less is more.

Another technique is to carefully select activities emphasizing *purpose* over *pleasure*.

Seeking purpose means you're seeking your better nature and striving to realize your full potential. It's the *Eudemonic* approach to life.

Seeking pleasure means striving for the maximization of pleasure and the avoidance of pain. It's the *Hedonistic* approach to happiness.

Humans generally find their highest level of happiness by leading a virtuous life and self-actualizing their talents. Now that doesn't mean you can't enjoy a good time now and then. It just means you have to have your priorities straight.

The more purpose you seek over pleasure, the more happy and successful you'll be because purpose is generally a stronger motivator over the *long term.*

Pleasure may be a strong motivator in the short term but does little for long-term motivation. If you seek long-term happiness and success, then getting distracted by the problems of pleasure seeking (or pain avoidance) can trap you in a rut.

A third technique combines the first two. That is, ask if what you're doing supports your *Life Vision* and your *Who I Am* statements you created in the BRAIN-RESET series.

These statements embody a *purpose* driven life as opposed to a *pleasure* driven life.

If the activity does not support either your *Life Vision* statement or your *Who I Am* statement, and the activity is not something you *must* do, then the decision to turn down or eliminate this activity from your life becomes much easier.

The fewer distractions you have, the fewer "problems" you'll have in the way of your desired outcomes. Remember, it's ok to reduce or quit something to pursue more worthy causes in your life.

A fourth technique is to focus on a goal and set a time limit, as opposed to merely starting tasks on a goal with no time limit.

For example. If you need to pack for a big vacation, give yourself thirty minutes to pack. Otherwise, you could easily take several hours to do this task.

Or if you need to shop for groceries, make a list, give yourself thirty minutes to shop, and be done with it. Without a list and a time limit you could easily turn that into a three-hour event.

Exercise is another great example. Give yourself thirty minutes of good exercise and then be done with it. You don't need to turn it into a two to four hour session, unless of course you're training for an athletic event.

At work, try making a to-do list for the week, and then assign time limits to each task. I have found it takes me about ten minutes to make such a list, and it saves me a lot of time during the week.

A good rule of thumb is to immediately do any task taking only two to three minutes to complete. That way it is done and out of the way and you can focus on more time-consuming projects.

For best results, make these techniques *permanent* habits. You'll be glad you did.

9 ASK QUESTIONS SO YOU DON'T MISS THE OBVIOUS

One of the biggest mistakes people make is assuming what is obvious to them is also obvious to others.

Wrong.

Here's another little surprise. It very well could be *you* who's not getting the "obvious."

There's a brilliant video demonstrating this phenomenon superbly. Two small teams of basketball players are passing a ball around. Viewers are instructed to count the number of times a team passes the ball. At the end of the video everyone proudly announces the number of passes they counted.

Then the instructor asks if they saw the giant gorilla walk across the basketball court. Everyone is confused because they didn't see a gorilla.

The same video is played again and this time viewers are instructed to look for the gorilla. Just as plain as day, there it is walking casually across the court. It even waves at everyone!

How could they miss something so obvious?

Because they were focused on something else entirely.

It's easy to miss the obvious when your mind is completely zeroed in on something else.

Investigators understand this phenomenon well. That's why they ask so many pesky questions that seem silly and obvious. They want to be sure they're not missing anything.

Good writers also understand this. They don't assume everyone has the same understanding so they state the obvious, sometimes repeatedly.

In order to boost your awareness and understanding of any given situation, you want to ask a lot of good questions. There are several techniques for this.

First, you want to identify your assumptions and then ask questions that can confirm or debunk those assumptions.

If the assumptions are confirmed, then they become *facts*.

If any assumption is debunked, that could alter your whole line of questioning.

The second tip is to ask open-ended questions and avoid yes/no questions. For example, "How did that make you feel?" or "What are your thoughts on this plan?" or "Tell me about a time when you were happy" as opposed to "Were you upset?" or "Do you like this plan?" or "Have you ever been happy?" When given an answer, go deeper by following up with questions like "What makes you say that?" or "Tell me more about _____" or "What do you mean by _____?"

A third tip is to avoid questions that put people on the defense.

For example, try asking "What's your plan to be on time?" or "What are your ideas to get back on track?" or "Tell me your thought process behind that decision" as opposed to "Why are you late?" or "What's the problem?" or "How could you do such a thing?"

Finally, use silence and don't interrupt.

When you're silent, people tend to want to fill the void by talking. The more they talk, the more information you gather. You want to avoid interrupting so that you can let them talk themselves out. The more they talk, the more you learn (even if you don't like what you're hearing.)

Asking good questions is an important part of your communication.

Remember that the automatic mind heavily influences your communication. You want to be cognizant of how you ask questions so you don't unknowingly following unchecked assumptions, ask leading or yes/no questions, put people on the defense, or interrupt.

It takes effort and practice to master asking good questions.

When you master asking good questions, you gain more knowledge to inform your own decisions, and you earn more respect from others.

10 RECOGNIZE ANALYSIS PARALYSIS

L istening to others has its limits.

At some point, you just have to make the best decision with the information available and live with it. If you have a lot of time to make an important decision, then take that time if you need to. Chances are you don't have a lot of time and getting caught up in "analysis paralysis" will not help you one bit.

Analysis paralysis is when you spend way too much time gathering information and trying to achieve certainty on *everything*.

It's often used as a form of procrastination.

It can also be used to resist change.

As a leader, analysis paralysis can be frustrating when you're trying to get things done.

As a team member, analysis paralysis on your part can frustrate others.

As a person trying to make an important decision in your life, analysis paralysis can hold you back from being your best self.

I'm not saying to go along with everything like a lemming. What I'm saying is that there's a time to decide—*do* or *not do*, and if not, then *what*—if anything?

The reason making a decision and following through with it is important is because the process of stewing over it takes up a lot of your valuable time and energy. It can also burn up your reserve of willpower. Your time, energy, and willpower are finite resources. They're not unlimited.

Remember, no matter what you do, you can't please everybody. Chances are there's going to be *someone* who doesn't like your decision.

Here's a little story that makes the point well.

A young boy and his elderly grandfather were walking with their donkey. Some people passed by and asked, "Why don't you let the old man ride the donkey?" So the old man rode the donkey.

Later some other people exclaimed, "You terrible man! Why do you make your poor grandson walk? Let him ride the donkey instead." So the old man dismounted and put the little boy on the donkey.

Later still, some other passersby blurted, "You fools! Why don't you both ride the donkey?" So the old man rode the donkey with his grandson.

Finally, some more people announced, "How terrible you are to burden that poor donkey with all that weight!" So the old man and his young grandson dismounted and began carrying the donkey. Soon the whole village was laughing at them.

Do you see how ridiculous this can get?

While listening to others and considering their input is encouraged, following their advice is not always wise. At some point, you must decide and move on.

Big decisions such as quitting your job *should* take time, but little ones, such as what to have for dinner or what color to paint your bedroom, are not worth agonizing over.

Eliminate the bad options and choose "good enough." Rarely is perfection required.

If you make a mistake, chances are you're going to be *just fine*.

It's ok to let someone else make the decision so long as you trust them. This is especially helpful if you have a lot of decisions to make and don't have a lot of time.

If you're on a team and you're using analysis paralysis to resist change, be careful that you're picking the right battle. Not everything is worth fighting over.

If you're a leader of a team locked in analysis paralysis, give them a time limit. Keep them focused on the goal and listen carefully to their concerns.

Working for leaders who struggle making decisions requires some work on your part. To handle this, make sure you've given them at least *three* options with the pros and cons of each. Then listen carefully and have an honest discussion about their intent and concerns. They will appreciate this very much.

Some leaders need good people like you to help them in this way, especially when they have many decisions to make. You influence the tempo and momentum of decision making and efforts overall. This makes you a valuable member of the leader's staff, and a more effective leader of teams.

11 ★ THE CURSE OF *SHOULD*

One of the fastest ways to create anxiety or induce a guilt trip is to use a sentence with "should" in it.

"I *should* do my homework."

"You *should* take out the trash."

"I *should* have resisted dessert."

"You *should* have visited your mother."

How did you feel after reading all that? Pretty de-motivating, huh? Now let's say these statements differently.

"I *want* to do my homework."

"You *want* to take out the trash."

"I *could* have turned down dessert (and it wasn't a priority at the time.)"

"You *could* have visited your mother (and there were other things going on too)."

"Should" is a de-motivator.

"Want" and "could" are *empowering*.

The difference may seem subtle, but it's not to your automatic mind.

When you use "want" and "could," your automatic mind feels more autonomous, as though it has more control. When you use the word "should," you feel as though some external force is in control. There's a sense of lost autonomy. "Should" is just plain stressful.

There's another reason to avoid "should," and that's to help you with *rational thinking*.

For example, "Those people *shouldn't* vandalize the school" or "He *should* be more helpful around the house" or "They *should* be more respectful of the flag."

I realize this will be hard for some people, so please bear with me.

You see, there's no law of the universe that absolutely allows or prohibits these things. Sure they violate state laws, or social laws of decency, but the fact of the matter is people *can*, and *will*, do these things.

Are they upsetting? You bet they are!

Are they unfair? Most likely, and that's probably one of your hot buttons.

Nevertheless, these things and many other "shoulds" and "should nots" *do*, and in many instances, *will* take place. The problem with these instances of "should" is they trigger you into a negative state, and we want to avoid that.

So how do we do avoid getting triggered into a negative state?

You do it by reframing with the word *prefer*.

For example, "I *prefer* those people not vandalize the school," or "I *prefer* he help out more around the house," or "I *prefer* people respect the flag."

Do you see what happens when we use the word "prefer?" We take the sting out of it. We're far less likely to be triggered into a negative state. Because at the end of the day, that's the truth anyway. Of course you "prefer" those things. That is completely true and rational.

What's *not* true and rational is "should" or "should not" because, again, there's no law of the universe that says so.

You'll want to get into the habit of using *prefer* in every instance that annoys you. "I *prefer* people drive with more courtesy." "I *prefer* my boss not be a jerk." "I prefer she not snort laugh like that."

Reframing in terms of *preferences* instead of absolutes is much less likely to upset you. Being upset is largely a waste of time, energy, and willpower—all of which are finite resources. You want to preserve these precious resources for more worthy things like your peace of mind, your goals, and your health.

12 IT'S TIME TO MOVE...

From the Land of Perpetual Victim to the Land of Joyful Victor.

You may not even realize you're in the Land of Perpetual Victim. Sadly, an awful lot of people live there and don't even know it. It's not their fault. It's just that people have to work to get out of it. But first they have to know they're in it.

A sign you've taken up residence in Perpetual Victim Land are *subconscious* fear, rage, and sadness leading to *conscious* anxiety, anger, and depression.

Often when we're consciously anxious, angry, or depressed, we don't understand why. We often make up a reason, but it's not the actual cause.

What's really going on is there's hurt from the past trying to get your attention, but you don't want to listen because it's too painful. So it just integrates itself into your personality without your awareness because it refuses to be ignored.

What's worse is these ignored hurts can further manifest into health problems, sometimes very serious ones.

Sadly, it's more "normal" to be in this land than not because few people get through life without some sort of trauma, abuse, or neglect.

It's bad enough to have been a victim of these things. What's worse is these experiences can dump some really toxic deposits in the program of your automatic mind.

Toxic deposits can look like "It was my fault," "I'm a bad person," or "I deserved it." You may not be aware of toxic deposits, but deep down in the back of your mind, they're there.

Toxic deposits are like leaking drums of radioactive sludge; they wreak havoc on your life.

What's worse is toxic deposits form an *unholy alliance* with your Toddler. We all know that everyone's Toddler is not flattering. So when toxic deposits and

24

unflattering Toddler combine, you have a real mess on your hands.

Strangely, your programming default is to stay in the Land of Perpetual Victim because it's familiar, therefore it's "safe." Clearly, anxiety, anger, and depression are not safe, so we need to get out of this place.

How do we get out of this land and *move* to the Land of Joyful Victor, where peace, success, and happiness are?

First of all, moving to the new land is a journey. It takes time and much self-reflection. I don't mean self-pity. I mean objective self-reflection in which you observe past events in your mind.

Observe the victim (you) not as yourself but as an *outsider*. Notice that you went through a tough experience. Pay attention to the toxic deposits that may have developed in those moments, such as, "It was my fault."

Now replace them with something loving such as, "You're a fantastic person. You did your best. That was a really tough time. It's over now. You're in a better place."

Notice how we didn't blame a perpetrator, even if they were to blame. That's because we want to keep the door open for forgiveness.

In this exercise we merely observe the *truth*. You're a fantastic person, you did your best, it was a tough time. That's because they *are* true.

What's also true is you're *victorious*.

Despite what you went through, you're still an amazing, wonderful, fantastic person. When you imagine yourself the *victor*, because victors get through tough times and difficult circumstances, your move to the new land is enabled.

Now on to your Toddler.

Yes, he or she is still unflattering *and* absolutely worthy of all your love. Make sure you separate toxic deposits from Toddler because you must deal with them *separately*. You treat your Toddler with *love, patience*, and *understanding* like you do a *real* toddler, giving it attention, settling it down, and asking it to help.

Your Toddler is victorious *with* you because the strong will of a toddler is an asset.

On the other hand, you treat your toxic deposits by firmly *confronting* them, and replacing them with healthy deposits. Your Reality Show is a very helpful tool to help you with that. So is *Ground Control*.

You want to expunge the toxic deposits while remaining best friends with your wonderful, albeit unflattering, Toddler. That's why understanding the difference between toxic deposits and Toddler is so important. You handle them differently.

13 UNLEARN LEARNED HELPLESSNESS

In the last lesson we introduced you to the Land of Perpetual Victim. We explained how people get stuck in this land because the default programming is to stay there where it's "safe."

The problem is getting stuck in this sad place leads to chronic emotional distress and sometimes physical ailments too. It traps you into believing that you're *helpless*.

When you're in emotional and physical distress, you're *suffering*. Suffering you think you cannot control leads to hopelessness, which then leads to depression.

When you're depressed, it's hard to be grateful, to appreciate little things, to think clearly, or to do things with energy. Your relationships suffer. Your work and hobbies suffer. Your mind and body suffers. Your mind stays stuck in negative thought patterns reinforcing ugly lie deposits.

You've "learned" to be helpless. You develop self-defeating patterns of thinking, emoting, and behaving. Your behavior then manifests the prophecy of the automatic mind—that you're really not smart, attractive, or capable – or *worse*, that you're a no-good, rotten person.

When the prophecies seem to come true, they reinforce ugly lie deposits in your automatic mind. The cycle continues and you get even *more* depressed.

As you can see, there's a lot going on here.

First, there's the ugly lie deposits. We already talked a lot about how to deal with those.

Second, there's Toddler, and we already talked about how to manage that wonderful little creature.

Third, there's SCARF (Status, Certainty, Autonomy, Relatedness, and Fairness.) We're going to talk about how SCARF contributes to your being trapped in the Land of Perpetual Victim and learned helplessness.

In the Land of Perpetual Victim, there's a tendency for one or more SCARF elements to become highly sensitized.

Everyone is different. Some people are very sensitive to perceived challenges to their Status. Some people require a great deal of Certainty so they're very controlling. Some people can't stand authority of any sort because of a heightened perceived threat to their Autonomy. Some people are extremely needy and dependent on others, indicating a heightened sense of Relatedness. Finally, there are people who overreact to perceived or real instances of unfairness because their sense of Fairness is hypersensitive.

The problem is when an overly sensitive SCARF element gets triggered, the automatic mind uses the trigger to reinforce an ugly lie deposit, stir up your Toddler, and lure you out of your right mind. A cascade of negative thinking and emoting results, causing real suffering. When we think we can't control this suffering, we feel helpless. Feeling helpless is part of being in the Land of Perpetual Victim.

There's an antidote to help navigate yourself out of this place. In order for it to work, you must be honest with yourself about which SCARF elements are most problematic for you.

Quiet reflection and discussions with people you trust can help you with this critical task. Admitting a weakness in any SCARF area does not make you any less of a fantastic person. It just means you're human because many people have sensitized SCARF elements. Over-sensitized SCARF elements will cause much trouble for you, and you don't need that.

The antidote to this problem starts with *Ground Control*: First, notice the thought and feeling. Chances are you'll notice irrational thinking in yourself such as, "they *should* not do that."

Second, take a deep breath. This important step gives you time and space to pull yourself back into an objective place.

Finally, exercise one or more of the options listed below appropriate to the situation:

#1 *Be curious.* "What can I learn from this?" or "I wonder if there's an opportunity here?"

#2 *Reframe in a constructive, rational way.* For example, "He should never talk to me that way!" becomes, "I *prefer* he use a more respectful tone when speaking to me."

#3 *Gratitude and appreciation* for anything that's good and right, even small things.

#4 *Visit your Happy Place.* Take a mini vacation in your mind.

#5 *Let it float by.* If "thinking" is just too much to do right now, it's ok. Just continue to notice, stay detached, and let it float by like a passing cloud.

#6 *Secret Option Six.* Coming soon in this series. It's potent, but there's more to learn first.

Reviewing your *Reality Show* is also encouraging and reminds you of who you *really* are.

All these techniques empower you and give you a greater sense of control. In due time, you'll understand you're not helpless after all.

14 LET'S ASK THE MIRACLE QUESTION AGAIN

In the last lesson, we talked about how being in the Land of Perpetual Victim and how over-sensitized SCARF elements contribute to learned helplessness. We then discussed the importance of recognizing and accepting that one or more SCARF elements may be over sensitized. We mentioned the techniques to help you navigate your way out of this situation.

In this lesson, we'll revisit the Miracle Question and how to leverage it as a useful technique to add to your toolbox.

Let's assume your over-sensitized SCARF element is Status. You know you get annoyed when you don't think people recognize or respect you. You become irate when someone calls you a name, puts you down, or clearly disrespects you. You come off as "entitled" to many people. Others simply avoid you because you don't listen to their views and believe you're always right. You rarely apologize for anything, even if you're clearly wrong. You may resort to name calling or threats to get people to give you the "respect" you think is owed to you. You react angrily and defensively to criticism, constructive or not. Being in charge or a position of authority in some way, shape, or form is important to you—at the expense of your relationships and personal growth. You may have a tendency toward narcissism and some people may have even dared to tell you such. You respond either by laughing at them contemptuously or becoming extremely angry.

Yes, I know I painted a pretty harsh picture. It's also a fairly accurate picture of a person with a hypersensitive sense of Status. If *any* of this rings true for you, then it's an opportunity area for you to improve.

Now to the Miracle Question.

If by some miracle this problem suddenly disappeared, what proof would you have to know the problem was gone?

29

For example, if someone wasn't giving you your "due respect," instead of reacting negatively, you'd hardly notice it. You'd smile and be pleasant anyway. Why? Because *your self-worth doesn't come from others*. It comes from yourself.

If someone called you a name or put you down, you'd take a deep breath, and calmly say, "Gee, what makes you say that?" You simply wouldn't care, much less resort to name calling in return.

You'd be a more considerate listener, resisting the urge to interrupt, and being more open to understanding their view. You'd avoid acting pushy or entitled, even if you *are* entitled by reason of being a paying customer, special member, or hold a certain title. You'd carry yourself with gratitude and grace. You wouldn't throw your weight, rank, or position around in order to get your way. You wouldn't brag or try to impress or gain the approval of others. *You are perfectly content and at peace with yourself no matter what the situation or how others treat you.*

These behaviors indicate the problem of a highly sensitive sense of Status have magically disappeared.

Here's the beautiful secret: it's not magic at all.

Think about any one of these situations and imagine if you could start practicing it *now*.

You don't have to be good at all of it right away. Just pick one or two areas and start working on them right away.

One of the best tools to help you with this effort is *Ground Control*. 1. Notice the thought or feeling. 2. Take a deep breath. 3. Choose one of six wonderful Option Items.

Now, if your thought is, "That rat ____!" and your feeling is "rage"—that's ok. It's the truth and it's best to be honest with yourself. No need to lie to yourself or sugarcoat anything because that's only counterproductive. So go ahead and call it like it is. The next two steps will help you break out of the negative state, because you being in a negative state doesn't hurt them at all. It hurts *you*.

Once you've honestly labeled the thought and feeling, take a deep breath and then say to yourself, "That person is not in their right mind; I'm a fantastic person; I'm going to be just fine."

Try answering the miracle question with any character trait or over-sensitized SCARF element you'd like to change. Write down your answers and to see which one you could implement today. You don't have to do everything at once, but doing one *now* will make a difference.

15 TRIAL AND CONVICTION IN YOUR MIND

When we're not sure how to take someone, it's natural to jump to the conclusion of *threat*.

We assume all sorts of "bad" intentions on their part. We actively look for evidence of "no good" to confirm our suspicions. We overlook contradictory evidence. We may even spin genuinely good intentions into something nefarious. We deem them wrong or faulty people based upon a court conviction in our own minds. This court conviction was a trail for which they had little to no chance to defend themselves.

This sort of conviction is not uncommon. It can happen with perfect strangers, people we know, and even those we're closest to. Chances are you've done this with others—judging them unfairly without attempting to learn the truth about them. Also, chances someone has judged you unfairly, you had no idea why, and they didn't bother to talk to you about it. It's an awful feeling.

Now, if you've ever judged someone unfairly because you felt threatened by them, you're *not* mean, nasty, racist, sexist, xenophobic, evil, rotten, or stupid. You're a nice person with a normal threat response. You're also aware of it and want to do a whole lot better, and you will.

On the other hand, if anyone has ever judged *you* unfairly because they felt threatened by you for whatever reason, probably one of the most difficult things to do is to refrain from judging them unfairly in return.

Sometimes it's because they *are* rotten people, but most of the time, they're ordinary people trying to get through life just like you. You might want to assume the former, and that would be a normal response. However, it's a whole lot better to assume the latter because that actually works in your favor.

31

How? Let me unpack it for you.

You know they've judged you unfairly. What's next in their mental court?

They look for every shred of evidence they can find against you. So if you assume they're a rotten person, you *will* tend to treat them with contempt. I promise, they *will* pick up on that contempt and then they'll become entrenched in their unfavorable view about you.

Instead, you want to avoid giving them evidence against you as best you can. You do that by empathizing, by putting yourself in their position, and by imagining how it's possible they could feel threatened by you. When you do that, your whole demeanor changes from contempt to openness and trust.

I'm not saying you're kissing up to them. You're merely holding your objectivity, maintaining your grace, and not going negative, despite *their* negativity.

This is advanced stuff because you will feel vulnerable. I promise, you'll be fine.

Look for indications of your contribution or AMUM (Avoidance, Misunderstand, Unapproachable, and Mindless) and own up to any of them. Should you need to review AMUM, it's in the COMMUNICATION series in volume one.

When they point out a perceived flaw, try not to get defensive. Instead ask, "What makes you say that?"

Remember that FIFI is listening and you'll want to be cognizant of her influence. Explain your FIFI without putting them on the defense. This method has a far greater chance of turning their opinion of you to a more favorable view, which is what you want. This is advanced stuff, and you're ready for it now.

When you catch yourself in a situation in which you're judging someone rashly, first of all, get yourself into a calm frame of mind.

Reflect on your AMUM and FIFI. *Wonder* about their FIFI without assuming anything. Then, when you're in a relatively relaxed state, ask them about their FIFI with an open mind, and with empathy. Remember to avoid anything sounding like a thinly veiled accusation.

You can express your FIFI, and you'll want to in order to facilitate mutual understanding. By following this guidance you'll be more likable.

People will appreciate you took the time and consideration to understand, as opposed to snap to judgment, which is not fair to them.

Nobody likes to be convicted unfairly. When you're fair with others, people trust you.

16 HUMILITY VS. THE MACHINES

In highly competitive environments, promoting oneself and driving other people hard is expected. This type of environment can be energizing and exciting when cultivated in a balanced, healthy manner.

On the other hand, some people and organizations take this concept too far in an unhealthy direction. That's when we see behaviors emerge such as arrogance, low empathy, and toxic communication.

A hyper-competitive environment in which everyone promotes themselves and drives their people extremely hard is called the Land of the Machines.

In this stressful place, people are not treated like humans but like machines (objects). People are afraid to admit mistakes and quick to blame others. Everyone jockeys to look better than the other guy. Bosses could care less about your ideas or personal challenges. Bosses take credit for your hard work, or try to diminish your work. In order to be considered for promotion you feel compelled to be a machine and outperform the other machines.

Acting like a machine and treating others like machines (objects) produces self-sabotaging behaviors such as arrogance, low empathy, and poor communication, which eventually harms your relationships, limits your growth, and derails your long-term career prospects.

Machines enjoy momentary successes such as getting their way, forcing certain instantaneous behavior, or meeting short-term goals. The cost for this short-term gain is expensive: broken relationships, uninspired and sub-optimal performance, high-turnover, burn-out, anxiety, depression, anger, dishonesty, disloyalty, inefficiency, and difficulty meeting long-term visions.

The trouble is many adults aren't much better than toddlers when it comes to immediate gratification. They want what they want now and worry about the future later. This hardly bodes well for ideal long-term outcomes, including yours. There is another way.

Humility.

Humility can be challenging because it requires a great deal of self-confidence and authenticity to do well. It's why you don't encounter many humble people, much less humble bosses.

Few people possess the self-confidence and authenticity to be humble. The good news is if you learn humility you can become much more competitive and successful in the long run than your non-humble, machine peers.

Humble people admit their mistakes or contribution to problems without being a doormat or martyr. They give credit to others while still looking good. They're flexible in their views without compromising their core values. They listen patiently to others, ask thoughtful questions, and genuinely try to understand others. They communicate respectfully. They assert themselves skillfully without bullying, threats, or belittling others. They speak of their accomplishments and celebrate appropriately without boasting, "rubbing it in," or treating others with disdain. When wronged, they don't feel the need to retaliate. They remain in control of themselves during the storm and don't expect humility from others. They have a realistic view of themselves, are teachable, and value other's strengths and contributions. Finally, humble people are confident and comfortable in their humility.

Humble people are much more likable and respected. As such, they possess more influence and power. They're better performers and get along better with everybody. They enjoy healthier relationships, greater loyalty, and more honest interactions.

People are inspired by humble people and tend to follow their behavior.

Humble people make far better leaders than machine people.

For all these reasons, humble people tend to enjoy more qualitative promotion opportunities and the achievement of long-term goals.

Humility is hard and takes constant practice. It's also an advantage when competing with machines.

Yes, machines can and do sometimes get ahead of their more humble peers. Don't envy them; at some point they will pay for it with their health and relationships.

Machines focus on the short term.

Humble people focus on the long term.

Unless you don't plan to live very long, it's much better to have a long-term view and strategy.

TWO FORMS OF PERFECTIONISM— CHOOSE CAREFULLY

There are two forms of perfectionism. One is noteworthy. The other is poisonous.

The noteworthy form of perfectionism is when you seek excellence in a given craft such as art, athletics, inventions, or any other talent or accomplishment.

You may not actually achieve perfection, but you strive for it anyway. It demands much dedicated practice (recall the ten-thousand-hour rule.) You don't arrive at perfection overnight, nor do you expect to. Instead, you get there with stretch goals, honest reflection on your strengths and weaknesses, continuous refinement of your practice, and building your automatic capabilities.

This kind of perfectionist seeking requires grit and resiliency. For most people, it's not work but passion. It's a noble thing.

The poisonous form of perfectionism is largely anything outside the context above.

For example, seeking perfection in how you park, dress, look, eat, speak, work, play, relate, drive, walk the dog, put away the dishes, and such. It's not a passion but an unhelpful obsession.

Perfectionism of this sort is correlated with fear of failure, rejection, and vulnerability.

People who suffer from this form of perfectionism tend to be hyper-critical of others, black and white about the world, risk averse, and less innovative and creative. They often have great difficulty connecting with others. They struggle to talk about their personal fears or insecurities. They obsess over mistakes and become depressed when they experience failure. They take setbacks and criticisms personally. They're less resilient of challenges, are highly defensive when there's no need to be, and jealous of others' successes. They tend to feel excessive guilt and shame over perceived flaws in themselves.

This form of perfectionism is poisonous to every aspect of one's life. It's also pretty widespread and not unusual at all.

If you think *some* of these characteristics describe you in any way, you are *not* a rotten, mean, evil, selfish, no good, hopeless loser. You're an amazing person who simply wants to understand, succeed, and be happy in life.

There's nothing wrong with that. It's just you're going about it the wrong way and need to make some adjustments. If you find you have perfectionist habits, consider having deposits in your Reality Show steer you toward better habits.

Poisonous perfectionism is linked to:

> FIFI (Facts, Identity, Feelings, & Impact)
>
> U-HIDE-CUPID (your hot buttons)
>
> SCARF (Status, Certainty, Autonomy, Relatedness, & Fairness)
>
> And last but not least, your wonderful and delightfully imperfect Toddler.

You'll want to reflect, understand, and manage yourself in the four areas above. Additionally, the tools you've already been given such as *Ground Control* (with six Option Items) and watching your Reality Show will help you re-wire the programming in your automatic mind contributing to poisonous perfectionism.

Poisonous perfectionism can be challenging for some people to change, so give yourself *time*. This is where giving yourself a little bit of quiet space every day to reflect on the thoughts going through your head, why you behave in a certain way, what triggered a hot-button in you, why that triggered you, and how you can better manage your thoughts and emotions. This is the time to have those little conversations with yourself, ensuring they're rational, true, and nice.

Noteworthy perfectionism, on the other hand, is encouraged!

Passion and truly enjoying what you do fuels the challenges and stretch goals you set for yourself to achieve noteworthy perfectionism. If you truly enjoy what you're doing, and others are cheering for you, then you know you're on the right side of perfectionism.

⭐ 18 BRAIN HYGIENE

Growing up, we learn certain hygiene habits.

We brush our teeth, bathe, and wash our hands after every bathroom break. Yes, *every* time. We exercise to clear out our pores and get our blood moving. We even go on detox diets to clean our internal systems. Well, now it's time to learn about *brain hygiene.*

Brain hygiene is cleaning out brain-clogging thoughts leading to being in your *wrong* mind. Pesky negative thoughts or unpleasant memories that keep popping into you mind *soil* your brain. They do this by distracting you, darkening you mood, and keeping you awake at night. Your brain just isn't operating as well as it could. We want to change this.

The key part to brain hygiene is bringing your mind to the present moment and space. Not the past, not the future, not your problems, just *here* and *now*.

This might sound silly but it's actually incredibly important. In fact, you might find getting your mind to *now* is quite difficult at first. You may find it nearly impossible to stop thinking about the past, something or someone that upset you, your big test coming up, whether or not you'll sell the house, dear Uncle Charlie's cancer, or your job interview. It's ok if it's difficult. You'll get better with practice.

What's more is as you improve your brain hygiene abilities, you'll find re-programming your mind to run the right thoughts and emotions you want to experience becomes increasingly easier. Since you completed the BRAIN RESET series, you may still be struggling to replace old ugly lie deposits with your new, healthier, nicer deposits. If that's the case, then brain hygiene will help.

There are many ways to practice brain hygiene. Meditation is a good way, and it doesn't matter if it's religious, spiritual, or just plain relaxing.

Other ways include yoga and tai chi—not so much the exercise, which is also quite good for you, but the focus on the position and movement that goes along with the exercise.

Unless you know how to do this on your own, it's a good idea to have an instructor or guide. There are some good apps and videos out there to guide you. Some are free. The better ones may cost a few dollars. I personally use the "Breethe" app.

Any activity that guides you to *clear* your mind and *focus* on something here and now, like your breathing, the sound of the birds, the feeling of the grass under your feet, the smell of the humid air, the colors of a flower, the position of your body, and so forth is practicing brain hygiene.

While doing any of these activities, you may find your mind heading straight to the badlands of your worries. When that happens, simply *notice* that that happened, without judgment and without engaging, and return to the activity of focus. Be gentle and nice to yourself.

You may find yourself doing this over and over again. You may find you can only sustain this effort for a few minutes. It's ok. A few minutes a day is usually sufficient anyway.

What's important is you keep trying. You'll get better over time and you'll enjoy other benefits. You'll find your ability to stay focused on your conscious tasks at home and work will improve because your mind won't wander so much. You'll find yourself with improved awareness abilities because your manual mind is learning to set aside the white noise of your worries and see what's *really* going on.

The benefits of brain hygiene accumulate in tiny doses over a long period of time to help transform your brain into something very different from what you had before.

Good personal hygiene helps keep you clean, healthy, and happy. Consider brain hygiene every bit as important as keeping your teeth, hands, and body clean.

It's not that you should *never* have a negative thought. It's that you need to give your mind a break from the pervasiveness of worry, anxiety, fear, anger, sadness, frustration, or other burdens. It's like bathing for the mind.

Brain hygiene helps give your mind a fresh start with more energy to take on your day. It is also advantageous to your physical health. We will cover much more of this topic in the SELF-CARE series.

19 YOUR FUTURE DEPENDS ON MOVING PAST THE PAST

Painful memories from the past can cause present day feelings of regret, anger, sadness, fear, or revenge.

Although events may have happened long in the past, we often still dwell on them, waiting for an apology, justice, or some kind of relief that never comes. This sort of distraction from the past does not help your present situation, much less your future.

We talked about brain hygiene in the last lesson and it will help if you practice it. With that said, tough memories require a different approach because you're not going to just "forget" about them. In fact, trying to forget could make matters worse because all you do is lock the emotions in the Super Max where they cause mayhem on your programming. You'll think, emote, and behave in self-sabotaging ways and won't understand why. We obviously don't want that, so instead, we'll try something different.

Reflect on the past event as an *objective observer* instead of as yourself. As the observer, empathize with the "you" in the scene, without judgment. Acknowledge the feelings of fear, rage, despair, hopelessness, disappointment, embarrassment, grief, shock, and tell yourself, "I'm so sorry that happened to you. It's over now. You're with *me* now and we have fantastic plans ahead."

Do you hear how that conversation is going?

A confident, caring, loving, you is looking at the you of the past, understanding your pain, and telling you to come home to *your* loving arms.

You know that fantastic feeling when you help someone feel better? You know that fantastic feeling when someone who loves you makes you feel better? Well, you get to be both at the same time.

39

This is a brilliant way to learn how to love yourself unconditionally. You can say something like "I love that child; he/she is such a fantastic kid; that little kid did the best he/she knew how" as the wise, loving adult you are when speaking about *yourself* as a child. You can say the same for when you were a teenager, young adult, or at any point in your life.

You don't just say these, though; you *mean* them and *feel* them. As you manually repeat these messages, your automatic mind eventually *believes* them. Over time, the belief grows stronger and the negative feelings of the past begin to fade away.

This is important because you don't want to be a prisoner of your past. Your present and future have nothing to do with your past.

Now some people may go so far as to *blame* their present and future circumstances on events from the past.

The problem with blame – even if it's absolutely justified – is it causes *you* to fail.

It's like a nasty double whammy. Not only did you get screwed to begin with, but your very act of blaming, even if it's entirely justified, piles on to make matters worse. Few things will keep you enslaved to the past more than *blame*.

I know it's hard to not to blame, and it's critical to avoid it.

Letting go of blame allows you to let go of the past. When you let go of the past, you open up your future to much better possibilities.

Additionally, letting go of blame allows you to *forgive*. When you forgive, you free yourself from the tremendous weight of anger and resentment.

Forgiveness frees up your emotional energy for more meaningful life experiences. Forgiveness is not about letting them off the hook, it's about freeing yourself of burden. You have better things to do in life than deal with dead weight burdens. When you're free from the burden of anger and resentment, you have different feelings. You see, your feelings, whatever they are, will dominate your present.

Dominant feelings tend to absorb your focus. Things you focus on *grow*.

We don't want to grow anger and resentment. Instead we want to grow peace, confidence, and gratitude. We want to grow in our love for ourselves and for others. Growing in this way is difficult if you are burdened by dead weight emotions.

Some of life's experiences are painful. You don't just "suck it up" or "get over it." It's a process and a journey.

It helps tremendously to know the process as well as the destination you want to reach in your journey. If your destination is not dwelling in your past, but a wonderful, joyful future, then it's paramount to let go of the past, love your past you unconditionally, and forgive.

20 NOBODY OWES YOU ANYTHING

Warning.

This lesson could trigger your hot-buttons under Status and Fairness. Please keep an open mind and understand the thinking advocated in this advanced lesson is for your own good.

You've progressed nicely now and I believe you're ready for this.

No matter what you've achieved or endured in your life, no one owes you anything.

When you work extremely hard at something, it's normal to think all your hard work should pay off—that something is owed to you and you're entitled.

When you grow up in a disadvantaged or abusive environment, there's sometimes a tendency to believe people should be extra nice to you and the universe should make it right – that something is owed to you and you're entitled.

Your hard-wired sense of Status and Fairness insists this is true. The trouble is our hard-wired features are rarely, if ever rational.

The reality and difficult truth is despite your hard work or disadvantaged background, absolutely nothing is "owed" to you.

It doesn't matter if you're a veteran, disabled person, minority, abused spouse, refugee, PhD, billionaire, world renowned scientist, politician, major religious figure, centenarian, or blue collar worker who spent thirty years at the factory.

No one owes you anything. Period. Full stop.

There are two reasons why it's important you understand and accept this truth.

The first is that it's rational. There's no law of the universe requiring anyone to give you anything. There may be common decency and decorum, but you know people disregard these things all too often. There may be government laws or organizational regulations, and they certainly do help your case, but they're no guarantee because laws and regulations often change.

You can *prefer* to be given your due, but to *expect* it is irrational.

The second reason is that a sense of entitlement creates problems for you.

When your expectations aren't met, you're likely to become triggered into a negative state of mind. A negative state of mind will not serve you well.

What's worse is when you expect the universe to deliver something it does not owe you, you're more likely to be *complacent*. That means you're more likely to be passive with your life as opposed to engaged.

But that's not the worst it.

The *worst* part is when you go around with an air of entitlement; people pick up on that and it almost always evokes a negative response.

If you've ever encountered someone who acted "entitled," you know it's a huge turn off. So if you go around acting entitled for any reason, even if you *are* entitled, you're going to turn people off—and that's not good.

Expect that all your hard work may not pay off. Work hard *anyway*.

Expect that you could lose everything you ever worked for in your life. A good reason to enjoy the journey as opposed to being fixated on the future.

Expect that people will not treat you with respect or dignity. Treat them, and yourself, with respect anyway. Model the behavior you prefer to see from others.

I'm not saying to not pursue your entitlements. What I'm saying is to exercise rational thinking, and don't let them become emotional dead weights in your life.

Life is not about what is owed to you. Life is about learning how to love unconditionally and enjoying every moment as a precious gift.

# 21 RECOGNIZE SELF-BETRAYAL

Self-betrayal is self-sabotage. You're hurting yourself, your happiness, and your chances for success.

What's more is we often don't recognize self-betrayal.

One way you betray yourself is by not doing something you know you should do. It can be something as simple as following up on an email or phone call, or taking out the trash on trash night, even though your spouse normally does it, because he or she is working late. It can be something as big as not ordering the recall on the defective product, or "overlooking" telling your spouse you just blew $5,000 on a lost bet.

Other ways you betray yourself are when you don't uphold your own values, when you communicate in a toxic way, or when you see others as objects.

For example, if you value respect, but then call your loved ones names, or speak curtly to the barista, you are betraying yourself as well as hurting others.

The reason why failing to do what you should, or not upholding your own values is self- betrayal has to do with the second law of the automatic mind.

The second law states that all communication, whether in thought or speech, no matter to whom or what it is directed, is absorbed by the automatic mind. Your actions are a form of communication. The way you treat others is a form of communication. All communication, even if you're directing it toward someone else, gets directed toward your automatic mind.

Let's say you don't follow up on an email or phone call you should respond to. Not only do you communicate to others that you're not responsive, which is not a good message, you're telling yourself that you're not very responsive to yourself. In other words, you might be aware of something about yourself you should respond to, like not being in your right mind, but instead of responding to it (Ground Control) you ignore it (not good).

Let's say you don't take out the trash when your spouse is working late. Or you call someone names, or treat someone unkindly. What you're doing in each of these cases is treating others like objects. Treating others like objects is not good for you.

When you treat others like objects, two bad things happen.

First of all, they know it. If you've ever been treated like an object you know it doesn't feel very good. People who are treated like objects usually don't go out of their way for you. Basically, you're treating them as though they don't have any feelings. Anytime you treat someone that way, they'll tend to resent you.

Second, is your automatic mind knows it too. Your automatic mind registers that it's also being treated like an object, because when you treat others as objects, it's tantamount to treating yourself as an object, per the second law.

What happens next is you lose awareness of *yourself.* You lose awareness of your feelings. You lock your feelings in the Super Max. Why?

Because objects don't have feelings.

What happens when you lose awareness of your feelings? Your automatic programming takes over with all those ugly lie deposits. Hot buttons get pressed, and you behave in a self-sabotaging manner.

I know you're not a saint, and neither am I. I've said more than a few unkind words in my day. I've shrugged off plenty of responsibilities and courtesies I *should* have done. I haven't always remembered my better manners.

I can say that I'm a better person today than I was yesterday, and you probably want that as your goal as well. You don't have to be perfect; you just have to want and try to be better.

Not treating others, and subsequently yourself, like an object can be a difficult habit to break. Many people aren't aware they have this problem and it's pretty widespread.

Some people think that to care about someone else's feelings means you have to give up control. That's simply not true. You can care and empathize and not commit yourself to solving their problem or saving their day. A mere expression of gratitude and empathy is all most people want anyway. They don't need, or even want, you to go out of your way any more than that.

Gratitude and empathy doesn't cost you anything, and it gains you respect. It reassures others they're not objects to you, and tells your automatic mind you're not an object either.

When you're not an object to yourself, but a loving, fallible human being, you are truly living.

22 YOU'RE MORE RELEVANT THAN YOU THINK

You are an important part of the universe. Everything you do and say has an impact on someone, which in turn has an impact on others.

It doesn't matter if you're doing the dishes at a restaurant, sweeping up a construction site, or sorting boxes in a warehouse. You make a difference with what you do.

There's a proverb called *For Want of a Nail*. It goes something like this.

A weary farrier neglected to put the requisite number of nails into the last horseshoe on the captain's steed. The captain rode into battle and the shoe fell off. When the shoe fell off, the horse stumbled. When the horse stumbled, the captain fell off and was killed by the enemy. When the captain was killed, the men were leaderless and lost the battle. When they lost the battle, the kingdom fell. The kingdom fell, *all for want of a horseshoe nail.*

Here's another way to look at things.

A number of masons were laying bricks for a structure. One mason was asked what he was doing. "I'm laying bricks," he answered. A second mason was asked the same question. "I'm building a wall." A third mason was asked. He proudly responded, "I'm building a school."

It would appear the third mason is the only one who really got it. He understood his work was important, even if that work was arduous and difficult. The others didn't seem to understand.

When you understand the relevance of what you do, you'll feel better about yourself. You'll do a better job, and people will notice.

Understanding your own relevance even in mundane tasks brings opportunities and promotions.

When you understand your own relevance, and conduct your work with pride and enthusiasm, people admire and respect you, even if you're in a low-wage job.

When people admire and respect you, good things are more likely to go your way. It's not that you're trying to show off. It's that you really feel the value of your work so you put more genuine energy and pride into it.

I remember visiting Okinawa and was impressed by the way ordinary workers carried themselves. The sanitation guys wore collared shirts and meticulously kept everything neat and tidy. Store workers smiled often and took great care to keep the store clean and organized. People everywhere were polite. I learned that Okinawans understand their role in the world and take great pride in doing things well. There's no such thing as a menial task. Everything is important and done with pride.

Imagine if you applied that sort of thinking to your everyday tasks.

First of all, you do make a difference, no matter what job you have. The detail and quality of your work does matter.

Remember the farrier who neglected a single nail? I doubt he thought it would ever matter, but the consequence was huge.

Remember the mason who was building a school? How do you think the quality of his work compared to that of the other masons? If you were going to hire a mason, which one would you prefer?

When you believe your work is relevant, no matter how menial the task, you'll do a better job.

People will notice.

Many people will even follow your example.

When people follow your example, then the whole workplace puts genuine pride and energy into their tasks. The result is better performance for the whole organization.

When the whole organization performs better, better job security and possibly more opportunities for the future arise.

You see, *you* can be contagious. Seeing yourself as relevant and putting pride into your work doesn't cost you a thing, but it can reap rewards you otherwise would not enjoy if you thought and behaved otherwise.

23 MANAGING INNER CRITIC

"What makes you think *you* can do *that*? Get your head out of the clouds."

"If you don't look a certain way, then you're worthless and unloveable."

"Mom said you were a selfish, spoiled brat and you still are."

These and other self-flagellating quotes are attributed to the "third element" of the automatic mind…Mr. or Mrs. *Inner Critic*.

As you can see, Inner Critic is not very nice.

Inner Critic makes you *think* it has your best interests in mind. Rest assured it does *not*.

Inner Critic is *not you*.

It is *not* your Toddler.

It is *not* your friend.

Inner Critic is *automatic programming*.

Remember from the BRAIN RESET series how life experiences and thoughts can deposit ugly lies into your programming? Well that's exactly what Inner Critic is – the programming output of all those ugly lie deposits.

Let me tell you something right now, you are an amazing, smart, loveable person no matter what anyone says.

Are you perfect? Of course not.

Are you a work in progress and doing your best? Absolutely.

Do you have your weaknesses and flaws, just as I do and everyone else does too? You better believe it.

Does any of that make you a horrible, rotten person? Not on your life!

Inner Critic is programmed to pounce on anything it can to slow you down and sabotage you. It's nothing personal. It's executing its programming.

One way Inner Critic sabotages you is it makes you hypersensitive to criticism. When Inner Critic hears criticism, it pounces saying "See? I told you! You're rotten! You're incapable! You're selfish! You're slow! You're worthless! You're ugly! You're a loser!" Hearing all that negative self-talk can put you in a negative state of mind really fast. It's also extremely upsetting to Toddler, who's rather sensitive to the bullying and taunting of Inner Critic.

It's very important to be aware when Inner Critic is talking because Inner Critic must be dealt with in a special way...

The most valuable tool you have for dealing with Inner Critic is *Ground Control* using Secret Option Six, which we will now introduce.

1. *Notice* the thought or feeling: You'll know it's Inner Critic talking if the thought is putting you down or making you feel bad about yourself. Other thoughts like judging others, expressing a want or preference, or assessment of a situation are not Inner Critic. Those are usually Toddler or stray voltage from deposits in your programming.

2. Take a long, slow, deep breath. Take several if you like.

3. Secret Option *six*. Bear with me because this is just an introduction. We'll do a deeper dive in the next lesson.

Secret Option Six is to say, "I am love" or "I choose love" repeatedly.

Why say *this*? Because *I am...* and *I choose...* are the most powerful words in the world. They create movement and change. They are *decisive*.

Why *love*? Because "*love*" is the most positive, good, and accepting *force* in world. *Love is what you are.* It is truly what you were made to be.

When Inner Critic is loud, it can be difficult to listen to your love voice.

You might initially feel uncomfortable saying this to yourself because of the Third Law, "The automatic mind resists drastic change."

When you directly confront your programming with something as provocative and powerful as "I am love," that represents a drastic change so your mind will resist.

It's important to keep saying, "I am love." I promise you, Inner Critic will shout back "That's ridiculous! Stop saying that!" It's important to keep saying it anyway, as well as connecting with the words.

Inner Critic is one of the most difficult automatic programs to purge and that's why we have so many wonderful, talented people who struggle so tragically to be happy and successful in their lives.

You don't need anyone's attention, approval, or acceptance. Only *you* need to accept *you*.

You will battle Inner Critic for the rest of your life, but it does get easier over time.

SECRET OPTION SIX

We're going to get into some really advanced material, and you're ready for it now.

There's one thing Inner Critic and SCARF elements have in common…

They're all about competition for *survival.*

If there's the slightest perceived threat to survival, Inner Critic and SCARF elements get triggered. Hot Buttons get pressed, and you enter the land of hate, anger, resentment, revenge, jealousy, anxiety, irritation, or even rage. You enter your *wrong* mind.

For tens of thousands of years, humans *competed*, often quite violently, for resources like food, shelter, mates, and choice possessions.

Competition is strongly imprinted in human genetics. It was critical to the survival of your ancestors, and they have generously passed this imprinting along to you. It's deeply embedded in Inner Critic and SCARF, which merely execute the genetic programming they were given.

When either perceive a competitive threat, they respond by triggering hate, anger, resentment, anxiety, revenge, jealousy, irritation, and rage. *These are the emotions of competition and survival.* They're the base, low frequency emotions of the carnal body.

Notice they're the *same* emotions that sabotage and cause problems for you.

Inner Critic does *not* want you to get comfortable or feel good about yourself. Why?

Because keeping you in an angry, anxious state of mind keeps you alert to your competition.

That was helpful a few hundred years ago when animals or other humans could sneak up and slaughter you at any moment, but that does not help you today. In fact, it's limiting and sabotaging you.

The same goes for SCARF. Any threat to your Status, Certainty, Autonomy, or Relationships was a competitive threat to your survival. Anything that was not Fair, where you were directly left out of the distribution of resources, was absolutely a threat to your survival. That's why any threat to these elements can trigger a strong response such as rage or revenge seeking.

SCARF elements are designed to put you in negative mindset because that's what made your ancestors competitive in a brutal world. That's what helped them *survive.*

Anger, resentment, revenge, irritation, rage, jealousy, anxiety and hate are the animal emotions of competition and survival. They all share a very low frequency vibration.

Remember you're always emitting an emotional frequency whether you want to or not. You will *attract* the frequency you give off, and reinforce it in yourself if you don't change anything.

Love, hope, joy, and forgiveness are the emotions of the human *soul.* There is no competition whatsoever. There is no concern over survival because the soul does not die.

Love and joy share a high frequency vibration. When you emit love, hope, joy, and forgiveness, you emit a high frequency that's *attractive.* Why?

Because people *crave* love and joy. It *nourishes* them. It breaks them out of their low frequency rut. It heals. It also heals *you.*

When you say "I am love" or "I choose love," you're rejecting the lure of competition and survival and accepting to trust the power of the Universe (or God, or Source, or whatever you like to call the source of your beautiful soul.) You're choosing your destiny instead of being a helpless victim of your survival emotions. You're rejecting Inner Critic and SCARF and embracing Toddler (who's not perfect but so what), Love and Optimism. You're grateful for all your blessings instead of focusing on the things you don't have.

Do you see why I waited until the WISDOM series to share Secret Option Six with you? It's a lot to absorb and think about, isn't it?

And now, here's the complete version of Ground Control.

☆ Notice the thought or feeling without explanations, judgments, or justifying them.

☆ Take a deep breath; let this simple yet vital act help reset you.

☆ Exercise one or more of the following Option Items:

1. Be curious: What's the lesson or opportunity? Ask good questions and listen.

2. Reframe: Put into more constructive or positive terms. Apply rational thinking.

3. Gratitude: Take nothing for granted. Appreciate everyone and everything.

4. Happy Place: Take a mini vacation in your mind. Your mind thinks it's real.

5. Let it float by: Without engaging or reacting, just let it pass by like a cloud.

6. Secret Option Six: "I am love" or "I choose love." Reject the competitive energy of your body, and instead embrace love energy of your soul.

THE THREE ELEMENTS OF THE AUTOMATIC MIND

This a power packed lesson. You may want to print it off and keep it as a handy reference.

Over the course of the past two volumes, I revealed to you the three elements of the automatic mind. Here's a summary.

In the BRAIN RESET series, we introduced you the concept of deposits, which represent all the beliefs in your programming. Deposits are your friend when they are healthy, rational, and positive. They sabotage you when they're unhealthy, irrational, or negative. Deposits direct the path of your thoughts and emotions and are embedded in your programming. The automatic mind automatically processes deposits to produce a thought or feeling. You may not even know you're having the thought or feeling unless your manual mind is paying attention. If your manual mind is paying attention and approves of the thought or feeling, it can reinforce the deposit through *gratitude* and by *noticing*. If your manual mind does *not* approve the thoughts or feelings, then it can regulate them, and the deposits behind them with Ground Control. The manual mind is powerful in determing which deposits ultimately get expressed and which ones don't.

In the NEURO-SCIENCE series, we introduced you to Toddler. Toddler is the "you" before your manual mind fully formed. Toddler is loving, curious, optimistic, and energetic. Despite these wonderful qualities, we often find Toddler locked up in the Super Max with all the icky emotions you don't like. Why?

Because Toddler has unflattering qualities. Toddler can be needy, dependent, narcissistic, selfish, and hypersensitive. We don't want to see or know this about ourselves so we lock it away out of sight. By not having attention from you, Toddler naturally gets upset. In addition, the poor thing is covered with all your hot buttons, and any time a button is pushed, it goes into tantrum mode.

Whenever Toddler enters tantrum mode, it puts you out of your right mind. The result is much worse if Toddler is locked away in the Super Max. However, if you acknowledge Toddler's feelings, love it unconditionally, and ask it to help you, the frequency and intensity of Toddler's tantrums are reduced. This doesn't mean Toddler gets its way. All Toddler *really* wants from you is *attention*. When Toddler gets enough attention (that is, not locked up in the Super Max and ignored) then Toddler is much better behaved.

In the WISDOM series, we introduced you to Inner Critic. Inner Critic is *not* you. It's not your friend, although it'll *pretend* to help or protect you. Inner Critic is simply bad programming. It automatically pulls out the ugliest deposits and mercilessly taunts Toddler with them. Toddler gets upset, and when combined with having no attention from you, Toddler enters tantrum mode. Inner Critic further upsets Toddler by harshly judging and condemning you. It calls you names and puts you down. By doing this, Inner Critic generates feelings of anger, fear, and sadness.

These negative feelings reinforce ugly lie deposits and vibrate out into the world, thereby attracting negativity to you. Inner Critic poisons your communications such that you harshly judge and condemn others. You may do so subtly through curt, sarcastic, or snide remarks, or you may do so overtly with cursing and name calling. Either way, the result is bad news. You merely attract more negativity, which does not bode well for ideal outcomes in your life.

So there you have it, the three elements of the automatic mind. While we speak of them as discrete elements, they actually exist in a blended state. It's like having a strawberry, chocolate, and vanilla milkshake all in one glass; just because they're all mixed together doesn't mean the chocolate isn't there, or the other two either.

You manage each of these three elements differently.

You use your *Reality Show* to help clean up your deposits.

You acknowledge and *love* your Toddler, and no longer lock it up in the Super Max.

You use "secret option six" on Inner Critic.

You use your manual mind in *all* these circumstances, exercising awareness, good communications skills, rational thinking and a healthy understanding of SCARF, Love, and Optimism.

In doing so, you put yourself on the path of becoming an authentic *leader.*

26 THE BEST LEADERS ARE FAILURES FIRST

What would you do if you were fired from a job several times, failed in several businesses, and went broke more than once?

Harlan Sanders created Kentucky Fried Chicken. He succeeded to become one of the most well-known franchisers in the world.

What would you do if a book you wrote was rejected by publishers thirty times?

Steven King continued submitting his book until it was finally accepted. The book was a bestseller, he published many more books, and is a world-renowned author.

What would you do if you joined the military as a captain and returned as a private, *and* you failed in business, *and* you lost several elections?

Abraham Lincoln ran for President of the United States and *won*. He is considered one of the greatest leaders in American history.

History, and the internet, is full of stories of highly successful people and great leaders who at one time were miserable failures, many of them failing repeatedly.

There's an old saying, the definition of "insanity" is doing exactly the same thing over and over again and expecting a different result. This saying is largely correct.

What brings success is *learning* from failure. If you learn from the failure and try again and fail again, well then you know that that doesn't work either. So you learn, change it up, and try again. You'll never know if you'll succeed unless you try.

If you don't try, then you *automatically* fail.

A lot of times when we experience failure or rejection, Inner Critic starts piping up. "See? I told you so! I told you, you're ugly, no good, and not worthy! Why bother trying again? Don't embarrass yourself."

It's a darn good thing Harlan Sanders, Stephen King, and Abraham Lincoln didn't listen to their Inner Critic, or we would not have the delicious fried chicken, thrilling novels, or the United States of America as we know it today. In fact, we would not enjoy a lot of things if Inner Critic had its way. We would not have light bulbs, iPhones, Oprah Winfrey shows and a host of other conveniences, inspirations, and delights if Inner Critic had won the day.

Here's an important question.

What are *you* denying the world because you're listening to Inner Critic?

Yes, that's right. You are *denying* the world something great and wonderful because you fear failure and rejection; because Inner Critic is in charge.

Failure is an opportunity to learn and try again.

Failure is *not* an excuse to blame others, blame your upbringing, blame the situation, blame the world, or blame yourself.

When you blame, you automatically fail.

You don't fail as long as you learned something.

You don't fail as long as you don't blame.

You don't fail as long as you keep trying.

Trying again means you continue to pursue your passions and dreams in life.

Trying again means you don't sit back and play helpless.

How about rejection? What do you do when you encounter rejection?

A lot of people avoid sales jobs because they can't take all that rejection. That's because they take it personally. They take it personally because Inner Critic is back there poking you right where it hurts every time you're turned down or told no.

Really good salespeople are adept at laughing in the face of Inner Critic, and turning rejection into a game. They know that after so many rejections they get closer and closer to yes, followed by a big sale. Rejection is viewed positively because each rejection brings them closer to a sale. The more rejections, the more excited and happy they become.

Tell Inner Critic to pipe down and leave you alone. Tell yourself "I am love" to escape the carnal mindset of competition and connect with your higher being. Then let your failures and rejections inspire you to try again.

27 AN INTRODUCTION INTO STRATEGY

In this lesson, we'll introduce the concept of *strategy*. Few people understand what strategy is, much less implement in. Truth be told, what seperates moderately successful people from highly successful people is strategy. Some people are naturally good at it, while others become just as good, if not better, once they understand and practice it.

Strategy consists of three key parts. The first is what's called the *End State*. The End State is the vision for how you want everything to be.

Let's say you're managing the Olympic Games in your city. The *End State* may be to provide a safe, secure, high quality experience for both competitors and supporters from start to finish. The more detail in the End State vision, the better.

The second part is the *Current Picture*. The Current Picture is the whole, current reality; the summation of all the details as they are *right now*.

Continuing with the Olympics example, let's say six months before the opening ceremony you notice problems in some areas, and smooth coordination in others. Some efforts are ahead of schedule while others are behind. From this Current Picture you know your End State will not be met unless you fix the problem areas and get them back on schedule. You'll want to engage the problem areas just long enough to get them unstuck, then return to the high level view to see the *whole* Current Picture. This time, you might notice problems emerging in other areas, so you'll engage your energy there for a time, just long enough to get them unstuck. You repeat this cycle until the End State is met.

Let's apply this concept on a personal level.

Your Life Vision statement and the movie in your Reality Show is your End State.

Given your End State, what is your Current Picture? Is it headed toward your End State?

For example, examine your health, mindset, relationships, communication, habits, and behaviors. Are they aligned toward your End State? If any one of these areas is out of whack, then your Current Picture is not heading toward your End State. You'll want to commit time and energy on the problem areas without getting so stuck there and neglect the other areas.

People struggle with success when they don't have a clear vision for their End State, can't see the Current Picture correctly, focus too much on certain problems while neglecting others, or get pulled into the *wrong* problems.

You can do everything right, but if you engage in the *wrong* problems, you will struggle.

People tend to get pulled into problems they're comfortable with addressing, and overlook the uncomfortable problems. These problems fester and become ongoing blind spots.

This phenomenon happens at work and in personal life.

Let's say you're an engineer who was just assigned as a project manager. You may be inclined to focus on engineering details as opposed to unfamiliar things like managing people, communicating across the board, watching the schedule, and minding the financials.

In your personal life, you might get wrapped up in social media instead of minding your health, talking to your spouse, or reading books.

The third part of strategy is the plan for how you expect to achieve the End State.

For example, let's say you want to become a medical doctor. What kind of medical doctor? Where? For whom? Get clear on your End State. If you're not sure, do research. Ask questions from mentors. Then make sure whatever you choose is aligned with the values and vision you set for yourself in your Reality Show. If through discovery learning you realize you need to update your Reality Show to support your End State, that's ok.

Next, come up with your plan on how to get there. It will likely include education, financial support, and how you'll maintain balance in your life. You'll want to discuss this plan with mentors and coaches to ensure you're not overlooking anything.

With all that said, you do *not* need a perfect plan. While plans are important, don't spend too much time and energy on this. Plans rarely survive life intact, so you need to be flexible. You just need enough of a sound plan to put you on the path. As you continually assess your Current Picture, you'll adjust your plans accordingly. Your plans, and the ultimate path to your End State, will very likely change over time. You can pretty much count on that.

We'll talk much more about strategy development and implementation in the LEADERSHIP series.

For now, it's important to understand that strategy isn't just for generals or big shot business leaders. Strategy is for you.

28 SEEK FIRST TO CONSOLE AND UNDERSTAND

I remember when my stepmother was dying from cancer, suffering through terrible pain, unable to walk, go outside, feed or bathe herself, she was more concerned about *my* migraine headaches than she was her own pain or impending premature death. She was more concerned about *my* stress in dealing with her illness while I was simultaneously preparing for my military deployment to Afghanistan. She consoled me, told me I was strong, and assured me I would get through this. Her example of seeking to console and understand others, even when she was in the clutch of a painful death, and not seeking to be consoled or understood herself, is the most powerful experience of my life.

There's a famous prayer from St. Francis that says, "Oh Divine Master, Grant that I may not so much seek to be consoled as to console, or to be understood as to understand." A famous quote from leadership expert Stephen Covey is, "Seek first to understand, then to be understood." The wisdom of these words are powerful. They can completely alter your life, and alter the lives of others for the better.

I heard this wisdom before but for whatever reason did not apply it very well. I was too caught up in my own issues and worries to put much energy into consoling or understanding others. Indeed, I had been that way for most of my life.

Apparently when I was three years old I slapped my stepmother in the face pretty hard because I preferred to have the mom I originally had. Growing up I wasn't always very nice to her and seemed to have a lot to complain about. I treated a lot of people like I did my stepmother and wondered why people didn't like me very much.

As my stepmother's illness progressed, she continued to be very polite and understanding of the nurses, even when the care was not very good. Her being polite and understanding, even to the most hardened nurses, seemed to draw a little more compassion out of them and it often worked in her favor. She never acted as though she were "entitled" to care or even to pain management, no matter how badly she felt. I know if I was in her position I would not have been so nice. I would have been pretty crabby.

She had no income except social security disability. She lost her husband (my father) to a heart attack years earlier, and lost her house to foreclosure due to medical expenses. She was in a tiny house that I rented for her because she was utterly penniless. Despite all that, she chose to find joy in a little goldfish. She chose to find joy in sitting by the door at Halloween to watch goblins and ghosts come to the door. She chose to find joy in the times she was not nauseous and could take a few sips of strawberry milkshake. She chose to find joy in hearing about my day at work, listening very carefully, and giving me encouragement.

Maybe her choice to console and understand others didn't save her life, but it did help the quality of her life. It also made a marked impact on others. She was a favorite among the nurses and hospice caretakers. She had a lot of friends and visitors because whatever love they gave her, they received from her threefold. She opened my eyes to my lifelong blindness up to that point of the value of seeking to console and understand others ahead of seeking it for myself.

Sometimes it takes a painful event to wake you up to your own ignorance. As difficult and painful as it was, I am grateful for it. I'm a different person now, much more grateful and understanding than before. At the same time, I'm still a work in progress. I still have a long way to go to be anywhere close to the model my stepmother was for me and others.

Yes, you have pain. Yes, you have disappointments. Yes, you have setbacks. Telling you to "look on the bright side" or "it could be worse" isn't going to help you one bit.

What might help is to consider focusing on others. Consider opening your heart and mind to others to hear their stories. Consider offering consolation for their troubles and congratulations for their triumphs. Consider giving this *gift* because that's exactly what it is, a gift. Giving feels good, and lifts you when you are low.

The second law of the automatic mind will perceive you giving this gift of consolation and understanding to *itself*, even though you're giving it to others. This has a positive and powerful effect on your mindset to help you persevere through your own troubles and achieve your greatest triumphs.

Seeking first to console and understand others is a karmic act, it eventually comes back to you.

29 PROCRASTINATION IS SELF-SABOTAGE

It will probably do me no good to cite the numerous studies showing how procrastinators experience poorer grades and performance than their non-procrastinating peers.

You've probably already heard of studies showing procrastination's ill effects on health and well-being.

You may have heard people brag about how they deliberately procrastinate because they "perform better under pressure," thereby stressing out their teammates who already have most of their work done.

I'm not telling you anything you don't know. Procrastination, in large measure, is not good for you and it's a form of self-sabotage.

There are many reasons why people procrastinate.

Some procrastinate because they have poor impulse control. Looking at cute puppies on social media is far more interesting than working math problems.

Some procrastinate because they subconsciously fear success. Their automatic mind says they don't deserve it so it does things like procrastinate to sabotage your success.

Some procrastinate because the task is uncomfortable or difficult, like Christmas shopping, cleaning the house, or doing taxes. The task can seem too much and overwhelming.

There are two tools you can try to beat procrastination.

The first is the one-minute rule. If there's a task that will take one minute or less to do, then do it *now*. A lot of times when we look at tasks we see one gigantic effort. In actuality, most tasks are series of little tasks.

For example, if your bedroom is cluttered and it seems like too much to clean it up, then break down the effort. Find *one* thing you can do right now that will take you less than a minute to do. Maybe it's putting all your dirty clothes in the laundry room. Maybe it's taking the trash out. Maybe it's making the bed. Maybe it's putting all your scattered change into a jar.

After you do that *one* thing in *one* minute you'll realize, "Gee, that wasn't so hard," and then look for the next one-minute task.

After just a few minutes you can make a big difference in your room. You can make a big difference in your office, your kitchen, your garage, your bathroom, or just about anywhere. One task, one minute, done repeatedly over hours or days can turn an overwhelming project into no big deal at all.

The one minute rule is good because it's only *one* minute. For those of you with short attention spans or who don't like the task at all, one minute is tolerable. Doing the project in one minute bursts is a whole lot easier than trying to do it all at once.

The second tool against procrastination is the Odysseus technique.

In Greek mythology, Odyssesus was the captain of a ship who needed to sail past the Sirens. The Sirens were dangerous beings who lured sailors with their irresistible voices and caused them to shipwreck on the rocks. Odysseus had his men tie him to the mast and swear not to untie him until they were past the Sirens, no matter how much he begged. He also had his men fill their ears with beeswax so they wouldn't hear the Sirens. As they sailed past the Sirens, Odysseus was enchanted by the Siren's sweet melodies. He thrashed about and begged his men to unbind him. The men would not unbind him until they were well beyond and sound of the Sirens and Odysseus had come to his senses. Odysseus's plan to thwart his future, irrational self worked and saved everyone's lives.

The Odysseus technique is where you create conditions now to prevent your future, irrational self from doing what you know you don't want to do.

For example, installing a breathalyzer in your car that prevents you from starting it if your blood alcohol levels are too high, or keeping your cupboards free from sweets and snacks to prevent you from unhealthy eating, or grouping all your social media apps onto a separate page and turning off all notifications to reduce the temptation to constantly check them.

What does this have to do with procrastination?

Often we distract ourselves with things we should not be doing in the first place. So if you apply the Odysseus technique and prevent yourself from doing those things, then you're more likely to stick to what you're supposed to be doing.

30 ✦ FORGIVENESS

Dr. Stephen Marmer is a psychiatrist with a masterful explanation of this difficult subject.

As Dr. Marmer explains it, there are three types of forgiveness. The type you apply depends on the circumstances.

The first type of forgiveness is *Exoneration*.

Exoneration is wiping the slate clean and restoring the relationship to the way it was before. It's usually what we think of when we say *forgiveness*, which is rather limiting. There's more to the definition of forgiveness, as we'll soon cover. Exoneration is not appropriate in every circumstance.

Exoneration *is* appropriate when:

1. The situation was an accident and the person is truly sorry
2. It was a child who didn't understand the hurt they caused
3. The person is truly sorry, takes full responsibility, and promises it won't happen again

In these instances, Exoneration (full forgiveness) is encouraged. To *not* forgive in these circumstances may indicate that you're the one with the problem, not them.

The second type of forgiveness is *Forbearance*.

Forebearance is something along the lines of "forgive but don't forget." The offender makes a partial apology while blaming you for their actions. You may be inclined to become defensive, but resist this temptation. Examine your contribution to the problem (Avoid, Misunderstand, Unapproachable, or Mindless) and apologize for your part.

If you truly bear no responsibility but still want to salvage the relationship, then you exercise Forbearance. In this case you stop dwelling on the offense without holding a grudge, but remain watchful since they may do this sort of thing again. In time, if the behavior is good then Forbearance can eventually become Exoneration.

The third type of forgiveness is Release.

Release is the most challenging form of forgiveness because the offender is not sorry, or only pretends to be sorry.

People who endured child abuse or were badly betrayed by someone they trusted often bear a great deal of hurt from the incident(s). In this case, you really don't want to continue the relationship, nor should you.

Release simply means you choose to no longer define your life by the bad things that happened. You no longer choose to hold on to the bad feelings you have. You no longer preoccupy your mind with the incident(s). You *Release* the negativity.

While Release is challenging to do, it's also important. By continuing to hold on to the negative feelings, you imprison yourself in your *wrong* mind (angry, depressed, fearful). As you know, being in a negative state of mind is self-sabotaging. It inhibits your growth, your happiness, and success.

Second, by continuing to preoccupy yourself with the offense, you continue to allow this person to hurt you. Why would you *let* this person or incident continue hurting you?

Your sense of Fairness and Status will resist because what happened clearly wasn't fair and depending on the circumstances could have been quite demeaning to you.

However, your sense of Autonomy, Optimism, and Love will pull you through.

Autonomy wants to be free from the bondage of the offense and from the negative feelings.

Optimism is cheering for you and sees a brighter future ahead.

Love wants you to be happy and is yearning to set you free.

So you see, you have friends inside your automatic mind who want to help. Let them help. Stop listening to ugly deposits and Inner Critic who are doing you harm.

You don't want to put your happiness on hold waiting for a condition such as an apology or reparations. You don't have time for that.

Your tools for helping you Release are:

1. Your *Reality Show* – Helps reset your automatic programming to replace the ugly movie in your past life with a fantastic movie you truly love.
2. *Ground Control* – Notice the thought or feeling, Breath, Option Item(s).
3. Brain Hygiene (meditation) – Helps you manage your thoughts and clear your mind.

31 GRIT

"Grit" is the new buzzword of the century. What is it really, and do you have it?

Grit is having a "never give up" attitude. It's the polar opposite of complacent or helpless.

Now, just because you give up on something doesn't necessarily mean you're gritless.

If you give up on something that's truly not in your heart or part of your values, that's understandable.

Maybe you tried out for a sports team, gave it a real go, and realized it just wasn't your thing.

Another reason to give something up is when you have too many things going on and you need to prioritize.

For example, if you're taking ballet classes, studying for your master's degree, working a full time job, writing a book, and raising several kids, you might be stretching yourself thin. Hopefully you wouldn't give up on the kids, but you just might put the ballet or the book writing on the back burner until you get your master's degree done. Or maybe you realize the value of the master's degree isn't what you thought so you drop out of school to enjoy your ballet and book writing more fully. That's ok.

Now, if you give up on something you *really* want to do and has value to you, but then you realize it's hard or extremely challenging, then that's another story.

Let me tell you something right now. Something being hard or challenging is *not* a reason to give up. That is tantamount to declaring "helpless." You are *not* helpless.

When something is hard or challenging, that's the time to bear down and dig in more. That's the time to focus your energy and prioritize your efforts. That's the time to discipline yourself and manage your time.

Wake up earlier. Think more. Get help. Find mentors. Do what you have to do, but do not give up.

Now, it does help to have a real interest in what you want to do. However, sometimes the thing you want to do may have some boring parts.

For example, let's say you want to learn a new language. It can be really boring at first, memorizing all the vocabulary and rules. Once you get through it, it gets easier.

Or let's say you want to learn to sail. There's a lot of stuff you need to learn in a classroom before you ever get in a sailboat. Are you going to give up your dream of sailing just because the class is boring? I sure hope not.

It's human nature for new interests to be fleeting. If you really and truly lose interest in your goal than that's understandable, so long as you didn't lose interest just because something got difficult or boring. If your parents pushed you through when times were tough, be grateful for that. If they let you quit at the slightest hint of difficulty, I'm sorry to say they did not do you a favor. You'll have to acquire your grit on your own, and while it's hard, it's doable.

When your goal is truly interesting and you can push past the boring and difficult parts, then it very well could become a passion. Keeping your curiosity high and not becoming complacent will help you continually improve. Continually trying new things, or experiencing familiar things in new ways, helps to refine your craft. It's what I call "pulling the string."

Part of having grit is being an optimist. Optimists look for specific causes of difficulties and assume they're fixable. They look to fix or get past the problem and keep going.

Pessimists assume causes of difficulty are pervasive and permanent, meaning they're not fixable. They use that as an excuse to give up.

Optimists enjoy better success and outcomes in life. They also tend to be grittier than their pessimistic counterparts.

Optimists know if they put in enough *effort* and *believe*, they will have success.

If you tend to be a pessimist or quit things when they become difficult, don't beat yourself up.

Instead, observe any negative self-talk and the resulting behavior. *I am…* and *I can…* are powerful words to help replace your negative self-talk. Reframe the situation into more positive terms. Take things in smaller steps. You'll get better in time.

32 WHEN THINGS GET TOUGH, *LEAN* INTO IT

The most common response to stressful situations is to tense up and worry. This is the worst thing you can do.

When you tense up and worry, you release harmful stress hormones impairing your sleep, energy, clear thinking, and communication. They also cause inflammation, weight gain, and impair your immune system. In short, stress hormones don't help you. The only thing they help you do is fall apart. Left unchecked, they will ultimately cause your demise. We'll talk more about this phenomenon in the SELF-CARE series.

In the meantime, there are three steps to help you avoid the "tense up and worry" trap.

The first is to not *awfulize* the situation.

Awfulizing is going on and on about how awful the situation is. Awfulizing puts you in a helpless mindset, and that's the last thing you need.

I realize that's very hard to do when your loved one was killed, you lost your job, your house was foreclosed, or some other very difficult situation. I'm not saying don't grieve. These are real losses that are truly painful. What I *am* saying is to not say things like "this should never happen" or "this is worst thing in my life" or "I can't take this." That is *awfulizing*.

Instead, admit you're sad or angry, because that's the truth, then say something such as, "I'm going to get through this. I will *learn* from this challenge. I will be *better* than before."

Now is a great time to call upon your good friend *Optimism*. We introduced you to her in the NEURO-SCIENCE series. She is eager to help when things get tough. Don't push her aside. Let her help. Just remember not to become complacent.

The second step is to think about a time when you experienced "good" stress. For example, moving into a new house. Starting a new job you're excited about. Getting married. Taking a vacation. Playing in the championship game. How did that "good" stress make you feel?

Did you feel energized by the challenge? Do you remember how excited you felt?

Recall those feelings and then try to apply that *same* mindset to your "bad" stress challenge. By bringing the same positive energy to the bad stress, you can actually improve your ability to get through with greater ease.

The third step is Brain Hygiene. You may not want to do this because your mind is running fast, or you *think* you can't sit still for a few minutes. That is all the more reason to do it.

Brain Hygiene is not about "forcing" you to calm down or be happy. It's about training your brain to not get fixated on things without your consent.

When you find you can't stop thinking about something, or can't stop worrying, that's your mind out of control. An "out of control" mind isn't good. When your mind is out of control, your thoughts and emotions go straight to the badlands and you'll surely tense up and worry.

In summary, the three step process to deal with your "bad" stress is:

1. Don't awfulize. Doing so puts you in a helpless mindset. Resolve to learn from the challenge and be even *better* than before. Open your heart to Optimism and let her help.

2. Remember your "good stress" energy and excitement and apply that *same* level of energy to your "bad stress." You can still admit you're sad or angry, because that's true. You can still grieve. What's different is you choose to give this "bad stress" the same positive energy as you would "good stress." It will help you get through it better.

3. Brain Hygiene daily. It'll help you get control of your mind, which is *crucial*. A few minutes a day, practiced consistently, is one of the best investments of your time, *ever*.

Stress is a part of life. If you're going through college and working at the same time, you know stress.

If you're a parent, you know stress.

If you have a job with bills to pay, you know stress.

If you have health challenges, you know stress.

If you have all of these (and some people do) you *know* stress.

These stressors are not going away. You can either let them harm you, or you can manage how you react to them and become this amazing superhuman marvel of calm, positive, energetic achievement. I sincerely hope you choose the latter.

Managing your response to stress is so important that you'll see this topic again in both the LEADERSHIP and SELF-CARE series.

33 DON'T APOLOGIZE FOR WINNING

For tens of thousands of years, humans lived communally. Very little was owned individually. Just about everything was shared. If someone came upon an abundance of anything it was shared with the whole family or tribe. It's still that way in many parts of the world today.

In fact, in many modern cultures and religions, if you seek more wealth for yourself, or if you come upon wealth and don't share it willingly with others, then you're a selfish, no good, rotten person. Who wants to be *that*?

If you grew up in an interdependent family, tribe, or community, you may find it very difficult to achieve the level of success you secretly desire in your heart. In fact, the idea of achieving wealth, health, or greatness of any kind may actually strike fear in you. Why?

Because of tens of thousands of years of genetic programming to share everything, and an upbringing that insisted you were wrong, mean or selfish if you didn't follow the norm.

If this describes you even just a little bit, there will be turbulence ahead.

Your life is changing, and that's the point.

You don't want status quo any more. Nor should you apologize for wanting to be your best self or wanting more in life without working so darn hard all the time.

On a race track, does a lead runner say, "Oh, I'm way ahead of the others. Maybe I should slow down and let the others catch up so they don't feel so bad." Or after winning the gold medal, do they chop it up into little pieces and share it with everyone? Of course not.

Assuming the runner didn't cheat, we can safely assume the runner won fairly.

We celebrate winners. It feels good to be a winner.

Will there be people who are jealous of winners or try to sabotage their success? Of course. Should that stop anyone from pursing more wins? Absolutely not.

Nor should it stop *you* from winning again and again.

If you become more successful than your friends, family, tribe, community members, or whatever, don't you dare apologize for it.

Don't hold yourself back to make others feel "better" about themselves. That's *their* problem, not yours. Don't own their problems.

If anyone threatens you in any way because you are pursuing your vision, ideal life, and being your best self, that is a huge red flag you may need to seriously re-assess your relationship with that person or group.

It doesn't matter if it's your parents, siblings, other close family, friends from grade school, spouse, religion, tribe, community, employer, or any organization. Relationships in life come and go. Relationships can help you grow, or hold you back.

Choose to nurture relationships that help you grow, and distance yourself from those holding you back.

I realize this could be a sensitive matter for you. Some of these relationships you cannot simply sever. You'll have to learn to manage them somehow.

Now, I assume you're not doing anything illegal or needlessly hurting others. That wouldn't be good and I certainly don't advocate it. Please keep that in mind as I continue.

Your genetic programming, your upbringing, and your current relationships can contribute to *your fear* of leading, standing out, or being successful. That is something to be *aware of.* It is not something to *blame.* Remember, once you start blaming, you automatically fail.

I used to feel guilty for having money or nice things, which was actually quite modest. Then I remembered how extremely hard I worked for it and didn't feel so bad about having it. Then family or friends would need financial help and I'd lose a substantial amount of net worth trying to help them with their never-ending problems. This went on for many years until I firmly decided not to be a prisoner of this "guilty" mindset any longer. I stopped helping these people and a crisis in their lives ensued. I was "blamed" for their crisis. They became angry with me and severed the relationship. I never heard from them again. Some of these people were close to me, but I had to let them go. Since I did, I've become more successful, less resentful, and a whole lot happier. I no longer feel guilty for my success, nice things, good health, working less, and enjoying life more.

Do I still contribute to charity and support causes I care about? Of course. But I no longer feel obligated out of guilt to do so.

What's more is I've become an inspiring role model for others to step out of their comofort zones, pursue their dreams, and lead. When others make that choice, more inspiring role models and leaders are created. So you actually do the world more good than you do by staying in you safe space and not pursuing your dreams.

34 FEAR, AND THE SABOTAGE ALLIANCE

You created your Reality Show to help manifest your Life Vision. You're using Ground Control to monitor your thoughts and feelings. You changed many habits for the better and are more mindful in your communication. This is all fantastic.

You may be focused on your goals right now, and that's a good thing. There's just one important matter to warn you about.

Sometimes when you're focused on achieving or having something, there's a *fear* of not obtaining it.

Fear can be a powerful motivator, but at a *cost*.

You see, fear is like the devil; he's more than happy to give you what you want so long as you give your soul to him.

What in the world does *that* mean?

It means that while fear gives you motivation, focus, and drive toward your goals, it also poisons everything along the way, thereby sabotaging yourself.

If you let fear help you achieve, then you'll either do so at the cost of your relationships, health, or other significant area of your life; or, fear will simply sabotage you so that you *don't* achieve what you hoped for. Let me explain.

Fear is in secret alliance with *Inner Critic* and ugly lie deposits to "protect" you. The alliance is giving you what you *really* want, which is *protection*, not the thing you're hoping for. Of course, you don't actually need or want this protection, but your automatic programming says it *does*. So the the alliance is happy to sabotage you for your own "good."

Fear is really bad news. It gives off a very negative frequency vibration impacting your thinking, emoting, speaking, gesturing, and behaving in icky ways.

Ideally we don't want to be fearful, but we are. Judging yourself or putting yourself down for being afraid only makes things worse.

It's better to *admit* you're afraid. Noticing and admitting your fear is the first step. What do you think the second step is?

If you said, "take a deep breath," you're right.

While taking that breath, remember not to judge or justify or engage the fear. All you're doing is *noticing* your fear and taking a deep breath. That is all.

As you can tell, these are the first two steps in *Ground Control*. Now you're certainly welcome to use one or more of the six options of *Ground Control*, but fear is such a negative emotion with an extremely low frequency vibration, it requires its *own* set of options.

The option you choose will depend upon the situation.

OPTION 1 is *Decide*. "I'm scared to death and I'm doing it anyway!"

Jumping out of an airplane for the first time is a great example of this.

OPTION 2 is *Research*. "Can I find other ways?" Or, "What are the most likely consequences?"

Let's say you're buying a house for the first time. If you're fearful of taking this leap, then researching other ways to invest and live may give you more choices. You can learn more about the risks and benefits of home ownership to help you feel less fearful about your decision. Just remember to not get stuck in analysis paralysis.

OPTION 3 is *Agnosticism*. In this context, *Agnosticism* means you choose to be happy either way. Sure you'll be disappointed if things don't go your way, but you'll recover.

Everything will be just fine, there will be other opportunities, and you're going to enjoy the journey and be happy anyway. This doesn't mean you're complacent or not driven. It means you're making the decision to *love* your life no matter what.

Courage is *not* the absence of fear.

Courage is doing what you know you must do *despite* your fear.

You may be scared out of your mind, and that's ok.

It's ok to have fear and acknowledge it. Ignoring it or wishing it away will only make it worse. So just go ahead acknowledge it. That's what's true and rational.

What's *not* ok is letting fear control you.

It's *not* ok to give into fear and let it have its way. That's like giving your soul to the devil. He will give you what you want (protection) but the outcome will not be pretty.

35 SOUNDBITE SOLUTION TEMPTATIONS AND YOUR GROWTH JOURNEY

Have you ever seen those internet ads that say something like: "Lose weight by not eating this one thing," "Attract the man/woman of your dreams by doing this," or "Become wildly wealthy by doing these three things"?

We want a solution so badly to our health, relationships, career or financial problems we're willing to fall for these ads that often do more to empty your wallet than to help you with your problems.

I'm sorry to tell you there's no silver bullet or just "three things" that will help you with most of the issues you're having in life. The proof is the size of the personal development industry. It's an eleven-billion-dollar industry and growing. Why?

Because good people, like you and me, are tired of the status quo. We're tired of believing what traditional authorities have to say about these matters. We want enlightenment to help us overcome and achieve. We want outside-of-the-box thinking. We want things to be simpler and easier. We're even willing to click on an ad with a ridiculous claim just to explore what the latest thinking is on the subject. We're willing to spend a lot of money to get it.

There's two things I have to say about all that. The first is I encourage you to explore and learn from others. I hope you continue building upon what you learn here. There's a lot of great stuff out there. With that said...

Be wary of expensive products or programs that insist you must go into substantial debt in order to benefit. I personally think these people are unethical.

What's worse is they'll have testimonials of people who "couldn't afford it" but emptied their life savings, took out a loan, or other risky measure in order to "invest" in themselves. They are now millionaires and "so glad" they took the risk.

Notice these companies will not tell you the percentage of people who actually "make it" but I will be happy to tell you. It's a very, very, *very* small number.

I know because I was one of those people who spent a lot of money on a promise and a dream and ended up losing badly. Worse, I did it more than once. How stupid is that? Yes, some do make it, but most do not.

Listen, I have two college degrees, am a retired USMC lieutenant colonel, and hold all sorts of other credentials to show how "smart" I am. The point is that "smart" people are victims of these scams too. I'm not saying don't do it. I'm saying, be skeptical and cautious of those who hold no hesitation about cleaning out your bank account.

I spent a lifetime test driving or even immersing myself in all sorts of personal development efforts. My whole point of writing these books is to help prevent you from making the same mistakes I did, and to grow and learn a whole lot faster than I did, because I did it the hard way. I don't want you to do it the hard way. It's much better to learn this stuff in a few months as opposed to decades.

Soundbite solutions usually don't last very long. That's because solutions to your struggle areas (weight/health/fitness/career/relationships/money/education/finances/etc.) really do require a *comprehensive* approach. That approach includes understanding your automatic mind, awareness of your thoughts and emotions, practicing good communication, implementing good habits (and eliminating the bad ones), continuous learning (never think you know everything), and striving to be a leader.

Yes, I said *leader.*

I'm not talking about being number one or being in charge of other people, although leadership can and often does include that.

I'm talking about being in charge of *yourself.* I'm talking about *leading yourself.*

When you learn to lead yourself well, you'll find that being number one or leading other people is a whole lot easier. In fact, I hope you consider striving to be number one or leading others. There's a shortage of great leaders, so much it's a crisis.

We desperately need good leaders. Now if that's not your calling, that's ok. However, to be your best self and achieve what you want in life, you must learn to lead *yourself.*

This next series is totally dedicated to the subject of LEADERSHIP. As the WISDOM series comes to a close, I hope you'll strive to continue your growth in wisdom—and to share your wisdom with others.

SUMMARY OF THE WISDOM SERIES

Congratulations! You've finished the WISDOM Series.

The WISDOM Series built upon the foundational learning from volume one. We revisited certain concepts, expanded upon them, and introduced some new concepts. We further defined and emphasized rational thinking, and how it can help you in your emoting, communicating, and behaving. There was powerful content in this series that if applied to your life, will align your Current State with your End State, no matter what your End State is.

To help remind you of key concepts, you may wish to print this summary and retain it for yoru records. It's a good idea to review it from time to time to help keep you on the right path.

Others are watching; you affect others wth everything you say and do. Perfection is not required.

Love is not a feeling but a conscious decision. It's a choice, not something that just happens.

Class is 100% about your *character*, not your wealth.

How you present yourself is your personal brand. Your morality is your reputation.

THINK before communicating: True, Helpful, Inspiring, Necessary, Kind. Set the example.

Being "right" is not important. Stop wasting energy on it or sabotaging your relationships over it.

Rigidity and chaos are extremes to avoid. Find the right place in the middle.

Navigate paradox with the "and" technique. Avoid "either/or" and consider both are right.

Manage commitments; learn to say no. Seek purpose over pleasure for long term happiness.

Don't assume you see the obvious. Ask questions and challenge your assumptions.

Analysis paralysis is a form of procrastination. Listening has limits. You can't please everyone.

Replace "should" and "must" with "want" and "could."

Avoid victim mindset and embrace victor mindset. Nurture your past victim to join you as victor.

Avoid helpless mindset. Leads to suffering, depression, self sabotaging behaviors.

Recognized oversensitized SCARF elements and resolve to work on them.

Use the Miracle Question to visualize yourself healed from oversensitized SCARF element.

Avoid jumping to conclusions about other's thinking, intent, or character.

If others judge you unfairly, be nice anyway. Otherwise you will reinforce their judgment.

Humility takes self confidence. Admit mistakes, give credit, flexible, don't bully, be respectful.

You can retain values, boundaries, dignity, and be humble at the same time. Don't be a martyr.

Machines are not humble. Think short term. Don't treat others as objects.

Avoid poisonous perfectionism; it's nonproductive; a form of fear of failure or rejection.

Embrace noteworthy perfectionisms; stretch goals; continuous improvement.

Practice brain hygiene with meditation, mindfulness, yoga, tai chi, being "present" activities.

Don't dwell in the past or place blame.

Nobody owes you anything. It's irrational. Avoid entitled attitude. Be grateful.

Treating others like objects, or not doing what you should is self betrayal.

Treating yourself like an object = locking up emotions in the Super Max.

Choose to take pride in everything you do, even the small, boring, or unpleasant things.

Inner Critic is *not* your friend. Makes you feel terrible about yourself. Discourages you.

Secret Option Six: "I am love;" reject competition; embrace love energy of the soul.

Three elements of the automatic mind: Deposits, Toddler, Inner Critic.

Use Reality Show to address Deposits.

Embrace and love Toddler; ask for its help; join you on journey.

Employ Secret Option Six against Inner Critic

Failure is ok when you learn; learning isn't failing; not trying is failing.

Strategy: End State, Current Picture, and plan. Plans will almost always change.

End State: Life Vision/Realtiy Show.

Current Picture: habits, behaviors, relationships, health leading to End State.

Poor impulse control and fear are forms of procrastination.

Do one-minute tasks; apply Odysseus technique to push past procrastination.

Forgiveness: Exoneration, Forebearance, Release.

Exoneration: person is truly sorry, or a child; restore relationship as before.

Forebearance: partial apology; let go of grudge but maintain watchfulness.

Release: they're not sorry, but you need to let go for your own sake, not theirs.

Grit: don't give up because it's hard; develop passion; optimism; effort is worth it.

Avoid awfulizing. Decide to learn and be better than before.

Fear allies itself with Inner Critic and ugly lie deposits to "protect" you and keep you "safe."

Be wary of any self-improvement program encouraging you to go into unsafe debt. Bad news.

PART 2
THE LEADERSHIP SERIES

INTRODUCING GEMS

The GEMS model of leadership is the synthesis of my thirty years of leadership training and development in the United States Marine Corps, a master's degree in leadership, a certification with John Maxwell, completion of several high level civilian leadership programs, and scores of courses and books on the subject.

I have led, mentored, and coached thousands of people.

I am a subject matter expert on leadership.

Simultaneously, I continue to learn every day because no true leader will ever say they know it all. It's a good idea to be skeptical of anyone who says they know everything about anything.

I like to use acronyms because they help people remember important points. GEMS is easy to remember, representing four maxims with deep meaning. It's much easier than many other numerous laws, principles, traits, or rules out there. I'll introduce each maxim in this lesson and then expand upon them in upcoming lessons.

The first letter is "G." It stands for *Get things done.*

Get things done is surprisingly absent from many other concepts put forth by experts on leadership. I think it's because *Get things done* is assumed. My position is that *Get things done* cannot, and must not, be assumed. *Get things done* is a key part of leadership. It's remarkable to me this key concept is overlooked so often. I have a lot to say on the subject, so there are several lessons dedicated to this maxim.

The second letter is "E." It stands for *Empower.*

You *Empower* yourself and you *Empower* others. This concept isn't new, but it summarizes a long list of other attributes and techniques. If you understand *Empowerment* you'll understand a great deal. There's no need to memorize a lengthy list of rules, concepts, theories, and such. It'll come to you naturally. There are several lessons dedicated to this maxim.

The third letter is "M." It stands for *Model.*

Remember when we introduced the concept of being a role model in the WISDOM series? As promised, we'll expand upon this subject in the LEADERSHIP series.

The fourth letters is "S." It stands for *Stretch.*

This word also embodies a host of concepts and principles. None of them are new, but the bundling of them into this one, all-encompassing word *is* new. Again, the purpose is to make things easier for you. If you understand the whole concept of *Stretch,* you'll understand a tremendous amount. I realize it may not make a lot of sense right now, but it will later. There are several lessons dedicated to this maxim.

> G E M S
> *Get thing done*
> *Empower*
> *Model*
> *Stretch*

If you don't memorize a single acronym in these books, do memorize GEMS.

If you're a parent, teacher, coach, supervisor, front line manager, police officer, fire chief, project manager, director, mayor, senator, lead chef, business owner, or any position leading people in any capacity, you'll benefit tremendously by memorizing GEMS, understanding the maxims, embodying the maxims, and living them to the best of your ability.

If you don't lead people in *any* way, you'll still want to employ GEMS in your personal life because GEMS will help you to *lead yourself.*

It'll be difficult for you to achieve your vision, ideal life, and goals if you don't learn to master leading yourself.

With that said, I do hope you choose to someday become "number one" in a field of your choosing, or to lead other people.

There are numerous leaders in name only and few true, authentic leaders.

If every "leader" read and applied the lesson of this series, maybe that would change.

In the meantime, let's focus on you and setting you up for leadership success.

2 GET THINGS DONE

At the end of the day, leadership of yourself or others is about getting things done.

Everything that follows (*Empower, Model,* and *Stretch*) supports *Get things done.*

Getting things done isn't simple. If it was easy, we'd have no problem with procrastination. Businesses and governments would never fall behind schedule or have cost overruns on major projects. Our kids' rooms would be nice and tidy, and their homework completed on time.

Of course, this is rarely the case.

There are several lessons on the topic of *Get things done.* We'll start off easy, then progress with more challenging concepts as we go along.

The first concept to introduce is the environment where *Get things done* thrives. Ideally, *Get things done* works best when the environment is neither too rigid nor too chaotic.

Let's start with what happens when the environment is too rigid.

Have you ever been in a place with a lot of strict rules and processes? It could be a factory, government organization, or even your own family. Rigid organizations leave little room for creativity, flexibility, or innovation. They're often very resistant to change. An organization like this is efficient at getting things done as long as circumstances never change.

The problem is that circumstances often *do* change. Market conditions, new laws, weather, new inventions, lawsuits, elections, and medical conditions are just a sampling of the large number of variables in the world.

Rigid organizations, and people, resist change. As the world changes, they're slow to adapt. As a result, they become ineffective, inefficient, or even irrelevant.

Often, bad outcomes happen because of failure to adapt in a timely manner. This is not an ideal environment to *Get things done.*

On the other end of the spectrum is chaos.

Have you ever been in place with no rules or processes? This could be a business, non-profit, state in anarchy, or again, your own family.

On the one hand, there's a high degree of flexibility. Chaotic organizations can often adapt quickly to changing circumstances. This is good for *Get things done.*

The problem is that while some things happen quickly, other efforts get caught in a quagmire. Often, chaotic organizations struggle to *Get things done* because of lack of structure and organization. *Get things done* is unpredictable and inconsistent. This is not ideal either.

The ideal environment to *Get things done* is where there is just the right amount of structure and organization to keep things consistent and predictable, with the right amount of flexibility to take advantage of opportunities or adapt to changing circumstances.

This works not only in organizations and families, it works in your personal life too.

If you have the *right* habits and routines (structure) you'll be more productive.

However, if you are too inflexible with certain habits and routines, even if they're good for you, then you may miss out on important opportunities or find yourself unable to handle a setback as smoothly as you'd like.

If you don't have good habits and routines then you'll be less productive. You might be more flexible to changing conditions like having to move, or taking on a new job, but if you don't maintain a certain degree of good structure then that flexibility won't get you far. You won't get as much accomplished as you'd like.

To become your best self, you'll want to optimize *Get things done.*

In order to lead yourself optimally, you'll want to find the sweet spot between rigidity and chaos, with just the right amount of structure and flexibility, to *Get things done.*

You may find yourself having to adjust between more structure and more flexibility. That's normal. When life is stable you can add more structure. When life throws you curve balls then you'll need more flexibility.

What about leading others?

Again, you'll want to find the right spot between strictness and leniency, and adjust between the two as the situation demands (within reason, be careful with inconsistentcy).

With that said, you're dealing with human beings so to optimize *Get things done* you'll need good skills in *Empower, Model,* and *Stretch.* We'll cover these maxims in detail later in this series.

For now, we'll continue the topic of *Get things done.*

3 PRIORITIZING WHAT YOU GET DONE

I have a different philosophy on prioritizing tasks than what some of my peers have popularized as conventional wisdom.

Conventional wisdom tells us to hold off on tackling unimportant and non-urgent tasks until we complete important and urgent tasks first.

Many people follow this model thinking they're doing a great job of prioritizing their work, then wonder why they fall further and further behind.

It's no surprise to me because I believe this model actually *causes* work to pile up. While I deeply admire many of my peers, I respectfully disagree on some matters.

I do not believe in *always* tackling important or urgent tasks first, with the exception of true emergencies like life or death matters.

The model I favor is the *cook-in-the-kitchen*. It doesn't offer a neat matrix or sequence of doing things. Instead, it's organic, fluid, and intuitive.

Think of a cook or chef putting out scores of meals in an hour. Every single meal has to be right. There's no room for mistakes on orders.

Cooks clean counters, put the spices away, and pull the meat out of the fridge, all while heading toward the grill to flip eggs. They take care of non-urgent and unimportant tasks *on their way* to handling the important task, which is cooking food on the grill. They're constantly in motion and have an innate sense of timing.

Imagine if the cook said, "Wiping the counters and putting spices away is not urgent or important right now. What's important is managing the grill, and what's urgent is flipping the eggs."

Fair enough. You know what would happen?

The kitchen would become such a mess that pretty soon the cook would fall behind in getting the meals out, or the meals will suffer in quality. Not good.

How do you apply this in your personal life or in business?

Any task, regardless of whether it's important, unimportant, urgent, or non-urgent taking less than one minute to do, especially if you can do it while on your way to a higher priority task, do it *now*.

You'll be surprised how many tasks take you only a few seconds to do. You'll be surprised at how much work you get done.

You might feel like you're expending more energy, and you are.

You're moving quickly from one task to another. Your mind is constantly scanning for opportunities to knock out a task, all while remaining mindful of the time and of your primary purpose. So while you're expending more energy, you're getting a lot more done. You'll feel much better about yourself and have more free time too.

For tasks taking longer than one minute, consider breaking them down into one minute tasks. Then tackle them one by one while you're accomplishing other more important or urgent tasks.

An example is cleaning your room or office. You don't have to do the whole thing at once. Just put your clothes in the laundry hamper while your computer boots up, or file some papers away at the office while you're on hold for a call.

I realize we mentioned this concept once before as a method to overcome procrastination. Well here it is again, and it's a critical part of *Get things done.*

For tasks that don't lend themselves to breaking down like that, like writing an essay or holding a collaboration meeting, estimate the time and put it on your calendar. Then commit yourself to your own appointment, and do your best to accomplish the task in the time allotted.

When all that's left are lengthy tasks, then yes, you'll want to tackle the urgent and important tasks first. For example, prioritizing writing your college essay over posting your entire vacation to Disneyland on social media is probably a good idea.

You see how this model does not lend itself to numerically ordering tasks or placing them into quadrants? Use your instincts and good judgment to *Get things done* as opposed to overthinking about what you should do.

Will you sometimes make a boo boo and burn the potatoes or drop the eggs on the floor?

Of course. Just as you might skid into a meeting a few seconds late or forget to pay the utility bill. Don't worry. You'll recover from that a lot more easily than you will from a mountain of "to do" items.

4 GET THINGS DONE AND END STATE

In the WISDOM Series, we introduced the concept of the End State and how it's a critical part of having a strategy.

End State plays an important role in *Get things done*. We'll discuss how in this lesson.

The vision of how you want everything to end is the *End State*. It can also be viewed as a collection of goals you want to achieve by a certain time.

An End State can be as simple as, "I want my hair to look like the person in this picture in two hours." Or it can be as grand as, "I want the dam built in compliance with regulations, safely, under $30M, within five years."

Declaring an End State is critical in helping you to *Get things done*.

It's a lot like "getting to the point." Instead of rambling on and on, just say or show what you want, then figure out how to get there.

People who articulate an End State for themselves are more likely to get the outcome they want.

Leaders who articulate an End State for their team or organization are more likely to get the outcome they want.

If you go to the hair stylist and said, "Please cut a little bit from the back, shave the sides but not all the way, color it dark brown with some blond highlights at the forehead, and…" I promise you, it will not end like you envisioned.

If you go to your organization and said, "Please mobilize fifteen dozers to the river, order three tons of #6 rebar, start filling out the environmental documents…" I'm certain you will get a lot of very frustrated people, and it will definitely not end well.

As a leader of yourself and others, concern yourself first about the *what*. Once you have the *what* firmly established, then concern yourself with the *how*.

For example, "We want to land a human on Mars and bring him back to Earth safely in the next five years with a budget of $3 billion dollars." Or, "I want to ride my own Harley Davidson motorcycle across the country in two weeks for under $5,000 before the end of the year."

If your *what* is something you've never done before, talking to experts can help you determine if your End State is realistic, or if you should consider adjusting it.

For example, experts on space travel say it's impossible with today's technology to make a trip to Mars and back within five years. They recommend tripling the time to fifteen years. Oh, and you probably better increase the budget to $15 billion. $3 billion won't even buy the rocket. ok, fair enough.

How about the motorcycle trip?

Your motorcycle-owning friends say you'll need at least $20,000 to buy a used Harley Davidson motorcycle, and unless you plan to sleep on the side of the rode and live off the land, hotel costs and food will cost at least $2,000. Finally, they may strongly suggest you plan your trip for summer instead of waiting until the end of the year, which is winter in most parts of the world.

When your End State impacts stakeholders like your kids, spouse, work team, employees, or students, it's a good idea to include them in the discussion and consider their input.

Also, when other people are going to execute the *how*, it's a good idea to include their input on *how* to get to the End State.

Sometimes asking for input is not always possible, like when the situation is an emergency or the matter is being dictated from above your level. That's not ideal, but sometimes it happens. Aside from that, you'll get much better results if you take the time to include others in the conversation and genuinely consider their input. They'll also respect you much more than if you dictate everything.

Remember, dictators activate resentment and all the negative neurochemistry that goes with it. It's like killing someone slowly with poison. That is not a happy ending.

Patient, authentic, empowering leaders like you activate the cooperative spirit and positive neurochemistry that goes with it. It's like growing ever stronger and vibrant with nutrients. *This* is the happy ending you want.

5 THE FIVE PARTS OF AN END STATE

In this lesson, we're going to unpack End State into its parts. An End State isn't quite complete without these parts addressed.

1. Scope: This is the big *what?* For example, "build a hotel" or "jump out of an airplane" or "bake a cake."

2. Quality: This is high level guidance on the *how.* For example, "in compliance with regulations" or "safely" or "without making a mess."

3. Cost: Ideally, how much do you want to spend to achieve your End State? You may not know right away, but you probably have an idea already of your budget. If research reveals the End State you envisioned will exceed your budget, then you may want to revise your End State. Sometimes there's no cost, or the cost is less than you envisioned. In that case, you can make your End State even more ambitious, if you want to.

4. Schedule: By what date or time do you want to achieve your End State? By next year, next month, the next hour?

5. Who: These are the people who stand to benefit or lose from your End State. These people are *stakeholders*. Rarely are you the only stakeholder in any End State vision of yours. Your End State will often include a number of stakeholders such as your family, friends, co-workers, teammates, employees, and so on. For example, if your End State includes "Enroll the kids in school…" then your kids are definitely stakeholders. Or, "Join the military" will include your spouse if you're married, or your parents if they already saved up for your college but now you're not going. Or, "Launch the new product" will certainly include your co-workers or employees.

A lot of times we don't want to think about or include stakeholders in our End State because we fear we'll lose control; or, we fear we'll spend too much time talking about it instead of getting things done; or, we feel they may object. These are understandable concerns.

The trouble is we often let our fears, as opposed to our better selves, dictate our actions. We become entrenched in what we want done instead of letting others have input and sincerely hearing them out.

When you deny stakeholders input, you trigger the yucky neurochemistry of resentment and disappointment. You may get that wonderful little dopamine hit in your brain of immediate gratification, but I promise, you *will* pay for it later, one way or another. So be careful about any approach that doesn't include giving a sincere ear to what your stakeholders have to say.

We'll have more to say about communicating with stakeholders later in this series. For now, it's important to understand that *Who* is every bit as important as *Scope*, *Quality*, *Cost*, and *Schedule* when it comes to your End State.

When you and everyone involved knows these five parts, you're much more likely to obtain the End State you envisioned than without these parts defined.

If you're working on a project and the End State is a long way off, it's a good idea to frequently remind yourself and your team of *Scope*, *Quality*, *Cost*, *Schedule*, and *Who*.

If you're leading a team executing the work to get to the *End State*, you definitely want to remind them of these five parts fairly regularly.

With that said, it's not ok to tell them *how* to do their jobs.

You can recommend, but don't bully them into doing things your way. Let them do things their way so long as the five parts are met and will meet the *End State*.

Having a clear *End State* is a whole lot better than rambling on and on about some obscure vision and not getting much done. That really irritates people and it won't serve you well on a personal level either.

In business terms, you may have heard the terms *vision* and *mission*, which can be confused with End State. They are not the same.

Vision is broad, and is about an organization *becoming* something. It will have the term *to be* in the statement. "To be distinguished in the market for organic floor cleaning products" is a vision statement. It is not an End State.

Mission is also broad, and is about what an organization *does* and *why* it does it. It often has *in order to* in the statement. "To deliver organic floor cleaning products in order to reduce the toxic chemical load in households."

End State is much more specific. It's about a single goal, or collection of goals, to form a grand whole. "To produce a product that cleans 95 percent of dirt and germs, focused on tile grout, safe for pets and children, in compliance with all safety regulations, ready for market within two years" is an End State.

Your End State provides critical input to developing your high level plan of action. That discussion is next.

6 GET THINGS DONE AND STRATEGY

Strategy plays an important role in *Get things done*. We'll unpack strategy more in this lesson.

Remember that End State is one of the three elements of strategy. The other two elements are Current Picture and the plan.

If you want your hair to look like a certain rock star, then your strategy might be to find a picture of that rock star. Then find several hair salons with the talent on staff who can produce *that* hairstyle (Scope and Quality). Then get pricing and schedules and select the salon that best matches your Cost and Schedule goals. Let's say your budget is $150 and your time limit is two hours. Finally, make your appointment and go to the hair salon to get the job done. Two hours and $150 later, your End State is met and you're the hit of the party.

Let's say your company must build a dam on a major river. You may have an End State in mind, but it may need refinement because this is a major undertaking. Your strategy will likely begin with hearing from the experts in your organization and then having *them* help you come up with a clear and realistic End State with all five parts defined. Next, you'll want to ask them to come up with the *how*, the detailed plan for achieving the End State. The final part of your strategy might be to hold regular meetings with your people to hear how things are progressing according to the plan, and to help them wherever and however help is needed.

Here we'll re-introduce the concept of the Current Picture relative to your End State. The Current Picture is how all the pieces and parts of the plan, right now, fit together to create a picture in line with, or progressing toward, the End State.

For example. After the dye is washed out of your hair, you look in the mirror and see your hair is the *wrong* color. Your *Current Picture* is definitely not lining up with your End State. Better say something now and get it fixed before the stylist starts cutting your hair.

Back to the dam. Let's say the design work is going well. The real estate easement work is on track, but the environmental contract is six months behind. Even if you're not an engineer or construction expert, the fact that a major component is six months behind schedule indicates a Current Picture that's not lining up well with the End State. A tactic on your part might be to engage more deeply with the environmental team to help them get back on track. Once they've caught up, you give them their space again and look at the Current Picture. Assuming the other components are still on track, your Current Picture should look more likely to achieve your End State.

Remember, your five components of an End State are Scope, Quality, Cost, Schedule, and Who. Your plan should ensure all five parts are addressed. Your Current Picture should look at the state of all five areas.

Ask for input. Generals and business leaders don't plan alone and neither should you.

Even if your End State is simple and involves only you, ask for input. For example, let's say you want to lose weight or get fit. It's a good idea to obtain expert advice, either by hiring a coach, or researching trustworthy articles on the internet.

If your End State is substantial and involves a number of stakeholders, and if you care about the long-term consequences, then you'll want to exercise the patience and excellent communication skills you possess to consider input from stakeholders.

With that said, I know you're a go-getter and want to *Get things done*. I understand completely, so I'll tell you the secret of the universe on the fastest way to *Get things done*, and how to sustain it.

That lesson is next.

7 HOW BEST TO GET THINGS DONE

When I worked in factory jobs, food service, or the military, I was expected to *Get things done* quickly. It seemed the harder I tried to move quickly, the more inefficient my movements, the more mistakes I made, and the longer it took to accomplish the tasks. I found this exceedingly frustrating.

I was a little slow to learn, but eventually I figured out that I had to *slow down* in order to go faster.

I had to slow down enough to be *mindful* of my movements. Greater mindfulness enabled me to move with greater efficiency, precision, and fewer mistakes. I was smoother in my execution.

The more *smooth* my movements, the more quickly I accomplished the tasks.

This was an important lesson for me. I realized the faster I tried to move, the slower I became. But, when I focused on the *smoothness* of my execution, rather than my speed, I became faster.

This not only works in factories, kitchens, and military units, it works in just about everything in life.

Let's say you want to get married and have a family as soon as possible. You've been dating someone you like for two weeks. What do you think will happen if you spring the "Will you marry me?" question now?

Chances are, you'll scare them away and you'll have to start all over again with someone new. Or worse, they say yes, you marry them, and they turn out to be a horrible spouse.

Springing the marriage question is probably something you'll want to time carefully in a few months after nurturing the relationship and making sure they're the right fit. Otherwise you could waste a lot of time and energy, and your dream of getting married and having a family could become a protracted mess or your worst nightmare.

How about doing a construction project?

Taking the time to *plan* and execute the work *safely* will do wonders to complete the project on time and under budget. Jumping into the work with little to no planning, and then trying to execute everything at a furious pace greatly increases your risk for mistakes and accidents. That is a perfect recipe for "late and over budget." Not good.

Smooth is *fast*. Now let's talk about balance for *sustainment*.

Have you ever sat on a chair or stool with uneven or broken legs? It's uncomfortable and chances are, you'll either fall out of it or not sit in it for very long.

Life is a lot like that. If it's out of balance, it's uncomfortable and you're not going to thrive in it for long. Chances are, you'll make a change, or *outside forces* will change it for you.

Working *really* hard and undergoing tremendous stress for protracted periods of time creates a strong imbalance. There's too much work and not enough time or energy to recharge the mind, body, and spirit, or tend to important relationships. Problems such as burn-out, health incidents, personal issues, and strained relationships will eventually occur. Your life will feel like you're falling out of your chair.

If you lead people and push them so hard that you upset the balance in their lives, you're likely to move ahead more slowly than you hoped as missed work, illnesses, divorces, burn-out, and high turnover become the norm. While some people are more resilient than others, you might find a lot of your good people are overly strained, you may want to consider balancing the demands to something more sustainable. You'll get a lot further ahead going at a sustainable and steady pace than you will at a furious pace punctuated by setbacks.

If you want to maximize *Get things done*, emphasize *smooth* and *balanced*. Slowing down just enough to be mindful helps increase your speed. Slowing down just enough to be balanced helps you sustain a steady pace without serious disruptions.

For those who are very driven, like me, these concepts seem unnatural because we just want to go, go, go. I get it I promise you after decades of experience leading people and organizations, smooth and balanced *is* the way to go.

8 IN THE LAND OF *GET THINGS DONE*, SIMPLE IS HARD

Company CEOs, government leaders, engineers, and design artists have one thing in common. They all agree that doing things simply is hard to achieve, even though simplicity offers tremendous advantages to *Get things done*.

A look at the United State's near 75,000 page tax code illustrates the point. Elected officials and voters alike have long advocated to "simplify" the tax code. Yet every year, more regulations and pages get added. Efforts to simplify the tax code are met with resistance by special interests. If the tax code was simplified to just a few pages, then far greater efficiencies, and cost savings could be achieved.

How about designing a rocket ship? The more moving parts there are, the greater chance for something to go wrong. For every possible thing that can go wrong, there needs to be a "back up" system, which only adds to the number of moving parts. If the rocket was simplified to just a few major parts, then it would be easier and less expensive to build with less risk.

One of the most challenging things leaders of all stripes face is keeping things simple. The simpler they keep the environment, the more they *Get things done*.

This concept doesn't just apply to big business or big government, it applies to schools, families, sports teams, churches, and your very own life.

Remember when we talked about the duality between rigidity and chaos? In between the two poles, there's an ideal zone were *Get things done* is optimal. As a leader, you work within the zone, trying to be as consistent as you can, while still optimizing outcomes.

There's a similar duality between simplicity and complexity. Simple is definitely more efficient, but it can come at a cost to *consideration*.

For example, if we simplify the tax code, then some stakeholders may benefit while others lose substantially. If we simplify the rocket to just a few parts, then we lose the benefit of certain capabilities like special cameras, or creature comforts for the astronaut who is out in space for a long time. If we simplify your life to just a room with a cot, not pets, no "significant others," and no pictures on the walls, then your life would be pretty boring.

Simple is fast and efficient while complex is slow and inefficient. On the other hand, simple does not consider all the other needs and wants, while complex usually does.

Do you see why simple is hard?

Like the duality between rigidity and chaos, simple and complex has its own ideal working zone.

Too simple and you may lose out on consideration. You'll be more efficient but you or others may not like the sacrifices you'll have to make. You may even trigger other's Hot Buttons related to Fairness and cause more trouble for yourself. That's not efficient either.

Too considerate and you may become too complex. You'll spend more energy trying to *Get things done* then you'll want to spend. You'll feel like you're pleasing everyone and no one at the same time. On top of that, you won't get much done. That's not good either.

If consideration is *very* important, that is you *must* have a cat, you *must* be fair to *all* your kids, or you *must* appeal to both Democrats and Republicans, then being simple will be challenging. It's not impossible, though.

To keep things simple when consideration needs are high, you'll need to bargain for it. You'll need to apply your best communication skills, particularly listening, and navigate in the ideal zone between rigidity and chaos. You may need to make some sacrifices or adjust your boundaries.

If consideration is not too important, then you'll want to take the time to think of the simplest solution. It's time well invested. Usually, the fewer number of movements, steps, pages or people in the environment, the simpler is. Less is more.

Focusing on strategic tasks and "packing light" will help you simplify your life and *Get things done*. This may come at a cost of some creature comforts, but you'll be more efficient in the end.

⭐ 9 SUMMARY OF GET THINGS DONE

Feel free to print this lesson and keep it as a handy reminder.

✓ PRIORITIZING TASKS: Use the "cook in the kitchen" model to maximize productivity, with less emphasis on task priority (situation dependent).

　☆ If the task will take less than a minute, do it *now*.

　☆ Break down lower priority projects into one minute tasks, then accomplish the tasks while working your higher priority efforts.

　☆ Tasks that can't be broken down, put on a calendar. Set aside a specific date and time to focus on that task alone without interruptions.

✓ END STATE: Start any major undertaking by defining your End State. Ideally, your *End State* should have the following four components:

　☆ Scope: This is the big "what." "I want the house built…" or "I want the garage cleaned…" or "I want to raise my GPA…."

　☆ Quality: Speak to both how you want to accomplish your End State, and the qualities you want in the "what." "…according to these plans…" or "…so that my car will fit…" or "…to 3.8 without cheating…"

　☆ Schedule: By what time or date should the End State be realized? "…in seven months…" or "…by the end of the day…" or "…by the end of my junior year…"

　☆ Cost: How much are you willing to spend in resources? Resources include money, time, and energy. "…under $300,000" or "…I will fix you your favorite dinner" or "…I will spend one month of my summer learning to study better."

☆ Who: Anyone who is impacted by the End State, or has a task in the execution of strategy. It can also include the people or talent you need to help you get to your End State. Stakeholders may include family, friends, co-workers, neighbors, the community, local businesses, team members, etc.

✓ PLAN: Your tactics for achieving the End State. "I will hire a contractor." "I will set aside the afternoon and ask the kids to help." "I will learn take a course on effective studying."

✓ CURRENT PICTURE: The status of the five elements relative to meeting the End State. You'll want to review your Current Picture often, and make adjustments to your plans in order to keep everything headed in the right direction.

✓ THE *ZONE*: Find the ideal zone between rigidity and chaos in order to optimize *Get things done.*

   ☆ Too much rigidity will hamper *Get things done,* especially when conditions change, and they will. However, insufficient structure and organization (rigidity) and you could become too chaotic.

   ☆ Too much chaos will hamper *Get things done.* There's too much disorder, inconsistency, and constant changes. Very little, if anything gets done. Not enough leniency and flexibility (chaos) and you could become too rigid.

   ☆ Ideally you want to have a structure and organization with a reasonable degree of flexibility.

✓ SIMPLICITY: Whenever possible, keep things simple. Reduce steps, pages, tasks, people, anything you can. If there are stakeholder needs or wants to consider then you'll need to find the right balance between simplicity and consideration. Generally the more consideration required, the more complex the solution will be. To keep things simple when consideration requirements are high, you'll need to bargain. When you bargain, there will be certain trade-offs to make in order to keep things as simple as reasonably possible and still *Get things done.*

10 E—EMPOWER

Empower is the fuel to *Get things done.*

If you or others are not empowered, it makes *Get things done* much more difficult.

Let's start with empowering *yourself.* (We'll talk about empowering others in the next lesson.)

The single most important tool you have to *Empower* yourself is your *mindset.*

Everything you learned from the BRAIN RESET series to this point is about empowering *you.* It's about re-programming your mind so it empowers instead of sabotages you.

If you believe you *cannot* do something because you're: too old, not smart enough, too busy, or whatever, you're not in an empowered mindset. You're not likely to get much done.

If you believe you *can* do something *despite* being: advanced in age, needing to learn something new, or needing to manage your time better, *that* is an empowered mindset. Your chances of getting things done are much greater.

Deposits, Toddler, and Inner Critic play a critical role in your mindset. All three of these elements reside in your automatic mind in a blended state. They influence each other.

Deposits are the beliefs embedded in your programming. They drive your thoughts, emotions and behaviors so they're extremely powerful. Some of your deposits may be wonderfully healthy, while others are ugly lies. The more wonderful, healthy deposits you have, the more empowered you are.

Toddler is your unflattering self who is absolutely deserving of all your love. When Toddler is locked up in the Super Max and cruelly ignored, you're not empowered because the tantrums of Toddler become much worse there. It's also not a very nice thing to do to a toddler.

Toddler *is you*—the you of long ago before your manual mind was formed. While Toddler is narcissistic, selfish, needy, and extremely sensitive, it is also sweet, loving, energetic, optimistic, curious and wants to help. When you *recognize* Toddler and *allow* it to help, you're empowered. You don't let it have it's way with the icky things. Instead, you acknowledge the icky in a nice way, tell Toddler you love him/her with all your heart, then ask it to help. It will gladly help. It wants so badly to be needed and loved. At the end of the day, that's all it *really* wants. Give *that* to your Toddler and he or she will empower you like you wouldn't believe.

Inner Critic is not you, and it's not your friend. It's simply bad programming. It lures you into a negative state of mind of anger, resentment, sadness, self-pity, blame, and the worst of all…*fear*. It offers nothing constructive. It's not trying to "motivate" or "help" you, although it may pretend to. It's the ultimate saboteur.

Inner Critic offers no empowerment whatsoever. All it does is bully and upset your Toddler and reinforce ugly lie deposits. When Toddler is upset and ugly lie deposits dust up, you won't be in your right mind. This is very important to understand because it's hard to be empowered with Inner Critic running amok.

Your *manual* mind is your best friend when it's awake and paying attention. If it's not awake and paying attention, then it's essentially asleep at the wheel while the automatic mind carries on with its programming. Now if you've been working hard to re-program your automatic mind, then this won't be as much of a problem. Still, you don't want to rely on auto-pilot too much because without reinforcement from the manual mind, you're automatic mind may regress from time to time. If it happens, and it sometimes can, don't sweat it. You know how to fix it now. Even the best leaders have to keep working at it.

When your manual mind is engaged, that is, you're *mindful*, it's one of the most empowering tools you have. Your manual mind can put a check on the shenanigans of your automatic mind, *and* can re-program your automatic mind.

So there you have it. You have the ability to empower yourself. This empowerment is critical to your ability to lead yourself and others.

Next, we'll summarize the many ways you empower yourself, and the then talk about empowering others.

THE MANY WAYS YOU EMPOWER *YOURSELF*

11

Here's a useful summary of the many ways you empower yourself. You're invited to print this page and keep it as a handy reference. Some of this summary comes from volume one.

You *Empower* yourself when you:

✓ Run healthy thoughts and positive emotions
  ☆ Leverage your Reality *Show* to keep healthy deposits in your programming.
  ☆ Implement *Ground Control* to manage what deposits get expressed and keep a lid on Inner Critic, using Secret Option Six.
  ☆ Exercise one of the three Fear Response Options (Decide/Research/Agnostic) to get past fear. Don't give into fear.

✓ Open your mind to learning and improving upon your knowledge and skills.
  ☆ Be curious and avoid judging. Ask lots of thoughtful questions.
  ☆ Practice active listening.
  ☆ Adopt or refine habits to improve your learning and skills.

✓ Adopt and practice *good* habits, while eliminating bad ones.
  ☆ Use Ground *Control* to maintain a high level of self-awareness.
  ☆ Practice *Brain Hygiene* (meditation) to clean up the clutter in your brain and allow it a chance to recharge itself.
  ☆ Adopt the specific habits you need to have in order to make your *Reality Show* come true.

✓ Communicate with confidence, love, and authenticity.

  ☆ Avoid toxic communication.

  ☆ Remember the Second Law of the automatic mind.

  ☆ Understand your and other's FIFI (Facts, Identity, Feeling, and Impact).

  ☆ Defuse tense situations with AMUM (Avoid, Mindless, Unapproachable, and Misunderstand).

✓ Nurture happy, loving relationships.

  ☆ *Notice* what's good about others and say so.

  ☆ *Empower* others (coming up next lesson).

✓ Have an End State for the big things you want to accomplish.

✓ Continuously *Stretch* yourself (we'll talk more about this in the LEADERSHIP series).

✓ Keep yourself healthy (the SELF-CARE series is entirely dedicated to this).

✓ Are resilient and gritty, no matter how hard things get.

  ☆ Put on your *Conqueror's Smile* and *Lean Into It*.

✓ *Balance* your life (work, family, leisure, mind, body, spirit—the SELF-CARE series will cover this too).

✓ Are *mindful* (manual mind is aware and present).

  ☆ *Ground Control…Ground Control…Ground Control*

✓ BE COACHABLE—never think you "know it all."

You don't need to memorize this. Rather, you want everything above to become *automatic*. If you notice you have a weakness in one or more areas above, then resolve to work on it as best you can. Remember, you don't have to be perfect. You just have to strive to be your best.

12 EMPOWERING OTHERS

If you lead people in *any* way, empowering others is just as important as empowering yourself.

It doesn't matter if you're not the boss or the supervisor. What matters is you're in a position to *influence* other people.

Any time you're in a position of influence, leadership is involved, even if you're the subordinate.

Being a co-worker, sibling, spouse, or friend automatically puts you in a position of influence.

Being a parent, boss, supervisor, manager, foreman, coach, teacher, or elected official, you're absolutely in a position of influence.

There are entire books and courses on the subject of empowering others as leaders. I have condensed the very best of what I know into just a few powerful lessons.

Let's jump right into it because this is something I am truly passionate about.

The number one way you *Empower* others is to make them feel *relevant*.

I remember struggling as a young adult to get by with all sorts of odd jobs: gutting fish in Alaska, working in factories, cleaning construction sites, laboring in food service, and operating amusement park rides. They didn't pay well. The conditions were often unpleasant, tedious, boring dangerous, or difficult. My employers treated me like an object instead like a real person. They didn't care one little bit about me, much less about my future. Indeed, some of these employers worked harder to find excuses not to pay me my full wage than they did to help me feel the least bit valued in my job. It was no wonder why I was unenthusiastic, gave only the bare minimum of myself, and was constantly looking for something better.

I had only a high school diploma, no valuable skills, and seemingly no future. The only thing I had going for me was a clean record, a willingness to work hard, and a lot of energy. These qualities made me a perfect fit for the Marine Corps. I joined and off to boot camp I went.

What I liked most about the Marines is that they *cared*. No, they did not give me a hug. They pushed me like I was never pushed before and held me accountable. They taught me the eleven leadership traits and fourteen leadership principles. They set me up for future success. They constantly reminded me I was an important part of a noble organization with a noteworthy mission. *That* is how they cared. No employer had ever done that before. No employer had ever bothered to make me feel relevant. The Marines did.

Don't get me wrong. The pay was still low and the conditions still arduous and difficult, but this time things were different. I felt *relevant*. I felt as though they actually cared about me as a person. I gave them everything I had. I worked as hard as I possibly could. I loved them, and yes I was willing to die for them. That is some loyalty. They had me for thirty years and I was grateful to give it to them.

If you think the Marines have an unlimited budget for training, that's not true. They accomplish their training on a shoestring budget, relying heavily on internal qualities such as strong role models at all levels, and a constant drive to learn and teach others. It's the Marines' organizational culture and leadership philosophy that brings out the best in people, even when wages are low and conditions are arduous, not their training budget.

It doesn't matter how big or small your team or organization is. It doesn't matter if you're running a household or a global corporation. If you make people feel *relevant*, 90 percent of them will respond very favorably, while 10 percent will not.

The trouble is, we worry more about the 10 percent, instead of nurturing the 90 percent. Don't worry about the 10 percent who are uncoachable, resistant to change, or even unethical. Don't put your valuable energy into them. Better yet, *let them go* if you can. Put your energy into the 90 percent who are hungry for growth and seeking legitimacy.

Even if you can't offer competitive wages or comfortable conditions, if you go out of your way to make people feel *relevant*—as though you care, as though they're learning and growing, as though there's a brighter future ahead, as though they're part of something worthy—they'll give you everything they have, they'll be loyal to you, and they'll stay with you longer.

Making people feel relevant does not have to cost a lot of time, money, or energy.

For those people and organizations who master this little gem, their ability to *Empower* and inspire others looks easy. They're ability to *Get things done* seems effortless.

What are the many ways you make people feel *relevant*?

Find out in the next several lessons.

13 YOU ARE MY WORLD

When you don't have a fancy title or gigantic bank account, making others feel *relevant* is the single most powerful way to influence other people.

Here's a fun story from Hindu mythology that makes the point.

Shiva and Parvati (two Hindu deities) were parents to Ganesha and Murugan. Ganesha was fat with an elephant's head, while Murugan was sleek and extremely athletic. Both argued endlessly with their parents about who was the favorite son. The parents, tired of the constant bickering, decided to end the matter once and for all. Whoever traveled around the world three times the fastest would forever win their affections as the favorite son. That evening, Murugan was highly confident he would win while Ganesha, in great distress, wondered what to do.

The next morning, Murugan mounted his beautiful peacock and bolted off to circle the world. Ganesha snacked on sweets and mounted his tiny mouse. Ganesha found his parents and began circling them, once, twice, then three times. He stopped and declared himself the winner. The parents confused asked how he was the winner. Ganesha answered effusively, "*You* are my entire world, and I have just traveled around my world three times!" Delighted and pleased with this answer, the parents declared "Yes, Ganesha, you *are* the winner, and you truly are our *favorite* son!"

Now there are many different versions of this story, but it makes the point. When you're trying to achieve something, it's a good idea to consider the interests of *others*. This is especially important when you're not endowed with advantageous gifts or abundant resources.

When you're in any position where you're not in charge, then making room in your life to address the interests of those above you is a powerful way to gain their favor. Some people may view this as "kissing up" and have a negative view of it.

111

It certainly can be problematic if done in the wrong way. You want to do this the right way, which is as follows:

☆ Do it with sincerity.

☆ Don't throw others under the bus (gossip, sabotaging others, or being manipulative).

☆ Have reasonable boundaries (not overly abdicating your own interests).

Now, taking an interest in the interests of others works in the *other* direction as well.

Let's say you're in charge of a group of people and you want them to perform their best. Taking a genuine interest *their* interests is a powerful way to make them feel valued and *relevant*.

For example, just about everyone has an interest in their *future*. If you take an interest in their training and development, and set them up for success so their future looks brighter, then chances are they'll perform much better for you than if you didn't care about these things at all.

Just because someone is not as or more successful than you doesn't mean they can't be helpful to you. It's a good habit to treat *everyone* like they are valued and relevant, even if they don't share your stature or success in life. There's two reasons for this.

First of all, for the sake of human decency, it's the right thing to do.

Secondly, you never know when you may need a favor from those very same people.

For example, treat the housekeeping staff at the hotel you're staying at as though their work is valued. You never know when you may have a medical emergency and one of them may take the extra effort to save your life simply because you made her feel relevant. A smile and a few kind words of appreciation does not cost you a thing, but it means the world to others.

When you make people feel relevant, you turn on a powerful neurochemistry in their mind activating their motivation centers. When you motivate others in a positive way like this, you *Empower* them.

That is leadership!

14 LEAD FROM A PLACE OF SERVICE

I remember a story set in the early 1900s about an explorer and his entourage traveling the jungles of Africa. The explorer commented frequently in his journal about their guide, an African native for whom their very lives depended. The guide helped find food and avoid poisonous plants. He helped find sources of hydration from unusual places. He helped them to avoid places where hostile tribes roamed. Through careful concern of every detail and total dedication to the team, the guide was admired and loved. Although the guide was a hired servant, who do you really think the *leader* was? The explorer may have been in charge but the real leader was the *servant*.

I remember when I picked up sergeant in the Marine Corps, I began working directly for officers for the first time. A wise senior-enlisted leader advised me to do whatever I had to do to make things easier on my commander and make him look good. That was exactly what I did. I went out of my way to ensure every detail was right, and to make things easy for my commanders.

In return, I was entrusted with a great many things. My commanders came to rely on me heavily to *Get things done*, and valued my advice. I was not in charge, but I was leading by serving to the very best of my ability.

With that said, I found it much easier to serve with verve and enthusiasm when my commanders were *good leaders*. That is, they listened, valued my hard work, and made me feel relevant. When I worked for poor leaders who were demeaning, unrealistic in their expectations, and saw me only as an object, I admit I didn't put forth my best. This was a lesson I remembered when I became an officer and began leading others.

The lesson is: not only can servants be leaders, the people in charge are much more effective leaders when they take on a servant approach. That is, they're focused on setting up their subordinates for success.

Now, some people may think that "setting up their subordinates for success" means demeaning, humiliating, or disregarding the feelings, opinions, and interests of their subordinates. Nothing could be further from the truth. In fact, that's a recipe for ensuring poor outcomes, particularly in the long term. You may achieve immediate, short-term results with that method, but you'll pay dearly for it later. Why?

Because leaders like that trigger the icky neurochemistry inclining their followers to be demotivated, unenthusiastic, angry and resentful. Nothing good comes out of that.

People appreciate an inspiring vision and honesty from their leaders. People generally know when they're being lied to or manipulated, even though they may hide this knowledge from their leaders.

For example, let's say you're a front line supervisor at a large retail store with about twenty or more minimum wage workers under you. Telling them to work harder or they'll be fired, and that they're lucky to have this job is definitely not going to ensure the best outcomes.

Instead, try letting them have some fun by making a bit of a competition between the day and night crew. Tell them how they impact the big picture. "Because of your hard work last week, we increased sales by 20 percent." Try giving them an incentive. "Because you helped increase sales by 20 percent you'll get an extra paid vacation day this year." Let them know you care about them. "We know this is not a job you'll have the rest of your life, but we want you to learn and grow from your experience here so you *can* get a better job. We want you to succeed, even if we lose you." Consider reading a lesson out of this book together every day with your team and having a quick chat about it. What a fantastic way to lead and mentor others while growing yourself at the same time! *That* is being an admirable role model.

When people are struggling with something, find out how you can help. Maybe they don't have the right tools, or need a little more training on a certain skill, or just need a helping hand when operations surge.

You helping them have the right tools, training, and working alongside them during surge times will earn you tremendous respect. *That* is servant leadership.

When your people see a future for themselves in your organization; when you mentor them; when you give them opportunities and a reason to stay; when they're treated with meaning, then they'll develop a passion or calling. They'll contribute more to your organization and work harder for you. On the other hand, if you treat people with no meaning, your organization will have no meaning to them. They won't work very hard and they'll leave at the first opportunity.

When you earn a reputation as a person or organization where people grow and feel valued under your leadership, you'll attract fantastic, enthusiastic talent willing to work hard for you, even if wages are low and conditions are arduous.

15 HOW TO PRAISE, AND HOW TO CRITICIZE

It doesn't cost you a thing or take more than a few seconds of your time to tell someone you appreciate their hard work, they're doing a good job, and their work is important.

Too often we take the people in our lives for granted without acknowledging their contributions. The vast majority of people enjoy hearing genuine praise. Even your boss, your parents, and your teachers enjoy hearing praise and thanks from those they lead. So praise isn't just offered to the people you lead, you offer it to those who lead you too.

Now some people don't accept praise very well and may disregard your praise. That's not a reflection on you at all. When someone doesn't accept praise well, it means their Inner Critic tells them they don't deserve it. Praise and thank them *anyway*, just try to do so in a more subtle way that doesn't get their Inner Critic all fired up. Trust me, even if they seem to resist, they secretly love and crave your thanks and praise.

Praising people doesn't mean you avoid offering constructive criticism. Just remember to praise in public and criticize in private. If you're offering constructive criticism of a whole team, then it's best to do so with everyone present, while remembering to appreciate them at the same time.

Notice effusively and publicly what is *right*, and do this *often*. Make it a consistent habit.

Notice what is not right with individuals in *private*, and with teams in a considerate manner without condemnation.

Consider an indirect approach first. Remind them of the scope, quality, cost, and schedule parameters and ask them what you can do to help them meet those parameters. Don't berate; instead ask how you can help them to achieve success.

One of the most challenging things to do is to criticize someone. There's a right way and a wrong way. We'll start with the wrong way first.

First of all, you don't criticize others by demeaning or humiliating them. If you were raised this way or taught this method growing up, I'm sorry to say you were taught wrong. This tactic will surely trigger the icky neurochemistry of anger and resentment. It is never a good idea to do that as a leader. Don't underestimate an angry and resentful person. It could potentially get ugly for you. Additionally, you utterly sabotage long-term success with that person.

Now for the right way. This method works in almost any situation.

Start by asking for permission to give constructive feedback. "Are you willing to hear a different perspective?" Or, "May I offer some feedback?"

Avoid the great eraser, "but." Often we start out with, "I think you did a great job in the meeting today, but…" Everything you just said was erased by the word "but." Try saying, "I think you did a great job in the meeting today. May I offer some constructive feedback? I noticed some of the numbers were off and there seemed to be some confusion about the graph…."

Make sure you're adding value and not just venting. Try to frame things from the "I" perspective such as, "I noticed that…" or "I feel that…"

Avoid making accusations such as, "You always…" or "You never…"

For example, "I notice when you're disappointed in my work you tend to ignore me. Is that your intent? I would prefer to hear your constructive feedback so I can improve." Or, "I notice when I ask you to stock the shelves you seem to procrastinate or not do it all. Can you tell me what's going on?" You might be surprised at what you learn. For example, answers to the above questions could be, "I don't know how to approach you when I'm disappointed in your work" or "I wipe the shelves before stocking them, and that's why I seem delayed."

Whenever possible, offer criticism face to face, or over the phone. It's not usually a good idea to offer criticism over email.

Email should be positive, and avoid negativity whenever possible. If there's anything "negative" you have to say, pick up the phone or make a visit.

It's a good idea to think through what you want to say in advance. You may even want to bounce it off a trusted friend or colleague.

Most important of all, keep an open mind. Be aware of how you may have contributed to the problem with AMUM (Avoid, Mindless, Unapproachable, Misunderstand). If you contributed in any way, admit it with sincerity. By taking this approach you're more likely to gain their willingness to be open and hear what you have to say.

Remember, make praise a habit. Praise even the small stuff. Praise publicly and enthusiastically.

Criticize in private, with consideration, and not over email.

16 — THE POWER OF *NOTICING*

"**O**h, Brian! You did it again! You know how much it makes my heart sing to see the laundry done when I come home from work!"

"You like that, huh?" He answers as I shower him with hugs and kisses.

This is one of many typical conversations I have with my husband. While Brian is truly my world, he did not start off in our marriage doing the laundry. Nor did I ever ask him to do it.

One day, he did a load of laundry. When I returned home from work I *noticed* by praising him effusively. Ever since, he's been doing the laundry. I make it a point to *notice* it every time.

Now I know some people will say, "He *should* do the laundry, especially if you're working and he's not." You could apply this sort of thinking to just about anything: "She *should* do this." "He *should* do that." "I *shouldn't* have to do that!" And on and on.

That is utter nonsense. Why?

Because it's *irrational*. There's no law of the universe dictating anything using the word *should*.

What if you're trying to *Get things done* and you really need people to do certain things consistently?

Remember, *smooth is fast* and *balance is sustainable*. Patiently waiting to see the right thing happen, and then *noticing* it with genuine appreciation (not expectation or sarcasm) *every* time it happens is the smooth and balanced way to *Get things done*. Why?

Because you *Empower* people. You make them feel relevant. You trigger all the feel-good neurochemistry that attracts them to *want* to do things for you.

119

Is it faster to *demand* what you want and give a threat or ultimatum if it doesn't happen? Yes it is. It's also the fastest way to trigger resentment and demotivate that person. You trigger all the icky neurochemistry that makes them want to get away from you, let alone do things for you.

There's a story of a shopkeeper who struggled to keep good help. One after another, he badgered his hired help to stock the shelves, sweep the floors, empty the trash, and so on. One after another, his hired help left and there he was again running the store himself while trying to hire someone new. He kept blaming the young generation. "They're so lazy and won't work." His wife advised him to try something new to keep his hired help. Taking his wife's advice, he *noticed* his newly hired help had swept the floor. He accomplished little of anything else the whole day he was there. The shopkeeper put on his best mood and praised the young man effusively for sweeping the floor. He then began stocking the shelves himself without commenting about how the young man should do it. The next day, not only were the floors swept, the shelves were stocked too! Now the shopkeeper was truly surprised and let out a burst of enthusiastic praise for the young man. This sort of thing went on until the young man was proudly running the store entirely by himself.

There's an old African saying, "The man who beats his donkey is soon walking."

Sadly, that's exactly what a lot of parents, coaches, and employers do. They badger their people, fail to appreciate them, and then blame others when things don't go well. They blame the people they lead for their "lack of motivation." They have no idea that over time they have flooded these people with the icky neurochemistry that turns them off from wanting to do much of anything. They got in this mess through constant criticism, badgering, and negativity. It's a culture of demoralized people where blame is the norm. It's a recipe for mediocrity at best and failure at worst.

Families, teams, and organizations who actively notice *anything* good, and do so consistently with genuine appreciation, turn on the good neurochemistry that motivates people to *want* to do more, work hard, and be more conscientious.

It's a culture of positive reinforcement, encouragement, and enthusiasm. It's a culture that *Empowers* people by making them feel relevant.

It's a culture that leverages the smooth and balanced approached to *Get things done.*

One does not arrive at this happy place over night. It takes time, conscious effort, and mindful leadership to get there.

17 MENTORING MAKES YOU AND OTHERS FEEL MORE RELEVANT

When you teach, coach, or talk to a loved one, friend, co-worker, or perfect stranger by listening and helping them think through their challenges, *that* is leadership.

Mentoring is not about telling others the answer; it's about helping them arrive at the answer themselves.

Keep in mind the three laws of the automatic mind as you mentor others.

First Law: *The automatic mind believes everything is real.*

Help them to envision a brighter future and positive outcomes. Some people really struggle with this. When you help them see better possibilities, they receive hope. Hope motivates people and motivation is powerful. You may even want to explain to them how all reality begins in the mind, and how they're more likely to create the reality they want for themselves by envisioning that reality often, even when setbacks happen.

On the other hand, the more they focus on negative outcomes, the more likely negative events are to happen. If they have trouble with staying positive, consider sharing the tools of *Ground Control* and brain hygiene (meditation). These tools are extremely useful for taming the wild and wayward mind.

Second Law: *All communication, whether in thought or spoken allowed, is internalized by the automatic mind.*

Help them pay attention to their self-talk. Are they putting themselves down? Are they making assumptions that aren't true? Are they saying things that limit themselves?

Help them understand how self-talk in social conversations also impacts them. These conversations feed directly into the First Law, for better or for worse.

Third Law: *The automatic mind resists drastic change.*

Understand that when others seem to resist change, the change they're contemplating might be more than they can handle. Try to help them scale things down into smaller doses.

On the other end of the spectrum are people who take on way too much, too fast. They're at risk of burning out. You'll want to gently remind them to pace themselves so this doesn't happen to them.

One thing you'll certainly mentor people on is *fear*. Consider sharing with them the options you now know about to deal with fear:

Decide: "I'm scared to death and I'm going to do it anyway!"

Research: Gather more information until you're more comfortable with what you're doing.

Agnostic: No matter the outcome, *choose* to be happy anyway and make the best of it.

With all this said, stay focused on the coachable. You'll find out pretty quickly if someone is coachable or not.

Uncoachable people respond unfavorably to mentoring, are negative, complain about everything, refuse to take responsibility, blame others, and make excuses. Some people are not ready to change and that's fine. Respect they have their journey and move on to people who can really benefit from your mentorship. It's best not to waste time or neglect yourself (or others) trying to help those who won't be helped. It's also important to get negative people out of your circle *quickly*. Some of these people may be very close to you and you'll have to figure out whether to sever the relationship or manage it from a distance.

As a mentor, remember to encourage your mentees in all areas of their life. Work-life balance is important. Family, personal relationships, and health directly impact performance at work and school.

If you're a teacher, coach, or work supervisor, you'll want to encourage and empower people in their personal areas, not just the work or school areas. By doing so, you'll improve performance at work and school. You don't have to get too deep with them, either. Sometimes all you need to do is listen for a short time. At other times you may want to ask them questions to help them see the path. Remember to avoid going straight to the solution as they are much less likely to act on the solution than if they come up with it themselves.

Now on to you. Do you have a mentor? Do you have someone in your life who is wealthier, fitter, smarter about something, or has better relationships than you?

If not, it's time to seek out relationships with people like that. If they offer to mentor you, consider it a great honor and *be coachable*. Be open to constructive feedback, open minded, and open to change.

18 EARN AND GIVE TRUST

Just because you have a title doesn't mean people trust you.

No matter what your position or status, trust is not automatic. Trust has to be earned.

Studies show people trust leaders who express a clear vision (not vague or constantly changing), actually *care* about people (not just pretend to care), and are of upright moral character. If a leader is lacking in any one of those three things, trust will be an issue.

Let's start with the vision. If your vision is a little unclear, it's ok to ask for input. No one is saying you have to come up with the vision all by yourself. In fact, it's much better to let others contribute to crafting the vision.

What's important for the leader to do is to *fully* adopt the vision, once everyone has agreed upon it, and stay the course. If the leader does not fully embody and live the vision by everything he or she says or does, then the vision becomes unclear. If the leader changes the vision to suit his or own ends, people are less likely to trust that leader. You want to be the kind of leader who facilitates the crafting of the vision, and then *lives* the vision by example. We'll talk more about this in the Model section.

The second part is caring about people, or empathy. Empathy means you listen and care about the well being of others. It doesn't mean you have to spend hours of your day playing counselor or save their day by fixing their car. You can do that if want, but if you lead many people you may not have time for that. Taking a moment to notice something good *is* caring.

Mentoring is a powerful way to show you care.

Another way to show you care is getting dirty yourself when your people need an extra hand.

When someone loses a loved one, a sympathy card signed by the group shows you care.

If you don't care and just *pretend* to care, that's actually worse. People pick up on phoniness. If they sense any phoniness from you, they won't trust you.

The third part is moral character.

Let me tell you something right now. *There's no such thing as separating your personal morality from your work.*

I realize a lot of people may disagree with this, but I'll go to my grave shouting this to the hills because I know from personal experience and thirty years in the Marine Corps that separating your personal morality and work morality is *impossible.*

Case in point, I was never surprised to learn a certain person being disciplined at work also had some sort of personal moral flaw (drugs, alcoholism, excessive gambling, promiscuous sex, child abuse, animal abuse, crime, etc.) The morality of your personal life absolutely impacts your work life. That's not a political statement, it's a solid *fact*. If people know about flaws in a leader's personal morality, trust will be a very big problem. Only those who share the immoral behavior of the leader will trust the leader. No one else will, and those outside the "circle" will be inclined to leave. We'll talk more about personal morality in the Model section.

You empower people when you're a leader who can be *trusted*. If they don't trust you, then they'll be fearful or resentful. They'll avoid or leave you, perhaps even sabotage you, and if they stay, then they most certainly won't do their best for you.

Now onto *you* trusting your people.

Let your good people help you get important things done and trust them it will turn out. Don't try to do everything yourself or helicopter over them. Don't demand everything be "your" way. If their solution works, but it's not your way, so what? Let it go.

Trusting your people doesn't mean you should abdicate your responsibilities or over-burden your people. You'll want to pitch in and help when they need you, or when you don't have much else to do. They should never see you just hanging out and relaxing while they're working hard. That is a big no-no.

You'll want to *inspect* what you *expect*. You want to ask questions, get out of the office and look at things, and spot check the details. You want to find the right place between the extremes of micromanaging (which is not trusting) or abdicating your responsibilities by being totally passive (never inspecting.)

Remember to give *feedback* during inspections. Remember to be enthusiastic in noticing what is right, and give *constructive* criticism on areas that will help them improve.

When you trust your people to get important work done, they enjoy working for you more and are more likely to do their best for you. Trusting your people is one of many important ways you set them, and yourself, up for success.

19 ★ WHAT *NOT* TO DO

Just as important as *what to do* to empower people, there's plenty of things *not to do* to avoid sabotaging yourself.

Remember, when you empower people, you multiply the potential for better outcomes.

When you don't empower, or worse, *limit* people from exercising their talents, you sabotage yourself by limiting their potential for best outcomes.

We've said this before, and it's important enough to say again, *do not* demean, put down, humiliate, disregard, name call, or use toxic communication as a leadership tool. If you were taught differently in your family or job, you were taught *wrong*. Period. Full stop.

When you lead a project, it's usually best not to focus on your personal areas of expertise or interest. Instead, it's better to focus on the areas of which you're uncomfortable, not an expert, or even find boring. Why?

Because these are the areas that will bite you, not the stuff you like or have expertise in. It's a great idea to ask questions, ask others to teach you what they know, and ask them how you can help.

With that said, don't helicopter or micromanage either. Helicoptering and micromanaging is watching every move, constantly making your people redo work to "your" exacting standards, and not trusting them to get the job done.

Do not take all the oxygen out of the room by doing most of the talking. Ideally, you should do the least amount of talking. Let others have their say before you.

Do not be the smartest person in the room, show off your expertise, or put down others' ideas and comments. People really don't like that, even if you *are* smart. No matter who you are or what your credentials are, you're not as smart as you think you are.

Do not take credit. Let your people shine and give them all the credit for everything that's right. You may graciously accept compliments so long as you recognize the hard work of your people in helping you achieve.

Do not blame. Even if it wasn't your fault, take responsibility for whatever "bad" thing happened and genuinely try to figure out how to prevent it from happening again. Seek input from your people. Trust me on this one; when you voluntarily take the heat for whatever "bad" thing happen, people know you're not at fault, and they love you for taking it on anyway. It's a great way to earn trust. When you start blaming, people become fearful and look at you as a coward. That's not good. If you make a mistake, own it, learn from it, and move on. If others make a mistake, don't waste time with blame; fix it and move on.

Do not procrastinate. People with a P (Perceiver) personality type will struggle with this more than the J (Judging) personality types who are naturally more organized. Good leaders know how to get in front of the bow wave and stay there. You can't do that if you procrastinate. Taking on the cook-in-the-kitchen model of completing tasks helps ensure you stay ahead of all your tasks, not just the important or urgent tasks. The cook-in-the-kitchen model works for both personality types.

Do not make excuses. I once worked in an organization that hired a fantastic person who hit the ground running. Six months later, performance evaluations were due. Her supervisor wrote a mediocre review on her because it "wouldn't be fair to those who worked at the organization longer." That's a lousy excuse to give someone a mediocre review when their performance was outstanding. There were a number of people I knew who did fantastic work but still received mediocre reviews because their supervisors "didn't believe in giving outstanding reviews on anyone." That's a lousy excuse too. There was a senior military officer who was well known for his sexual harassment of women. His leadership turned a blind eye and when it *finally* got to be too much, he was merely asked to retire. No punishment. The reason? "We don't want this to get out in the public" and "He was a good officer until he was caught." In the meantime, military people of much lower grade were courtmartialed for far less crimes. I could write a book about the lousy excuses leaders give for not doing the right thing. Don't be one of those leaders who gives excuses. People will lose respect for you and think you're cowardly, even if they don't show it outwardly.

By eliminating these behaviors from your leadership toolbox, you *Empower* people.

If you've ever exhibited one of these behaviors in the past, that does *not* make you a rotten person or a rotten leader.

You likely didn't know better, had poor role models, or were taught wrong.

Now that you know better, *forgive* yourself, continue to strive to do your best, and move on. It does absolutely no good to wallow about your mistakes from the past. Instead, focus on making the present and future better.

20 CARE-FRONTATION

"Care-frontation" is a word I learned from motivational speaker Lisa Nichols. It's a great word to describe an important way to empower others, by holding them accountable in a *firm* and *loving* way.

As a leader, you have the power to help develop others and change their lives for the better.

As a parent, coach, teacher or manager, you have a *duty* to develop others and set them on a path for success.

Here's a typical care-frontation conversation:

Mom: "Did you finish your homework?"

Son: "No."

Mom: "Then why are you playing video games? You know the rules of this house. No video games until your homework is done."

Son: "I needed a break."

Mom: "You need to do your homework, then you can take a break. If you need help with your homework, let me know and I'll help you. Now turn off the video game, and let's get your homework done. What are your assignments?"

Yes I know. This is hardly a revelation for parents. The point is to emphasize the "care" in care-frontation.

Notice how Mom is not losing her temper or putting down her son.

Notice how she uses "rules of the house" instead of "I told you…" Doing that helps to reduce the tension of competition between the two.

Notice how she offers to help and asks about his assignments.

Notice how she offers to *listen*, not to his excuse but to his *challenge*. He may be procrastinating because the homework is a little too challenging for him. By asking him about his assignments, she can learn more about what's *really* troubling him and help him navigate through it.

Here's another example.

Manager: "Have you been keeping public affairs informed about the project's status?"

Worker: "I emailed them last month."

Manager: "I thought we agreed you'd update them weekly. What happened?"

Worker: "I got distracted with other things."

Manager: "I really need you to keep public affairs updated or else they start calling me with questions. What do you think about setting a reminder in your calendar? Is there anything I can do to help you?"

Again, notice the "care" in this discussion. The manager is keeping his cool and not putting down the worker. He offers a suggestion (using a calendar reminder) and asks the worker what he thinks without demanding the worker use it. Finally, he asks if he can help. The question is deliberately open ended to allow the worker to open up. This becomes the manager's opportunity to learn more about the perspective of the worker.

What if the worker responded with, "I already have a calendar reminder. I guess I could use a little more clarification on what public affairs wants. It seems to change every week and I have trouble keeping up with their changing demands." Now the manager has information to help smooth out the problem. This works a lot better than beating up on the worker.

Care-frontation done *consistently*, with genuine care, is how you leverage your "frenemey," Certainty, in a healthy way. Remember Certainty from SCARF? We talked about her in the NEURO-SCIENCE series in volume one.

Whether or not we're in a leadership position, we naturally want to be certain of the outcomes. The higher the need for Certainty, the more we tend toward controlling and impatient behavior.

Think of how you typically respond to controlling and impatient people. I bet you find it annoying and you're probably not your best.

On the other hand, no care-frontation is clearly not caring. Not caring is the opposite extreme to controlling and impatient behavior. It's just as bad. People will feel disconnected from you.

If you want the best out of people, you must give them the *best* of yourself.

21 EMPOWER WITH A CLEAR PHILOSOPHY

While a student at Command and Staff College, an advanced military leadership school, I learned the concept of having a "philosophy of command." It contains the commander's beliefs about leadership, and sets high level expectations and boundaries for the organization. From 2009-2011, I was assigned to Afghanistan as the Officer In Charge (OIC) of robotics maintenance and distribution for U.S. and coalition forces. The organization profile consisted of military, government civilian, and contractor staff; engineers, robot repair specialists, and logisticians; and facilities spread across a country the size of Texas. I found having a "philosophy of command" was critical to communicate my expectations and beliefs to a large, diverse, complex and widely dispersed organization. My philosophy was simple, limited to ten points, and one page in length. It clearly stated my beliefs and expectations for everyone.

1. We support the warfighter. Our needs come second. All of your actions, words, and priorities will reflect this number one rule.

2. Only I may say no to a warfighter. Direct all unsupportable requests to me.

3. Be part of the solution, not the problem. Find a way, not an excuse, within the rules of ethics, safety, and good sense.

4. Live morally pure and demonstrate the highest ideals of good character. You can't keep a secret here. Immorality hurts you, those around you, and our organization. Leave the smut, drugs, and bad behavior out, or you'll be out.

5. Share your knowledge and skills. If you stand out as an excellent robotics technician and no else around you imporves, there's something wrong.

6. Supply and maintenance management discipline – know and live by it. Be meticuluous, detailed, and accurate. The cost of our robots and parts

131

is enormous and our nation's taxpayers expect us to exercise the higest degree of stewardship. Don't disappoint them.

7. Make others and the organization look good. This is the "front sight post" – focus on it and you'll be surprised how much you make yourself look good. Watch what you do and say at all times with due diligence for the outcomes.

8. Everyone is a human being first. I promise to treat you with humanity and fairness. I expect you to do the same with others. Your family and your health are very important to me. Please talk to me if you need help. Everyone gets bumps in the road now and then.

9. Your thoughts, ideas and suggestions are welcome. I'll give you a sincere audience, and once a decision is made you must support it fully and move on regardless of your personal feelings on the matter. We won't agree on everything.

10. Know and understand my intent. You're all very smart and I expect you to take appropriate initiative and decisive action in support of that intent. I encourage you to seek clarification anytime you're unsure. I have an open door, email, and phoneline. I will respond to you.

I made posters of the philosophy and hung them at every site. I personally lived by my own rules and reinforced my philosophy daily through my communication and actions. I let the philosophy empower my people so they could run with the ball. I gave my people wide latitude and authority to operate, acquire resources, and make decisions. I met with them weekly to learn their perspective, and share with them my perspective from the theater level. Sometimes I would give them direction, but most of the time we collaborated on our next big move and shared ideas on best practices.

In two years we grew the robotics program by over 3,000 percent, saved over $120M in acquisition and logistics costs, and accomplished more than what had been accomplished in all of the eight years prior, *combined.*

That kind of success would have been impossible if the people in the organization were not *Empowered.* There's absolutely no way on earth I could have achieved that on my own.

When people have clear expectations and boundaries, they're empowered to move further and faster than if given vague ideas or suggestions.

What do you think about having a philosophy on how you teach, coach, parent, or manage people?

On how to lead yourself?

Some examples are coming up next.

22 A PERSONAL LEADERSHIP PHILOSOPHY

As a person, I believe in:

1. Being *aware* of self-limiting emotions such as anger, fear, resentment, hatred, jealousy, anxiety, sadness, helplessness, revenge, self-importance, self-pity, regret, worry, unworthiness, shame, guilt, and lack.

2. Enhancing self-empowering emotions such as love, joy, happiness, confidence, forgiveness, patience, gratitude, contentment, openness, trust, acceptance, and abundance.

3. Being *aware* of self-sabotaging behaviors such as toxic communication, AMUM (Avoid, Mindless, Unapproachable, Misunderstand), procrastination, locking up Toddler in the Super Max, listening to Inner Critic, negativity, complaining, blaming, competing (unless you're playing sports or a game), neediness, seeking recognition, rushing, desperate, dishonest, defensiveness, inconsiderate, arrogant, conceited, shy, timid, dramatic behavior (unless you're in theater), interrupting, controlling, need to be "right," judging, or bullying.

4. Enhancing self-empowering behaviors such as active listening, humility, positivity, expressing appreciation, consideration, owning my mistakes, brain hygiene, continuous learning, *Ground Control*, managing fear, watching my *Reality Show,* embracing Toddler (loving him/her unconditionally), counteracting Inner Critic, and healthy communication.

5. Surrounding myself with positive role models and avoiding negative people (or manage my relationship if avoidance is not possible.)

6. Investing in my self-improvement, whether it's health, skill enhance-

ment, education, or any area important to me. I don't make up excuses as to why I can't invest in myself. I find ways to make it happen.

7. Balancing my life between career, health, personal relationships, work, fun, and spirituality. I avoid allowing any one area to dominate my life for a long period of time to the degree that other areas are sacrificed or harmed.

23 ★ A FAMILY LEADERSHIP PHILOSOPHY

As a family, we believe in:

1. Speaking to and treating each other how we ourselves want to be treated. We do not shame, belittle, name-call, hit, disregard, dress-down, humiliate, harm, or deliberately hurt each other. We treat each other with dignity and respect.

2. Owning our mistakes, and forgiving those who own their mistakes without bringing them up again or their past mistakes against them.

3. Maintaining our self-awareness. If we get too upset to speak calmly and respectfully, we take a "time out" to gather ourselves. When others need to have a "time out" we allow them space and time without following or badgering them.

4. Completing our assigned daily and weekly duties without having to be told, and to do so with quality, a grateful attitude, and due consideration for the needs of others.

5. Listening to each other without interrupting, and giving each other opportunities to speak their minds, ideas, and feelings.

6. Encouraging and supporting each other in our dreams and aspirations.

7. Not taking unfair advantage of each other or being manipulative or deceptive.

8. Supporting each other's health and well-being through sound nutrition and exercise.

9. Supporting each other's emotional and spiritual needs through empathy and mentoring.

10. Being the best version of ourselves, and serving as positive role models.

11. Being open to constructive criticism and to not getting defensive.

12. Being considerate and respectful in our delivery of constructive criticism. We do not criticize in ways that truly do not help.

13. Not blaming. If we have an issue about something, we bring it up in a calm and considerate manner. We listen openly and patiently to those who bring up issues.

14. Being mindful in our communication and behavior, and to understand each other. We do not avoid each other or behave in a manner as to be unapproachable.

As parents, we believe in:

15. Setting appropriate boundaries for safety and security, and sound life habits for our children, while allowing for autonomy and growth toward independence.

16. Providing our children with enriching experiences to help them grow into well-adjusted and successful adults.

17. Fostering a growth mindset in our children, and coaching them in pursuing their passions. We actively model this behavior for them.

18. Loving our children unconditionally, even when they do wrong or disappoint us.

19. Setting an excellent example of a healthy and happy marriage.

20. Setting an excellent example of a healthy, productive, balanced, and happy lifestyle.

As children growing up in this household, we believe in:

21. Trusting the wisdom of the boundaries and expectations set by our parents and obeying their rules, even if they're inconvenient. We do not attempt to circumvent or deceive them.

22. Adopting a growth mindset and persevering through worthy efforts, even if they're difficult or boring.

23. Talking to our parents whenever we have a problem or struggle, and not letting problems fester or discourage us.

24 A CLASSROOM LEADERSHIP PHILOSOPHY

As a teacher, I believe in:

1. Being open minded about education tools, techniques, and best practices in order to improve my teaching skills, and realize better outcomes in the classroom.

2. Being aware of negative thinking or emoting on my part, as that can limit my own and my students' learning and growth.

3. Enhancing positive thinking and emoting on my part, as that will empower me as a teacher and help my students to learn and grow.

4. Modeling healthy emoting and behaving when faced with frustrations, challenges, difficulties, or other upsetting things. I stage at least one demonstration of this daily.

5. Actively listening to and learning from my students, as this is modeling behavior for them.

6. Avoiding toxic communication or any treatment that shames, humiliates, embarrasses, or discourages students. When I see this behavior from students, I quickly care-front it.

7. Readily admitting my mistakes, and modeling behavior for humility and forgiveness. I stage a demonstration of this at least once a week.

8. Exercising "care-frontation" to enforce boundaries and expectations for behavior and performance from my students.

9. Modeling behavior for appreciation and gratitude. I demonstrate this several times a day.

10. Noticing what's right and saying so often. I will not simply notice what is wrong.

11. Fostering a growth mindset in my students, and encouraging them to persevere through learning that is difficult or boring.

25 A SPORTS TEAM LEADERSHIP PHILOSOPHY

As a coach, I believe in:

1. Being open minded about coaching tools, techniques, and best practices in order to improve my coaching skills, and realize better outcomes on the field.

2. Being aware of negative thinking or emoting on my part as that can limit my and my players' improvement and performance.

3. Enhancing positive thinking and emoting on my part as that will empower me as a coach and help my players to improve and perform.

4. Avoiding toxic communication or any treatment that shames, humiliates, embarrasses, or discourages players. When I see this behavior from players, I quickly care-front it.

5. Exercising "care-frontation" to enforce boundaries and expectations for behavior and performance from my players.

6. Readily admitting my mistakes, and modeling behavior for humility and forgiveness.

7. Modeling behavior for appreciation and gratitude. I demonstrate this several times a day.

8. Noticing what's right and saying so often. I do not simply notice what is wrong.

9. Fostering a growth mindset in my players, and encouraging them to persevere through practice that is difficult or even boring. I will not bully or shame them to comply.

10. Coaching my players in their personal lives, as this often translates into performance on the field.

139

26 A WORK TEAM LEADERSHIP PHILOSOPHY

As a front line supervisor or team leader, I believe in:

1. Leading by *serving* to the best of my ability, and by actively setting my people up for success.

2. Being open minded about leadership tools, techniques, and best practices.

3. Being aware of negative thinking or emoting on my part as that can limit my and my peoples' growth and performance.

4. Enhancing positive thinking and emoting on my part, as that will empower me as a leader, and empower my people to perform.

5. Being open to constructive feedback, to really listening, and not getting defensive.

6. Avoiding toxic communication or any treatment that shames, humiliates, embarrasses, or discourages people. When I see this behavior from my people, I quickly care-front it.

7. Exercising "care-frontation" to enforce boundaries and expectations for behavior and performance from my people. I do not confront with disdain or anger.

8. Readily admitting my mistakes and modeling behavior for humility and forgiveness.

9. Not taking credit, but rather giving credit to my people for everything that goes right.

10. Taking responsibility for anything that goes wrong, even it's not my fault. I do not blame.

11. Modeling appreciative and grateful behavior. I demonstrate this several times a day.

12. Actively listening and learning from my people.

13. Noticing what is right and saying so often. I do not simply notice what is wrong.

14. Fostering a growth mindset in my people, and encouraging them to persevere through challenges.

15. The power of our team to change the company and make a hugely positive impact.

A COMPANY LEADERSHIP PHILOSOPHY

A s a business, we believe in:

1. Growing and developing our employees so they leave as better people than when they came. Hint: use this book as a tool, give out copies, and conduct frequent, short learning sessions.

2. Fostering a culture of role models and servant leadership from front line supervisor to CEO.

3. Doing the right thing by our people, our customers, and the environment.

4. Ensuring our leaders are above reproach in their ethical and moral behavior. We do not make excuses or cover up for poor behavior, especially from our leaders.

5. Trusting our people to achieve great things while providing them the tools and encouragement to do so.

6. Fostering a balanced, healthy lifestyle for our people.

7. Fostering a culture of active listening, mindfulness, learning, and growth.

8. Providing an inspiring vision that our people can be proud of and get behind.

9. Eliminating toxic communication and modeling healthy, respectful communication.

10. Openly admit our mistakes, make reparations, and foster healing.

11. Modeling "care-frontation" as opposed to confrontation in our relationships.

12. Educating our people on GEMS, and implementing GEMS at every level of leadership.

13. Encouraging our front line supervisors to implement a *Group Reality Show.*

14. Valuing people, ideas, and then things.
15. Our own power to change industry, institutions, and societies in a hugely positive way from our company.

EMPOWER YOUR GROUP WITH A GROUP REALITY SHOW

28

If you want to motivate and synchronize a group of people so they work much better as a team, a *Group Reality Show* is a powerful way to achieve this. A *Group Reality Show* is also a highly effective tool for establishing and reinforcing culture and habits for success.

A *Group Reality Show* is similar to a personal *Reality Show* in that it challenges limiting beliefs of the group, and programs the group with empowering thoughts and behaviors. We covered making a personal *Reality Show* in the BRAIN-RESET series of volume one.

The biggest difference between a *Reality Show* and a *Group Reality Show* replacing *I* with *we*.

If you lead a family, classroom, sports team, work team, or company, you can greatly benefit from creating a *Group Reality Show*. You create it similarly to creating a personal *Reality Show* with some minor differences. I'll give you the step-by-step instructions in the next two lessons. First, some things you need to understand.

Let me warn you, some of you may think the steps to building your *Group Reality Show* are too "touchy feely." It *can* be if you as the leader take it too far. On the other hand, avoiding the discussion of emotions with your people creates a blind spot and contributes to poor communication. These issues will severely limit and sabotage you as a leader if you continue to avoid the topic of emotions, and that's not good. Don't let *your* fear limit yourself or the group. Do your best to navigate the emotional terrain, and, no, you don't have to be perfect. You just have to make a sincere effort, and trust me, people will see your effort.

You need to go through this journey as a group so you all understand what's really going on in the mind of the *group*. This awareness is just as critical for the group as self-awareness is for yourself. We want to start building the group's awareness of its collective mindset, and build *your* awareness of the group's mindset so you can better lead them.

A *Group Reality Show* works best with a relatively small group, like a family, classroom, sports team, project team, squad, or platoon-sized military unit, or other work-related team of less than fifty people. This is a guideline, not a hard and fast rule.

If the group is too large, then you'll have too many people hiding in the shadows and not participating in the process of building the *Group Reality Show*. If they're not part of the process, then they won't feel compelled to "go along" as well. When the group is too large, then usually a few, dominant people speak up and push the agenda, so then your *Group Reality Show* reflects the wants of those few, dominant people while leaving the others out.

After you've developed your *Group Reality Show,* you'll want to hang it in plain sight, or have it run in a loop on a video screen.

Next, assign each and every person to "monitor" one or more deposits. Their job is to focus on that particular deposit for the week. If you have a lot of people, you may assign multiple people to the same deposit, or you can just rotate the others through later.

At the beginning of each week, or time period that works best for you, gather around the *Group Reality Show* and view it together. As you go through each deposit, ask the "deposit monitor" to give his or her opinion on how well the group is doing with that deposit.

For example, are they really *believing* or *doing* it? Or, are they struggling with it? What can they do together as a group to try to make it better? Sometimes there's no better answer than "we'll keep trying." That's ok.

Continue through each deposit in this way spending about one minute on each deposit. You don't need to say or discuss much unless there's a particular deposit your group wants to talk about. If you have twenty deposits in your *Group Reality Show,* then the whole conversation should take less than thirty minutes. This is time well invested in promoting team work. Once your conversation is over, assign everyone a new deposit to monitor. If they have an idea on how to improve upon the deposit, or add a new one, let them make changes. That's ok. In fact, the more you change the pictures and make improvements, the more everything stays "fresh" and likely to stick.

Are you ready to make a *huge* difference in the performance of your group?

Then let's get started on building this thing.

29 BUILD YOUR *GROUP REALITY SHOW*, PART I

Step One: *Get the group's buy in to create a Group Reality Show.* Ask your group to give it chance. Explain that what you're doing is creating the "movie" of the group's goals as though they have *already happened.* You'll need their help to produce the movie. You have learned that teams who create a *Group Reality Show* and engage in it regularly can actually make the movie come true. It's the latest tool in leveraging group psychology to accomplish incredible things they never thought possible. "Let's do this before our competitors do!"

Step Two: *Assess the group's emotional baseline.* The reason for doing this is *not* to hold some sort of group counseling session. The reason is you need to have a clear understanding of the prevailing emotions of the group. In this exercise, you might learn they tend to be pessimistic with a willingness to change or try again. Or you may find they're overly optimistic with a poor understanding of what it takes to succeed. What you learn from this session will help guide you in building your *Group Reality Show.* For example, if you notice your group tends to resist change, you may want to encourage the group to develop deposits helping them to be more flexible with change (without coming right out and saying, "You guys are resistant to change so we're going to have a deposit that says such and such.") What you'll do here is lead a discussion about the group's *best* and *worst* moments, and how those moments made everyone feel. Try to come up with several sentences starting with "When we did _____, we felt _____", or, "When _____ happened, we _____". For example, "When we won the game, we felt... elated, happy, like maybe we didn't deserve it, weird." Or, "When we lost the big contract, we felt...shocked, disappointed, unsurprised, fearful." It's a good idea to write it out on a white board where everyone can see. Some group members may have difficulty expressing how they feel, so be patient with them (you may use the word list from the BRAIN RESET series if you'd like). Or, they may come right

146

out with everything at once. That's fine too. Listen to what everyone has to say *without judgment*. That is extremely important. Finally, make sure *everyone* gets a good chance to speak their mind.

Step Three: *What organizations or people does the group admire?* Ask your team, "If we could be just like a certain organization or person, who might it be?" Often the team might not know right away, so it might help to ask individuals for people they admire and why. It doesn't matter if they say "Mom," "Uncle Buddy," "Beyoncé," "Donald Trump," "PETA," or the "Lakers." Let them say who they want and give their reasons. Ask questions such as, "What qualities do you admire about them?" "What habits do they have that make them admirable and successful?" "When things get challenging, what is their thought process?" Give each person a chance to speak and write their answers on a board where everyone can see them. Then you may want to say something such as, "These are all good choices. I wonder if any of them stand out as a role model for our team to follow. What do you think? Let's try to pick out the top three to five." It's ok if the people or organizations your group picks as your top three to five are totally unrelated to what your team does. What matters is you're capturing the *thinking*, *traits*, and *habits* that your team will want to model after. These attributes will form the basis of many of the group's deposits, of which they'll create later.

Step Four: *"We are at our best when we are...."* Ask this question of your team and try to get each person to come up with one or more answers. Write everyone's answers on the board. The answers can be anything at all. "We are at our best when we are... anticipating what needs to be done and doing it, communicating often, showing up on time, supporting each other, thinking positively, flexible and innovative, hopeful of the future, etc." Try to come up with about twenty statements. If you have more, great. The answers to this question will also form the basis for many of the group's deposits, which they'll create later.

Step Five: *What are your group's Magic Words?* Remember when we did this exercise for your personal magic words? You will do this in much the same manner. One way to do this is to give everyone a printed handout of the word list in the Magic Words lesson from the BRAIN RESET series in volume one. Ask everyone to take a deep breath, and then state words that resonate with them. Write these words on the board. If a number of people say the same word, put a tick mark next to that word to show how many people picked that word. Once you have all the words on the board, ask the group to select which words are Important (#3), Very Important (#2), and Most Important (#1). Aim to have an equal amount in each column without feeling the need to be perfect. Your #1 words are what you'll want to have in your group's Vision Statement, which we'll cover in the next lesson.

30 ★ BUILD YOUR *GROUP REALITY SHOW*, PART II

S tep Six: *Draft your group vision statement.* When everything is said and done, what do want your group to be and to have achieved? Outputs from Step 2 will help determine what emotionally drives or dampens everyone. For example, being the "best" at something may not motivate the group, but being the "go to" people or having a reputation for being the most reliable *may* be their motivator. Outputs from Step 3 will help determine who/what you want your group to model after.

You'll want to ensure your vision statement helps your group become what it admires. For example, if your group admires someone who was courageous in doing the right thing, then you'll want to emphasize "doing the right thing" in your vision statement somehow. Outputs from Step 4 gives you clues to what behaviors will help you achieve your vision. They help answer the "how?" Outputs from Step 5 are the words that resonate the most with your group. You'll want to leverage these words in crafting your vision statement.

An example vision statement for a work team could be: "We strive to set the benchmark in both speed and quality of work. Through continuous improvement and cheerful flexibility, we adapt quickly to change to retain our edge. We are extremely proud of the work we do, and we support each other to become our professional and personal best."

Step Seven: *Draft your group's deposits.* Using the outputs from your previous work, you'll want to draft about fifteen to twenty-five deposit statements. Your deposits will state what you want to be as a group, but said in the present tense as though you had already achieved it. Deposits will also describe behaviors that a group like yours, having achieved what it has, will have. For example, "We are leaders in innovative ways to train." That is the statement of what your group wants to be, said as though you had already accomplished it.

Statements like these will largely come from your Vision Statement. Supporting deposits might include, "We continuously seek ways to improve. We share our ideas and listen to the ideas of others. We welcome constructive criticism. We do not get comfortable with status quo."

Statements like these will mostly come from your answers completing the statement, "We are at our best when we are…" It is a good idea to collaborate with your team on building the deposits, as opposed to trying to do it yourself. That way there's buy-in from the team and they're more likely to go along with what the deposits suggest. There are examples of group deposits following this lesson.

Step Eight: *Gather deposit photos/videos.* For every deposit, what might be a representative photo or video that speaks to the group? Let your team members choose. Over time, your team may revise the wording of the deposits and the photos and videos that go along with them. Or you may keep them as they are. That is completely up to you and your team.

Step Nine: *Create your board/slideshow/video.* There are several ways you can create your *Group Reality Show.* The low-tech way is often called the "vision board" technique. You may use a large corkboard, piece of cardboard, or other suitable material as the backdrop. Write your deposits on sticky notes or index cards, or you may use a printer, and place them on the board. Then place the representative photo next to the deposit.

It's a great idea to do this as a team and make it a fun team project. You may be as creative as you like. You'll want to place your *Group Reality Show* in a visible location with enough room for everyone to gather around it periodically. For the extra motivated, you may make copies and hang them in several locations. Or you may copy the deposits and accompanying photos, and place one deposit and photo in different locations. Just make sure there's at least one location where all the deposits and photos are in one place. That way you can gather around it at a frequency of your choosing and chat about it. What deposits are sinking in? Celebrate and congratulate yourselves for that success. What deposits are the group struggling with? Without blame, how can the group overcome the challenge?

High-tech ways of creating your *Group Reality Show* include making a slideshow from software such as PowerPoint, or creating a video from software such as iMovies. You may put the show to music, which can be a nice feature. There's also nothing wrong with using high-tech techniques while having a vision board version hanging in the common areas. Again, at a frequency of your choosing, your whole team will want to gather and watch the *Group Reality Show* all the way through. Identify the deposits that are sinking in and celebrate your success. Chat about the deposits that you're struggling with, and collaborate on how as a team you can make things better. Remember that as a leader, you have a lot of influence on these discussions.

EXAMPLE DEPOSITS FOR YOUR *GROUP REALITY SHOW*

We are confident and poised in our demeanor.

Our habits are precise and productive.

We are organized and disciplined.

Each individual works hard to make others look good.

We are open minded and ready for learning new things.

We learn something new every day.

Each of us is a deep, sincere listener.

Each of us seeks to improve our health.

We love sharing ideas on how to become healthier .

We forgive everyone who has hurt us.

We resonate with the world's positive energy.

We know when to surge and when to recharge ourselves.

We are bold and make a positive impact.

We continuously seek better ways of doing things.

We respond to setbacks with calm confidence.

We see challenges as opportunities to learn.

We are masters at adapting quickly to change.

Our quality and speed of execution improves continuously.

We learn something new about ourselves every day.

We are grateful for the opportunity to train hard.

We are mindful of our thoughts and emotions.

We welcome constructive criticism as valuable.

We notice the best in people and tell them so.

We are quick with appreciation and compliments.

We are articulate and well spoken.

We are curious about others and seek to learn from them.

We seek to understand others.

We are receptive to new ideas.

We are aware of our emotions and how they impact us.

We are aware of our emotions and how they impact others.

We listen to the better side of ourselves.

We enjoy celebrating every little win.

We see trends and patterns that others don't see.

We hold no grudges and continually look forward.

We are gracious, even when we are hurting.

We are happy, even if others are jealous.

We do what's right, even if it's forgotten the next day.

We do what's right, even if no one knows.

We are grateful, even when things don't go our way.

We are flexible with our preferences.

When we don't know something, we seek to learn.

We enjoy sharing ideas on how to be more productive.

We are responsible for our own group culture.

When our thoughts are negative, we are aware of them.

We reappraise negative situations in a more positive light.

We are mindful of communications and actions.

We continuously challenge ourselves.

We seek to eliminate unhelpful habits.

We seek to improve the flow of our day.

We support each others' improvement.

We celebrate each others' successes.

We avoid blame and stay focused on solutions.

We understand and appreciate the importance of our work.

We are a world-class team.

We are highly admired and respected by others.

We "care-front" to help keep our team members accountable.

We are exceptionally creative.

We do the little things that help us achieve our goals.

We manage our time expertly.

We move quickly from task to task.

We stay on task and complete them quickly.

We enjoy our work and working with each other.

We handle setbacks with grace and resiliency.

We remain calm during upsetting situations.

We persevere through challenges.

We follow through in what we set out to do.

We improve in some small way every day.

We find ourselves "in flow" often.

We can learn anything, even if we struggled in the past.

We see criticism as a chance to learn something new.

We push through our fears with calm determination.

Each of us spends a little time daily to think quietly.

We listen more than we speak.

Each of us seeks to better connect to those we care about.

We forgive ourselves for our own wrongs.

No matter what anyone says, we are good people.

We have courage to engage in tough conversations.

We stretch ourselves continuosly and relevantly.

We are energetic and synchronized.

Each of us seeks to improve ourselves.

We help each other improve in our communication skills.

We help each other improve in our technical skills.

We help each other improve in our leadership skills.

We are all in service of each other.

When things get tough, we pull together and lean into it.

We are highly successful and sought after by others.

We seek to make a positive impact and lasting legacy.

We can change the organization from our team.

32 SUBORDINATES WHO LEAD BETTER THAN YOU ARE *GOLD*

Some people develop faster than others.

If you're a leader of a team, it's not unlikely one or more people under your care may be better leaders than you.

This is *not* a threat, but a golden opportunity for growth and learning. Such people are rare and worth their weight in gold. Here's a story that makes the point.

When I became a lieutenant in the Marine Corps, I was assigned as a platoon commander. I was in charge of over sixty young Marines, most under the age of twenty-five, and a platoon sergeant who was older, wiser, and quite frankly, a much better leader than me. While I was the one "in charge," he was very much the *real* leader. Everyone knew it, including me. He was supportive and never undermining. He was respectful and the perfect example of a servant leader. He spent much of his time mentoring and grooming me to be a better officer and leader. He taught me how to stay focused on what was important and how not to get distracted by "shiny objects." He taught me to know when to engage, and when to stay out of the way. Finally, he taught me how to read the emotions of the group. That was probably the most important part.

I led a platoon of truck drivers. They did not *feel* important. "Truck driver" was not a prestigious job. In their mind, the only thing worse was being a cook. They drove long hours in extreme heat and cold. They had to get up earlier than Marines in other jobs due to the nature of their work. Most of them were assigned as truck drivers because they weren't very "smart." They were unmotivated and unenthusiastic about their job. Needless to say, their performance was mediocre. When you hate your job, and you don't feel relevant, you're not going to perform well. That much I understood.

I did not have the benefit of a *Group Reality Show*, so I made do by explaining to them the importance of their role with the "want of a nail" story. I explained to them how their trucks are the most glorious site for a platoon of infantry Marines to see after a twenty-mile hike or a week in the field. I noticed what they did right and "care-fronted" them on the things that needed to be addressed. All that was nice, but the one thing that really turned the platoon around was my platoon sergeant's idea to train them…*hard*.

He took them to the field and taught them combat driving, herringbone formations, responding to convoy ambushes, expeditionary recoveries, field repairs, navigation, employing vehicle-mounted weapons, and camouflaging. He volunteered the platoon to participate in exercises with motorized infantry. He had them load their vehicles on and off landing craft on the beach. To the chagrin of the sergeant major, he worried less about shiny boots and more about their mindset and skills as "combat truck drivers." The Marines *loved* the hard training. They loved the relevant challenge, and they loved the opportunity to do cool things every once in a while. Their performance skyrocketed from mediocre to on-fire. This one man turned the platoon around in a way I never could have done.

Of course, all along, I was learning from him too. He explained to me my role in all these circumstances, let me serve my role, and then privately critiqued me afterward. He was always careful not to take over my role, but rather to support me and help me be successful. The experience served as a valuable lesson that it's *very* advantageous to have people who are *better* leaders, serve under you.

Many years later when I entered civilian life, it became apparent that many people tend to be intimidated by someone who's a better leader, or they feel threatened by them. I noticed older people who were fantastic leaders but wanted to "downgrade" in their job, but for a variety of reasons were often turned down for employment. I suspect it's because the hiring managers were intimidated by the greater leadership experience of these people. When I see this happening I want to care-front them on the incredible opportunity they're losing. They could learn, grow, and improve the performance of the team all at the same time.

If you know someone who's better than you at something, that's *more* a reason to hire them than not.

You empower your people when you hire the best leaders you can find, even if those leaders are better than you.

33 ✦ A SUMMARY OF HOW YOU EMPOWER OTHERS

Remember, the most powerful way you empower others is by making them feel *relevant*.

In review, here are the ways you make people feel relevant. Feel free to print this lesson and keep it as a handy reference.

- ✓ Praise and thank people. Show genuine appreciation and *notice* what's right.

- ✓ Create fun and meaningful competition. Give others an opportunity to shine.

- ✓ Tell people the impact of their work, especially on the big picture. Help give their work *meaning*.

- ✓ Be *honest* with people. Don't be manipulative or disingenuous. Never lie or withhold critical information that others really should know.

- ✓ Help people grow and set them up for success, even if they might leave you.

- ✓ *Engage* to help your people succeed when they're struggling. Seek to make things smoother for those over you. *Serve* others.

- ✓ *Do not* diminish people by:
    - ☆ Being the smartest person in the room.
    - ☆ Being dismissive, or putting down other people and their ideas.
    - ☆ Contributing to communication problems with AMUM (Avoiding people, not being Mindful, being Unapproachable, or Misunderstanding others).
    - ☆ Using toxic communication, bullying, or threatening others.

✓ Be a role model by striving to be the best version of yourself (this is the "M" for "Model in GEMS).

✓ Offer a clear and inspiring vision that others can truly feel good about supporting.

✓ Communicate a clear End State, remind them of the five components of the End State, and let others help you figure out how achieve it. Be careful about offering solutions. Give others their autonomy and let them take the credit.

✓ Be an excellent listener.

✓ Practice "care-frontation" as opposed to confrontation.

✓ Hire people who are better than you, especially in the areas where you're weak. That includes leadership.

✓ In collaboration with your team, create a *Group Reality Show.* Watch and discuss it together periodically.

✓ Give your people relevant challenges and training that is hard and stretches them. We'll talk more about this in the Stretch section. Stretch is the "S" in GEMS.

34 M–MODEL

When I was about eight years old, my mother tried all sorts of remedies to get me to behave myself. I tended to disobey, talk back, and would not sleep at night. I would not do my chores unless I was told, and I was a little too loud and hyper for other people. Then one day, she told me something that really made me stop and think.

"Valerie, do you know what it means to be the oldest child? It means your younger brother and sister are watching you, and they'll do what you do. If you behave badly, they'll behave badly too. If you're good, they'll be good. I really need your help. Can you be good and help me so they'll be good too?"

That little conversation changed the path of my life. Sure, I still went sideways from time to time, but I didn't stay there long. I felt the responsibility of being a role model to my younger siblings. I loved them dearly, even if I didn't always show it, and I didn't want to let them down. I also felt a sense of relevance and importance because I was helping my mother.

Fast forward twenty years, and I'm a Marine Corps captain leading thousands of junior enlisted Marines through training at the School of Infantry. I was their company commander, the most senior person many of them had ever met. Class sizes ranged from 350 to 450 Marines at a time, and they all watched me closely. It didn't take me long to notice a large number of them, especially the female Marines, mimicking me; not in a bad way but in a way that clearly showed they were looking for their identity as Marines by modeling me. They mirrored the way I walked, talked, carried myself, word choices, moods, gestures, and even the way I put my pack together for our training hikes. If you've never been surrounded by four hundred reflections of yourself for an extended period of time, I'm telling you it's both nerve wracking and a shocking realization of the power of being a role model. I knew it was important before, but I took it *much* more seriously after this experience.

It has taken me many years to come up with the perfect formula for being a fantastic role model for others. I wish I had known this much sooner, but that's ok because I learned by being and doing, noticing what worked and what didn't. I will share that formula with you now.

The formula for being a fantastic role model is: VEGEMS/C. It stands for:

V—VISION

E—ENERGY

G—GRIT

E—EMPATHY

M—MORALITY

S—SELF CONTROL

C—COMMUNICATION (Common Denominator)

As you can probably tell, the GEMS shown in the role model formula is not the same GEMS as the four leadership maxims (Get things done, Empower, Model, and Stretch). But it's nice to have a similar acronym so it's easy to remember.

Notice that *communication* is the common denominator to VEGEMS. It means communication plays a key supporting role in every part of VEGEMS. Communication includes verbal, non-verbal, words, deeds, and self-talk.

I understand some of you may be a little spooked about being a role model. Instead of viewing it as something scary, view it as an exciting challenge. Understand that in order for you to become the person who's more successful, wealthy, popular, fit, healthy, and likable—the person of your own personal *Reality Show*—you will need to become a role model for…*yourself.*

Does that mean you become a different person?

Yes. That's the whole point! We're trying to let go of our "old" self and become the new, amazing, confident, smart, fit, wealthy, and successful self.

You did not come this far on this amazing journey to chicken out. So let's do this.

35 V–VISION

When I was deployed to Iraq in 2004, I met a young Iraqi interpreter who I'll never forget.

This young man's country was shattered by war. His entire family was killed. He was utterly broke with the exception of the income he earned as an interpreter (it wasn't much).

He lived in the dirt alongside the Marines, regularly getting shot at, with an Al Qeada bounty on his head. After all he had been through, you'd think he'd be a little down.

To my astonishment, he was the happiest, most energized and optimistic person I think I've ever met in my life. He was 100 percent certain he was going to become an American citizen, live in Texas, and become a millionaire. He carried himself with supreme confidence and certainty that the destiny he envisioned for himself would occur, in time. There was zero doubt in his mind.

At first I thought this was a little over the top, but after meeting and chatting with him several times, there was no doubt in my mind either. I secretly became his cheerleader, and I think he had a lot of people rallying around his vision and cheering for him. I'm certain he's living in Texas today doing great things, with a bank account much larger than my own.

There's just something about a person with a fantastic vision that's admirable and inspiring.

When you have an attractive vision, people cheer for you. People are drawn to you and often they want to *help* you. They may not benefit one little bit, but if the vision is inspiring and a great story, they want to be a part of that story, even if it's a small part. It makes them feel good to contribute, and *that* is their benefit.

Most people go through life with hardly any vision for themselves. It's sad and doesn't lead to ideal outcomes. However, when people see *you* with a vision and striving to make it happen, it inspires them. It gives them the hope and courage to have their own vision. Their vision may not be as grand as yours, but's it's a vision nonetheless, which helps them become the best they can be. They *model* you in that they put forth a vision for themselves.

What I just described is an example of a grand life vision. It's a great thing to have, and not everyone has it. That's ok, because there's another kind of vision that works wonderfully as well: your moment-to-moment vision. We usually understand it as *optimism*. I refer to it as an optimistic vision. It's different from your grand life vision.

An optimistic vision is, no matter what happens, everything is going to be just fine.

An optimistic vision is the *decision* to be happy and grateful no matter what the circumstances.

This doesn't mean you don't have a good cry because you lost a dear friend. It means you don't stay there, awfulizing everything, pitying yourself, and being a total wet blanket for everyone else. It means you get it out of your system quickly, then start looking for the lesson and opportunities.

An optimistic vision means leaning into the challenge of change as opposed to *resisting* it.

An optimistic vision means continuing to find, and outwardly express, all the things for which you're grateful.

Do you wake up in the morning and *decide* you're going to have a great day? If things don't quite happen the way you wanted, do you *decide* everything's going to be ok anyway?

An optimistic, moment-to-moment vision is just as inspiring as having a "grand" life vision. People are drawn to you and your vision. They want to help you. They see your example and consider it for themselves.

Of course, it's best to have *both* a grand life vision *and* an optimistic vision. Having both turns you into a gigantic magnet of good things. People admire you and want to help you. People want to share in your vision. Your vision gives people hope and brings out the best in them.

Do you see how this seemingly small thing of having a vision can become contagious?

Do you see how it can change *your* life and the lives of others?

Having a vision is role modeling behavior for others to follow; however, if that vision is communicated in an unenthusiastic manner, or not communicated at all, it won't do much good. You want to have no small amount of *energy* behind that vision.

That discussion is next.

36 E—ENERGY

There was once a sergeant who worked for me who grew up in the poorest part of the Deep South.

He could barely read or write. His spoken English was often riddled with grammatical errors. His teeth were in poor condition. He was soft spoken and shy except when he was in front of a platoon of Marines. Here he became a different person.

The man came alive with a passion and energy that made *me* want to re-enlist all over again. He told stories of his deployments to different countries, and the fighting he did in Somalia. He explained to them why seemingly boring things like keeping your rifle clean, keeping track of all your equipment, digging fighting holes, and studying your "knowledge" was so important. He told great stories to back up his assertions. He was enthusiastic about even the most mundane things.

"You see that cover [hat] you all have? Well that cover was *made* to fold up and put in your pocket. Do it now!"

"Yes, staff sergeant!" they'd shout back. Then they'd sit in the grass and listen to another one of his riveting stories. He was passionate about being a Marine, even if a lot of things Marines did were dirty, boring, and arduous. His energy was contagious, and his Marines quickly responded to his positive energy.

He was a master at "care-frontation," never belittling or berating his Marines. Even though he yelled, there was passion and concern behind his yelling, not anger or disdain. He had females in his platoon, yet he simply called them "Marines." He did not treat the female Marines any differently than the males. He gave them the same positive energy and held them to the same expectations. They loved him for this. His platoons consistently had the highest level of energy and the highest level of performance.

He did not have a grand life vision, but he had a strong, optimistic moment-to-moment vision. No matter what awful thing happened—bitten all over by bugs, utterly exhausted, getting *shot*—everything was going to be just fine. He was going to be happy *anyway.* He's the kind of guy who if he stepped on a land mine and lost both his legs, he'd lift his head with a great big smile and give you the thumbs up. He was invincible with his energy, and if you caught his energy, you felt invincible too.

Have you ever heard the saying, "The guy isn't smart, but he makes up for it in enthusiasm?" There's a lot of truth in that saying. By staying positive and energetic, you can overcome a lot of shortcomings.

Energy fuels vision, whether a grand life vision or optimistic, moment-to-moment vision.

Energy is a form of communication.

If you're low energy and unenthusiastic, it will definitely show up in your spoken words, non-verbals, and actions. You can fake it if you like; there's nothing wrong with that. In fact, faking energy and enthusiasm can help reprogram your automatic mind so in time you truly are enthusiastic. I'm actually a big fan of "Fake it 'til you make it." It's a technique that really works, and there's neuroscience to back it up. Many of the greatest leaders did exactly that.

If you are high energy and enthusiastic, it'll reflect in your spoken words, non-verbals, and actions. It will reinforce the positive programming in your automatic mind. It will send out strong, high frequency vibrations of high energy, courage, joy, love, hope, and optimism. These frequencies overpower lower frequency vibrations associated with low energy, fear, anger, sadness, hate, and pessimism.

People operating at a lower frequency will start to synchronize with your higher frequency. In that case, your energy is contagious.

People already on a high frequency will be attracted to your high frequency. In that case, your energy is a magnet.

Do you see how having positive energy can make you an exceptional role model?

Do you see how you can change your life and the lives of others with energy, enthusiasm, and a high frequency vibration? Even if you're not very smart or grew up in a disadvantaged situation, energy can make up for a lot.

Energy is critical to have a lot of if you're going to demonstrate the next key part of the role model formula.

That discussion is next.

37 G—GRIT

Believe it or not, I spent most of my life struggling to be *average*.

I struggled terribly in grade school. I was bullied and had poor social skills. The teachers treated me like I wasn't very smart. Once I achieved sixth grade, my parents could no longer help me with homework because it surpassed their knowledge. When I arrived at middle school, they literally put me in the same classes I had in elementary school. I protested and insisted they put me in the more advanced classes. I put up quite a fight and they relented. I was placed in the more advanced classes and barely got by with C grades. It wasn't that I wasn't applying myself. I was trying hard. It was the best I could do given I had no help.

Athletically I wasn't much better. I played soccer and softball in grade school, but I was not good enough to make any sports team in middle school.

In high school, I managed to convince the school to put me in "advanced placement" classes. I always felt like an imposter with all the smarter kids. I pretended as though I belonged there. I challenged myself to run for sophomore class president and was stunned when I won. The school formed a girls' soccer team for the first time in its history, and because they barely had enough players for a team, I easily "made" the team. I did ok. I was no star player by any stretch of the imagination. I managed to graduate high school, making the honor roll by a whisker, and get accepted to university. In the meantime, I enlisted in the Marine Corps Reserves, hoping they could push me to "above average" and to have a means to pay for college.

In college, my grades took a serious nosedive. I was competing with some of the smartest people in the world and I was definitely not one of them. It took me seven years to complete a four year degree. My goal was to go to medical school, but my grades and test scores were too low. No medical school would accept me. Another option was to become an officer in the Marine Corps, but my SAT score was too low. I studied extensively, re-took the SAT test, and barely earned a "passing" score by about a tenth of a point. I then went on to the officer training schools, exerting extraordinary effort, only to pass with average scores.

Why am I telling you this? Because the moral of the story is to not quit. The kid who seemed most unlikely to succeed would grind through life, enduring every setback, and progress forward in small steps that added up over time. At this point of my life I am a retired Marine Corps lieutenant colonel with thirty years of service, hold a master's degree in leadership, hold professional certifications in project and program management, and have led and mentored thousands of people around the world to accomplish incredible things in difficult conditions at unlikely odds. I did not achieve all that because I had it easy. I most certainly didn't.

Yes, there are people who had it far worse than I, and achieved much more. The reason I use myself as an example is because I'm truly as ordinary and average as they come. There's nothing special or extraordinary about me. Despite that, I was able to achieve what I did because of one thing....*grit.*

I know there are people with grittier stories than mine. The point is you don't have to be an extraordinary person to have grit. You don't need to have a "rags to riches" or "rock bottom" story. It's ok to be an ordinary person, like me. It's *not* ok to quit on yourself. It's *not* ok to let others dictate your future. *That* is the point.

Grit takes a lot of energy.

It's hard to persevere when your energy levels are low, you're unenthusiastic, and emitting a low frequency vibration. You want to have high, positive energy to grind through the setbacks of life and not quit on yourself.

One of the best ways I've found to stay positive is to hang out with positive people and avoid negative people as much as possible.

You also want to overcome *fear.* A lot of times people quit on themselves because of fear of failure.

Remember, the three ways to push past fear are:

1. Decide: "I'm scared to death but doing it anyway."
2. Research: Learn more to increase your confidence.
3. Agnostic: Decide that whatever the outcome, even if you fail, you will choose to be happy anyway. At worst, you'll learn from the experience, and that in itself is worth it.

Grit is part of the role model formula because people admire those with grit.

As mentioned earlier, grit a significant amount of energy. It also takes courage, and strength.

When people see grit in action, they know what it looks like and can better emulate it. That is the whole point of being a role model, to give people an example to follow.

38 E–EMPATHY

Former U.S. President Teddy Roosevelt once said, "People don't care how much you know until they know how much you care."

Many people feel they don't have "time" or "energy" to care.

They think caring obligates them to take action. They have too many obligations already so they avoid caring. These are false paradigms.

In politics, caring might mean one must alter his or her political stand on certain matters. So people avoid caring on some of the most shocking and sad abuses against humans and nature in order to avoid agreeing with any aspect of a political party of which they don't identify. This is also a false paradigm.

All these false paradigms will limit your progress in life and limit your leadership abilities—*if* you subscribe to them.

Often we subscribe to one of these paradigms when we're overly stressed. We become more absorbed in our own problems, leaving little room for empathy for others. This is a particularly common problem with managers, busy spouses, and parents.

Being in an overstressed state is bad news for you. In the SELF-CARE series, we'll talk about stress and how to manage it so it doesn't sabotage or kill you (yes, it's *that* serious).

For now, just understand that allowing yourself to become overstressed will limit your capacity for empathy.

You'll think you don't have the time or energy to care so you just won't bother. If that happens, you're sabotaging yourself in ways you cannot even fathom.

A lack of empathy in a relationship is like death by a thousand cuts. While the process is slow, death is certain. If a lack of empathy continues uncorrected, then at some point it *will* result in people quitting, a divorce, a child running away, or worse.

A lack of empathy in the world creates a miserable existence. You see it every day in the news. The abuses against humanity and nature can seem overwhelming. There is often the feeling of, "I can't solve it so I won't bother to care."

Empathy is a form of *awareness*.

It does *not* mean you agree or sympathize.

It does *not* mean you must take action.

It means you're aware of the point of view of others, and you can see things from their perspective.

It means you take a little time to listen and understand.

The fact you did that much shows you care. You're an exceptional person for doing that.

Just because you don't *act* does not make you a bad person. You most certainly can if you want to, but you don't *have* to. Your life is full of so many things and you must prioritize and even say no to some noble causes, but you can still *care*. You can still have empathy. And you know what? For many people, just having your empathy is all they really want.

It's difficult to have empathy for others if you don't first have empathy for *yourself*.

If you lock up Toddler in the Supermax, and let Inner Critic run amok, then your capacity for self-awareness is significantly reduced. When you don't have self-awareness, you don't really know your own perspective. If you don't really *understand* your own perspective at a deep level, then you really don't have much empathy for *yourself*. That's why self-awareness is so important because it actually increases your capacity to care about *yourself* and others.

When you have empathy for others, your communication and body language will show it.

Remember, you don't have to sympathize, agree, or take action. Please get that terrible paradigm out of your mind. You just have to listen and sincerely understand their perspective.

When you understand others' perspective, *they* feel empowered.

They feel relevant.

They feel as though you're someone they can *trust*.

You get to enjoy all that influence because you took a moment to empathize.

People love leaders who can see things from their perspective.

Empathy is also powerful role modeling behavior for others because when others feel empathy from you, they're more likely to be empathetic themselves. The result can be contagious.

In the next topic, we'll talk about what happens when leaders have no empathy, no awareness, and no moral compass. As you can probably guess, it's not a pretty outcome.

39 ★ M—MORALITY

"**L**ook, I know we *all* do it, but we just can't have pornography on our government computers anymore."

This is a quote from one of my commanding officers back in the 1990s. When he said that in front of a room full of military officers, I was filled with disgust for this man. The only other female officer in the room and I looked at each other knowingly, *we* were most certainly *not* part of the "we."

First of all, it was shocking that it was revelation to anyone you shouldn't have pornography on a *government* computer. Secondly, my fellow female officer and I realized we were being led by a pervert. I cannot speak for the other male officers because sadly, they seemed to be as oblivious about these obvious matters as the commanding officer himself. Why?

It's not necessarily because they were bad guys, it's because they were being given a bad example by an immoral man. They were following his lead.

Ultimately, this commanding officer was relieved for poor performance and inappropriate behavior. He was one of a number of examples where immoral behavior in his personal life affected his professional life. I saw this happen too many times to count.

I am telling you, with all the love in my soul, this law of the universe:

You cannot separate your personal morality from your professional life.

Period. Full stop.

I know you're not a perfect person, and you don't have to be. I'm not saying you have to join a religious order or anything like that. Most importantly, I'm not here to preach to you. I'm not going to tell you what's right or wrong. That's something only you can determine for yourself in your own heart.

What I will advise you to do is to give the matter of your personal morality some serious thought.

If you were in charge of a group of people and those people learned of your personal morality, *what would they think?*

What if your personal morality made the *headline news?*

I know what *I* thought when I learned of the personal morality of some of my leaders. I also remember the impact on my loyalty and performance. When I was disgusted with them, I did the bare minimum, and yes, sometimes I wasn't very nice and even sabotaged them a little bit. I was not interested in making them look good. I'm not saying it was right of me. What I'm saying is this is a normal human response.

However, when I *admired* the personal morality of my leaders, I was energized and worked a whole lot harder for them. I went out of my way to make them look good. I have found this response to be true not just with me, but with people in general. It's a fairly common and widespread phenomenon.

In countries where corruption is high, ordinary people suffer the most.

Corruption is a system where personal morality (most of it very bad) enters full bore into the professional life. Political and business leaders are not trusted by the people, and for good reason. Their leaders are terrible at solving problems and seem only interested in enriching themselves.

It's difficult to effectively lead people whose moral compass and integrity is stronger than your own. You lose credibility and trust. You lose influence and respect. You lose support and their willingness to go the extra mile for you. That is not ideal.

When you at least *strive* to have a sound moral compass, that is, you're fully honest and humble, living a relatively clean life (you don't have to be perfect because no one is anyway), not harming others for self-gratification, and making a genuine effort to do the right thing (even if you get it wrong sometimes), people *admire* that.

Admitting your shortcomings and challenges, and genuinely trying to be a better person, people admire that.

It's the honesty of your shortcomings and the sincere effort to be a better person that makes you a role model. Perfection is not required.

If and when you master a moral challenge in your personal life, consider coaching others with the same challenge. No one is perfect and we all need a helping hand now and then.

40 | S—SELF CONTROL

In the AWARENESS series, we examined our Hot Buttons, the strength of our Hot Buttons, and how we typically respond to a Hot Button trigger.

Here's a reminder of the ten Hot Button categories: U-HIDE-CUPID.

UNFAIR: Situations and people that seem inequitable or unjust.

HOSTILE: Behavior toward you or others (verbally, psychologically, economically, socially, physically, or other) that feels like a significant and dangerous threat.

INCONSIDERATE: Behavior that to you appears abrasive, curt, cold, rude, aloof, condescending, dismissive, or other manner that seems inconsiderate of you or someone else as a person. It doesn't rise to the level of a dangerous threat, but it still gets under your skin.

DISRUPTIVE: Or, inconvenient. Situations that slow you down, create more work for you, or adversely impact your goals or interests.

EMBARRASSING: Situations that seem to put you in an unfavorable light.

CONTROLLING: People who are overly demanding or micromanaging.

UNRELIABLE or UNTRUSTWORTHY: People or organizations who have demonstrated to you to be unreliable, undependable, or cannot be trusted.

PAINFUL: Physical pain, illness, or incapacitation.

INDECISIVE: Or uncertainty. People who are indecisive or over-analytical. Situations lending to uncertainty so that decision making is difficult.

DISAPPOINTMENT: Situations where expectations are unmet.

There's nothing wrong with having Hot Buttons, even strong ones. Hot Buttons are a normal part of life. Hot Buttons by themselves do not sabotage you.

What sabotages you is allowing a Hot Button to put you out of your right mind, sap your empathy, or cause you to say or do something you regret.

Being a hot head or allowing yourself to be vulnerable to Hot Buttons makes people feel uncertain and uncomfortable around you. They find it hard to trust you because they don't know if you're going to go off on them, embarrass them, make a scene, or hurt others.

If you're a hot head leader, then people will fear and resent you as opposed to being inspired by you. You get a lot more out of inspired people than you do from fearful and resentful people.

I'm not saying you can't get upset, because some things in life are upsetting. What I'm saying is to exercise enough self control to *respond* as opposed to *react*. Good self control requires strong self awareness skills, and we've been working on those skills for quite some time now. Remember to use those new skills in your favor to think and push through Hot Button events with more thoughtfulness and grace, rather then allowing them to pull you into a negative state of mind.

Remember, emotions are contagious. If you allow yourself to enter into a negative state of mind, your negative emotions will vibrate out into the world and incline others into a negative state as well.

I'm not saying you can't ever have a negative feeling such as fear, anger, sadness, disappointment, annoyance, and such.

In fact, it's healthy for you to openly admit you have these negative feelings. It's the first step in Ground Control and is critical to self awareness.

What you don't want to do is dwell there, and you don't want to say or do something you will regret. *That* is *self control.*

If you're a parent, teacher, coach, or manager, you can expect people (especially children) to model your self control.

If you're a parent who tends to lose your cool often, you can expect your kids to struggle with self control.

If you're a manager who loses your cool often, you can expect people to fear and not trust you, all while they actively seek another job.

On the other hand, if you're a model in self control, even when all your Hot Buttons are getting pressed, and you're the one calming others down when things get heated, people *love* that.

People really admire a leader with self control, so much so they'll try to emulate it.

41 C—COMMUNICATION

Communication is the common denominator under VEGEMS (Vision, Energy, Grit, Empathy, Morality and Self Control).

Below is how Communication is the vehicle by which these role model attributes are implemented.

VISION. A beautiful vision is not something to keep secret. You'll want to communicate it to the right people who'll be inspired by your vision and cheer for you. People love to get behind a great vision, even if it's not their own. To inspire others to help with your vision, you'll want to communicate it with conviction and passion. An inspiring vision, communicated in a skillful way, is enormously powerful.

ENERGY. Your energy is a form of communication. I'm not saying you have to bounce around like a puppy all the time. What I *am* saying is you're positive and optimistic, even when things aren't going well. Sure, you'll have bumps along the way and you might not *feel* energetic sometimes. What's important is you get your rest, gather your composure, and turn your energy back on again, even if you have to fake it.

Faking it is a powerful way of reprogramming your brain to feel it for *real*. Faking positive energy requires willpower because you're using your manual mind, so don't beat yourself up if you can't sustain "faking" positive energy for too long at first. Give yourself some time and rest and keep working at it the next day. At the same time, you don't need to overdo the "fake energy" bit either. That will feel awkward to you and to everyone else. You'll eventually stop doing it and go back to your old, grouchy self. Just turn your energy up a *little* more than you're used to until it starts to feel natural. Then turn it up just a *little* more.

You might start simply by acting just a little perkier in the morning, smiling, and saying good morning to people. After about a month of this behavior it'll become more automatic and less forced. Next, you might choose to view everyday annoyances like making a mistake on the computer, spilling your coffee, or getting caught in a traffic jam with a little less negativity and a little more cheerfulness. That behavior may take a little longer to set in, so be patient with yourself. Over time, a little bit adds up to a lot. You'll become a person whose positive energy is *contagious* to those with low energy, and a *magnet* for those with high energy. The more positive energy you bring into the world, the more influence you have to *Get things done*, and *Empower* yourself and others.

GRIT. Your self talk plays a *huge* role in grit. Self talk is a form of communication. It's the conversation you're having in your own mind. If that conversation is negative, making you feel bad about yourself, and questioning you're abilities, then you're not likely to stick with difficult efforts important to your life vision. For example, if learning business is hard for you, positive self talk will help you persevere and prevail. On the other hand, quitting something that does *not* contribute to your life vision is also gritty. For example, quitting smoking, a bad relationship, or ceasing to watch three hours of television every night requires positive self talk too.

EMPATHY. Listening is the second most powerful form of communication and is critical to showing empathy. Listening requires focus: the ability to set aside all the noise in your busy mind and really hear what's being said. It's a *crucial* skill to develop. Brain Hygiene is a powerful way to improve your ability to focus so you can be a better listener. Remember, you don't have to agree or take action. You just have to listen with genuine interest, and without trying to "get your point across." It's about *them* being heard. Not you.

MORALITY. Your actions are *the* most powerful form of communication. You can have a fantastic vision, high energy, lots of grit, be a empathetic listener, and possess great self control, but if your personal *morals* are in the toilet, and people know it, you lose a lot of credibility and trust. Immoral behavior in a leader is like a giant hole in a beautiful, majestic ship; no amount of rearranging the deck chairs or playing jazz music is going to stop the sinking.

SELF CONTROL. Your decision to communicate in a positive or negative way speaks to your self control. Some people can't seem to control themselves and communicate in toxic ways. *Don't* be one of *those* people. You want to exercise much good self control to communicate in healthy ways. For example, care-frontation can indeed be direct and "in your face," *but* it doesn't have one iota of anger, hate, disdain, shaming, or fear. Care-frontation is confident, loving, sincere, and passionate. It also takes no small measure of self control to keep it from turning into *confrontation*, which is loaded with toxic elements.

42 A SUMMARY OF MODEL

Before we get into the summary, it's worth noting what's *not* part of the formula for being a good role model.

To be a good role model, you do *not* need to be: perfect, everything to everyone, number one, in charge, loud, a doormat, extraordinary at anything, famous, highly intelligent or educated, saving the world, in great health, a spiritual guru, have a rock-bottom or rags-to-riches story, or achieved anything great. I can fully attest that I am or have *none* of these qualities, and yet am still a powerful role model for thousands of people—not by my own saying so, but by *theirs*.

The *most* important part of being a good role model is to constantly *strive* to be a better person. Don't become complacent. That really is the heart of it.

If you're *totally comfortable* with who you are, your relationships with others, your success in life, your health, and you're *totally satisfied* with the status quo, then you're no longer striving. When you're in *that* state, people aren't likely to look up to you because you seem to have it easy, with nothing they can relate to. When people can't relate to you, your influence as a role model is greatly diminished. If you're in that state, at least strive to share your secrets with others, the story of how you got there, because certainly there had to be strife with that. Then people can at least relate to the striving "you" of the past and learn from it.

I'm not saying beat yourself up or give Inner Critic a foot in the door about *anything*. I'm not contradicting the message to love yourself (and your wonderful Toddler) unconditionally. I'm not advocating worship of the future and contempt for the present. None of that is healthy. What I'm saying is to be happy no matter what while continuing to challenge yourself and seek improvement. *That* is what it means to be a good role model.

VISION

✓ Grand life vision—or—Optimistic, moment to moment vision—or, better still—*Both*

ENERGY

✓ Positive, high vibrational state (love, joy, enthusiasm, optimism, hope, curiosity).

✓ "Fake it 'til you make it" is a powerful way to reprogram your automatic mind.

✓ Be careful not to overdue the faking bit or it could backfire.

✓ Increase your energy in small doses until it feels normal. Then increase some more.

GRIT

✓ Persevere on the habits and efforts contributing to your life vision.

✓ Seek to *quit* the habits and efforts detracting from your life vision.

EMPATHY

✓ Self awareness is crucial to empathy for *yourself,* which is crucial to empathy for *others.*

MORALITY

✓ You cannot separate your personal morality from your professional life.

SELF CONTROL

✓ It's ok to have Hot Buttons. It's not ok to let them control you. Respond, don't react.

COMMUNICATION

✓ Share your vision.

✓ Energy *is* a form of communication. Keep it positive.

✓ The quality and positivity of your self talk matters.

✓ Listening is a critical skill requiring focus. Brain Hygiene helps.

✓ The most powerful form of communication is you actions. Morality matters.

✓ Care-frontation (healthy), not confrontation (toxic).

43 S—STRETCH

I use the word *Stretch* to represent a number of things. In short, Stretch means to constantly seek improvement.

Stretch demands a willingness to change because you cannot improve if you resist change.

Stretch means changing bad habits for better ones, and being open to constructive criticism.

It's great to *Get things done, Empower* yourself and others, and serve as a fantastic role *Model,* but if you get complacent and don't continually *Stretch* yourself and others, you *will,* in time, become stale, outdated, and eventually, *irrelevant.*

I remember working for an organization with a remarkable history of achievement over the past 150+ years. They accomplished incredible feats of engineering during the first seventy-five years. Somewhere in the middle of their life span they started to grow complacent, resting on the laurels of their past achievements, believing the way they've always done things in the past would surely lead them to success in the future.

Over time, their performance in project and program management slipped further and further behind industry standards. Today they're paralyzed with indecision, lack of strategic vision, and tremendous difficultly completing projects within scope, cost, and budget constraints.

The senior leadership is absorbed with petty problems and trying to please *everyone.*

Their middle managers, many who've been with the organization for decades, think they're doing "just fine" and resist most efforts to modernize or adopt industry standards for project and program management.

Their junior people have a rather high turn-over rate because they soon realize that while the organization has a distinguished history and noble mission, it's stale, lethargic, slow, and complacent. They don't want to work for an organization like that so they move on.

Middle management blames the high turn-over on low pay scales and not enough perks, as opposed to their *own* uninspiring leadership.

Senior leadership merely throws up their hands saying they're a government agency and have no control over salaries and perks. Meanwhile, they do little to *Stretch* themselves or others to keep their organization fresh, innovative, and inspiring. They've become *complacent* leaders.

This is an example of how a lack of Stretch in your leadership will cause your slow demise.

Stretch means challenging status quo, even if it has worked in the past. The world is changing so fast that if you rely on what worked in the past too much, you'll quickly become overrun by those who have a better way of doing it.

You might think you're doing a "great" job at something. I assure you there's probably a better way of doing it. If you get complacent and don't strive to find better ways, it's just a matter of time before you're not doing a "great" job anymore.

It can be difficult to challenge long entrenched processes and policies. It takes courage and persistence to achieve even small measures of success, especially when you're challenging a large organization, majority of people, or government agency.

Stretch is hard, that's why many people and leaders shy away from it.

Stretch pushes us out of our comfort zones, that's why we *fear* it.

Stretch requires us to change, that's why we *resist* it.

Stretch is one of the four leadership maxims because without it, you and your organization cannot compete in a fast changing world. You'll become irrelevant and that's not good.

There's a *right* way and *wrong* way to Stretch yourself and others.

Those discussions are next.

44 THE RIGHT WAY TO STRETCH YOURSELF

When you look at people with amazing abilities, like playing the piano at Carnegie Hall, speaking multiple languages, or winning an Olympic medal, remember they didn't get there overnight or by complacency.

They got there by constantly *Stretching* themselves.

Little by little, day by day, they added a new challenge or goal. They practiced and *focused*. They adjusted their personal habits to augment and support their primary goals. They were willing to change in significant ways in order to optimize growth and master their chosen craft. In most cases of achieving some great thing, the ten-thousand-hour rule applies.

The good news is you don't need to pursue some lofty goal to benefit from Stretching yourself. You can reap tremendous rewards in your life by Stretching in the right way for the right reasons.

For example, you're already Stretching yourself by implementing anything you learned from this book series. Resetting your brain, increasing your self awareness, communicating in healthier ways, practicing Brain Hygiene—if you weren't doing any of that before and you are now, you *are* Stretching yourself. You have every reason to be proud of that. You know why?

Because, sadly, a lot of people give up and don't even try. That you've made it this far means you're not a quitter.

Choosing to Stretch yourself takes courage and a willingness to be uncomfortable. It also requires a willingness to *change*.

Change is the essence of life. Your body creates about ten million new cells every *second*. Birds molt, trees drop their leaves, seasons change. Kids grow, parents age, and new ideas alter our lives almost daily. I find it funny how some people are so resistant to change. To me, being resistant to change is like being resistant to life.

Of course, change for the sake of change, or change that doesn't result in growth or renewal is *not* good. For example, picking up a smoking habit is not a good change.

On the other hand, seemingly bad changes such as finding out you have a disease, losing your job, or your house catching fire, as painful as those events are, can serve as powerful growth opportunities. You may commit yourself to much healthier habits, start a business, or live in a new neighborhood with better opportunities. It all depends on how you choose to view these events and how you *navigate* them. In this case, Stretching yourself to navigate the difficulties in positive ways becomes a much more viable option as opposed to crying victim and doing nothing.

When you're in the thick of a difficult change, the option to Stretch and learn, or do nothing and play helpless, becomes crystal clear.

The *right* way to Stretch yourself is to focus on the habits and tasks that matter, and to add small challenges and goals exceeding what you've achieved before, slowly over time.

For example, if you want to read more books, start with two books a year, then maybe one book every three months, then one book a month. To achieve that, you will need to schedule time in your day for reading. You may need to give up watching TV sitcoms, playing video games that don't teach you anything, or surfing the internet on unproductive efforts.

The *wrong* way to Stretch yourself is focusing on habits and tasks that don't matter, or trying to do way too much too soon.

For example, reducing your sleep time by a small amount every week until you only sleep four hours a night (so you have more time for other things) is a terrible idea. You'll become a safety hazard on the road, a grouch to be around, and you'll wreck your health (more on that in the SELF-CARE series). Reducing your sleep time is the *wrong* thing to Stretch. Or let's say you want to run a marathon next week, and you've never run more than three miles in your life. While running a marathon is a noble Stretch goal, the way you're going about it with little to no training is bound to lead to less than ideal outcomes.

Once you achieve a Stretch goal, you'll want to challenge yourself with another Stretch goal. It doesn't matter what the goal is as long as it's meaningful to you. It can be quilting, throwing a football, brewing your own beer, doing pull-ups, learning history, or anything you like.

The important part is that you're always growing, learning, and improving in *some* way.

45 THE RIGHT WAY TO STRETCH OTHERS

"**B**ut you don't listen to your parents. What makes you think you'll listen to the Marines?"

That was the reaction from my stepmother when she learned I enlisted in the Marine Corps.

As an eighteen-year-old woman with no marketable skills, not very smart, and few resources, I knew I was at a disadvantage entering into adulthood. The only way I was going to make something of myself was to find ways to learn and grow no matter how grueling. In high school, I talked my way into classes well above my intellect and forced myself to get through them. I had just been accepted to a university known for it's academic rigor and knew I was in for a rough time. I enlisted in the Marine Corps Reserves because I thought it was the fast track to adulthood, to learn new skills and become "somebody," and to have a career to fall back on in case school didn't turn out (which is ultimately what happened). My story is similar to many other people who want to grow and learn, to be "somebody," and to feel *relevant*.

People *want* to be Stretched in ways that help them learn and grow so they can better pursue their vision and interests.

As a leader, when you attempt to Stretch others, you'll have much better success if you tie the effort they must put into the Stretch to *their* life vision and interests.

If you cannot, or are unwilling to do that, then your attempt to Stretch others will merely appear like autocratic bullying. They'll resist and you won't get the best out of them.

Merely saying that others *must* obey your demands to Stretch because you're the parent, teacher, coach, manager, or "in charge" works to obtain *compliance* for a short period of time. This scenario is marked by confrontation. In this case, you're not really Stretching anyone but rather bullying them and causing resentment. They sense you don't really care about them so they feel like objects. They will merely do what you tell them to do for now, and no more, until the time comes when they can get away from you. And trust me, they *will* eventually get away from you. I'm not saying you can't be direct and give orders. I'm saying to do so in a caring way *without* threats, anger, shaming, or disdain. Treat them like human beings, not objects.

To gain *commitment* (not just compliance) and truly gain their best performance for the long term, you'll want to appeal to their self interests. You'll want to explain how the Stretch relates to their life vision. It helps if you've already built some rapport with them so you know what their life vision is. Then Stretch them with meaningful tasks and achievable goals that push the limits of their capabilities, but don't exceed them (don't overwhelm or break them). This scenario is marked by care-frontation. In this way, they feel like they're truly learning from someone who cares, and are growing in a way that makes them feel relevant.

For example, let's say you're a school teacher. Compare the following two statements.

"If you don't turn in your homework, I'm going to fail you in the class." As opposed to…

"Doing your homework will help you understand how to build a robot, race car, or rocket ship."

Here's another example from a work manager. Compare the two statements.

"Your new production goal is now a thousand units a day. We'll fire anyone who fails to achieve this." As opposed to…

"Competition has become so intense that we need to produce a thousand units a day to stay ahead. I'm hoping you have ideas on how we can achieve this. You'll save our company from decline if you can help us with this problem."

Hmmm, who would you rather work for?

As parent, teacher, coach, or manager, you have a duty and obligation to Stretch others. Most kids and adults of all ages *want* to grow and learn. That's why they seek out leaders and organizations who can help them.

If you, as a leader or organization, can't or won't help your people learn and grow, then you won't attract the best talent and you won't get the best performance.

Stretching others requires a willingness on *their* part to change, to face the risk of failure, and to go beyond their comfort zone. It's much better to *inspire* that willingness as opposed to force things upon them. That's how true, transformational leadership works.

46 ⭐ A SUMMARY ON STRETCH

The number one reason I remained with the Marine Corps for thirty years was because they continued to Stretch me with new challenges and opportunities of interest to *me*.

Even though the work was arduous, dangerous, dirty, and sometimes boring, there was enough beneficial learning and growth to make it worth the grind. The pay started off low, but there was upward mobility and a pay increase with every promotion. After nine promotions (twenty-seven years later) I was earning the equivalent of a six figure income in the civilian world. I would have left the Marine Corps much sooner if I wasn't being Stretched, and then recognized or promoted for having met the challenge of those Stretches. Consequently, the Marine Corps usually has no trouble retaining their best talent or recruiting highly-motivated people. That's because their Stretch methodology works. It's why they enjoy a world-class work force.

I realize that may not sound very impressive to a lot of people. Yes, there are people who didn't work nearly as hard and earned a whole lot more than I did. Good for them, but that's not the point. The Marine Corps certainly is not for everybody, and, yes, they have their share of "issues." The point is there was no other organization willing to Stretch me and offer me opportunities for growth and advancement like the Marine Corps—and I worked for many organizations, not just the Marine Corps. I didn't stay with these other organizations very long because they didn't *earn* my commitment. I had no reason to stay. The point is, when you Stretch people in ways meaningful to *them*, you get long-term commitment *and* high performance. *That* is the point.

If you're a manager of an organization with few advancement opportunities and uncompetitive salaries, there are still plenty of ways to earn people's commitment and performance, thereby reducing turnover and increasing revenue. You'll want to invest in personal development and leadership training for your most junior people, allowing them to become "intraprenuers," and giving them a stake in the outcomes. (Intreprenuers are people who care as passionately about your business as you do.) By Stretching your people in ways meaningful to *them,* and making them feel highly relevant, you not only keep your best talent longer, you attract people who are keenly interested in having the experiences you offer.

Here is a summary of the Stretch maxim. Feel free to print this page as a handy reference.

Stretch means:

☆ Constantly seeking improvement. Don't become complacent.

☆ Challenging status quo, especially entrenched processes and policies that don't work well anymore. This takes courage and careful navigation.

☆ Being open to constructive criticism and thanking people for their honest feedback.

☆ Having the courage to change, risk failure, or be uncomfortable.

☆ Stretch yourself:

☆ Lofty goal not required, although lofty goals are fantastic. You just need to find something about yourself to improve. The very fact you're implementing the lessons from this series of books is a marvelous Stretch for yourself.

☆ You'll want to adjust personal habits and routines to meet your Stretch goals. Focus on habits that matter.

☆ Keep your Stretch goals realistic, healthy, and achievable.

☆ Stretch others:

☆ When Stretching others, make it relevant to *their* interests, not just yours.

☆ Stretching *correctly* is marked by care-frontation and making people feel *cared* about. *Incorrect* Stretching is marked by confrontation and treating people like objects.

☆ Stretching others requires *them* to be open to change, risk failure, and endure being uncomfortable. You'll need to navigate *all* of these elements and guide them through.

☆ Keep your Stretch goals for others realistic, healthy, and achievable.

☆ Leaders have a duty to Stretch others and *themselves.* Don't become complacent.

47 LEADING CHANGE

There are numerous books, workshops, and subject matter experts on the topic of leading change. Why?

Because people tend to resist change and for good reason. Change is fraught with uncertainty and hammers on all the hard-wired elements in your automatic mind—SCARF.

Status doesn't like change because it could mean a perceived drop in your Status.

Our frenemy, *Certainty*, does not like the uncertainty change brings one little bit.

Autonomy doesn't like change it didn't agree to.

Relatedness is uncomfortable because your friend/foe line up could change.

If the change is perceived to be unfair, then *Fairness* will get triggered. When Fairness gets triggered, it puts people in a negative state of mind. That's usually bad news.

Do you see why there's an entire *industry* on leading change? Change is hard to do.

People *fear* change, mainly because they perceive a *loss* of some sort headed their way.

Fear of loss is one of the greatest fears people have.

The loss can take just about any form: freedom, prestige, money, lifestyle, relationships, possessions, livelihood, health, and comfort.

When leading change within yourself, and you're fearful (which is normal; there's nothing wrong with that) it may help to reflect on what you fear you might *lose*.

For example, if you fear you may lose some relationships, that could mean: 1) a drop in Status with certain people, 2) people who were once friends may become foes, and 3) a reaction by them that is unfair to you. They could react by shaming you, betraying you, or abandoning you. Shaming, betrayal, and abandonment can be seriously wounding to the heart and ultimately, *that* is what you fear.

Remember the three ways to deal with fear are: 1) Decide—"I'm scared to death but doing it anyway." 2) Research—take the time to learn more. 3) Agnostic—Choose to be happy no matter what.

When leading change with others, it helps to understand the loss they fear, even if that loss is not something you relate to or find rational. It's not about what you think of the loss; it's about what *they* think. This is where your empathy skills become important. Remember, to have empathy, you don't have to agree or take action. You just have to listen sincerely.

If you're in a position in which you can collaborate with your people and get their ideas and buy-in for the change, that is ideal. As best you can, try to blend people's interests by finding win-win solutions, as opposed to compromising where both sides feel they are "losing" something.

Often you may be asked to implement a change for which you and your people had zero input. You personally may not like the change, and at the same time it's important you implement the change with all the verve and energy as though it were your idea. Why?

Because people will cue off you. If you have a bad attitude about it, then so will everyone else and that just makes things worse. If you have a good attitude about it, then others will likely model your behavior and that will help everyone to move on.

For those who *really* have issues with the change, lend them your ear. Let them vent to you privately while you listen with empathy. Then calmly inform them, "I know you don't like this, and I need your help to implement it. Please don't make this worse by having a bad attitude. I'm hoping you could give me some ideas on how we can implement this quickly so we can get past this."

In the Marine Corps, change was so frequent we had a saying about it, "Semper Gumby" which means, "always changing." When a change we didn't like came rolling down, which was quite often, we simply shook our heads, said, "Semper Gumby," implemented the change with energy and verve (a lot of it *fake* but that's ok; everyone knew it was fake, which actually made it quite humorous), and moved on quickly. We did not dwell on what was "lost" or hold grudges against the senior leadership for all the changes. We kept looking forward and saluting, smartly knowing we were part of the finest fighting force on earth, and making a positive difference in the world no matter how many changes came rolling down.

48 THE THIRD LEADERSHIP OPERATING ZONE

In *Get things done* we mentioned two zones: the zone between *Rigidity* and *Chaos*, and between *Simplicity* and *Complexity*.

As a leader, if you go too far in any direction (too simple, too complex, too rigid, or too chaotic), you'll experience less than ideal outcomes.

Navigating yourself into, and staying in the ideal zone is not easy, which is why many people struggle with leadership. Even the best leaders struggle with finding and staying in the ideal zone. The more you learn and put into practice, the easier it gets.

Now is time to introduce you to the third zone: the zone between *Doing* and *Being*.

Doing and *Being* could arguably fall under *Empower*, and *Model* (from GEMS). It could also stand on its own in the SELF-CARE series because of its significant connection to *health*.

Given that true transformational leadership of yourself and others requires a careful balancing act within this zone (in addition to the two you already know about), I felt it was best to speak of it here.

My personal, most difficult challenge in leading myself and others was in *this* very area. Until recent years, I was rarely in the ideal zone. I was all work and very little play. Work-life balance was virtually non-existent for me. I spent the vast majority of my time *Doing* and very little on *Being*. Needless to say, I was not very fun to be around, struggled with my relationships, and experienced health consequences as a result.

What's worse is I often imposed my commitment to *Doing* on the people I led. I put a lot on their plates and had little appreciation for their need to decompress or be with family. A lot of that had to do with the pressure I was under from my own leadership. Most of my own leaders had little to no work life balance either. I had become just like them.

I tended toward non-useful perfectionism, and putting so much on my own plate that the stress became enormously unhealthy. My attitude was, "I can sleep when I'm dead," and indeed lack of sleep nearly killed me several times. I had zero time or patience for Brain Hygiene and very little time for relationships. It took me decades to learn the error of my ways.

Too much *Doing* is contagious. Many people have this problem which is why they struggle with relationships and health. What's more is after a certain point, the more you *do*, the less you get done. It's like a law of diminishing returns.

You're not a robot. Humans need to just *be* in order to rejuvenate themselves. You need to enjoy the sunrise, spend time alone reflecting, listen to the birds, conduct Brain Hygiene, and chat with loved ones. If you struggle with your relationships and have health problems, you might have an imbalance with *Being*.

On the other hand, too much *Being* will hamper your ability to *Get things done*. Now some people dedicate their lives to *Being* (such as religious monks), and there's nothing wrong with that. The difference between them and ordinary people is they have no ambition to have families or run a business, nor could they because they could not *Get things done* with all the *Being* going on.

To be a true transformational leader and role model, you want to balance *Doing* and *Being*. For most of us, *Doing* is not the problem. It's the *Being* we lack.

There is such a thing as *Doing* disguised as *Being*. For example, taking care of your family by cooking or cleaning is not *Being*, it's *Doing*. Enjoying a great moment with your family, like going fishing, star gazing, or making s'mores is *Being* so long as you truly enjoy it too and you find it rejuvenating.

Spending quality time for yourself is *Being*. It doesn't have to be lengthy, and no it's not selfish. You want to have *some* time for yourself, just for you, in your own honor, every day.

Doing is critical to *Get things done*, but you don't want it to rise to the level of bad stress or feeling like a threat. You'll want to calibrate it so it all stays in the "good stress" zone, where it feels energizing and exciting as opposed to burdensome.

This isn't the end of the *Doing* and *Being* discussion. We'll talk a little more about it in the next lesson, and much more about it in the SELF-CARE series.

49 SUB-ZONES WITHIN THE THREE LEADERSHIP OPERATING ZONES

In review, the four leadership maxims are:

G—*Get things done*
E—*Empower*
M—*Model (Vision, Energy, Grit, Empathy, Morality, Self-Control)*
S—*Stretch*

Ideally, you want to exercise all four maxims to the best of your ability. To do so, it helps tremendously to operate in the "sweet spot" of the three leadership operating zones.

The three leadership operating zones are:

Rigidity <<<<< >>>>> *Chaos*
Complexity <<< >>>>> *Simplicity*
Doing <<<<< >>>>> *Being*

Within each of these zones, there are a number of sub-zones. I'll share them with you by means of introduction for your awareness. A detailed discussion of the sub-zones is beyond the scope of this book, but will appear in my more advanced material on leadership.

The diagram on the following page summarizes the three leadership zones and their sub-zones.

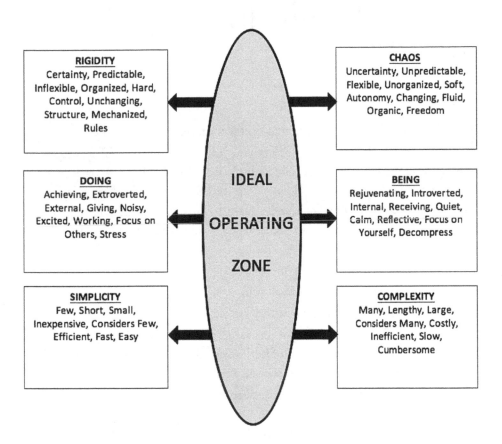

Diagram of the three leadership operating areas. The space between the two extreme ends is the ideal zone.

50 LEAD FOR CHALLENGE, NOT THREAT

L eadership is full of challenges that on the surface, *feel* like threats.

For example. Others may reject your ideas, or even you. They may resist change, or perhaps *you* have trouble with change. There may be setbacks such as an unfavorable decision, an accident, or a health incident. Red tape, daunting bureaucracy, betrayal, sabotage, the list goes on. Finally, there's the uncertainty of knowing what to do. Leadership seems to be a pain. Perhaps that's why a lot of people avoid it.

There's just one teensy weensy problem.

Avoiding leadership is giving in to *fear*.

What happens when you give in to fear?

Giving in to fear is like selling your soul to the devil. He'll keep you "safe and secure" from the "terrifying" world of leadership, all while wrecking your relationships and ruining your chances for success and happiness. Some deal.

Giving in to fear and avoiding leadership is bad news for both you and everyone else.

We have a critical shortfall of good leaders in the world because too many people give in to fear. You and I both know that must change, and we're on a mission together to make a difference, starting with you striving to be the best version of yourself.

As you grow as a leader and progress in your hero's journey, you'll expose yourself to what *feels* like threats.

You'll feel more vulnerable and that is indeed scary.

You may be tempted to worry, nag, complain, judge, control, quit, lash out, or react defensively. These are the behaviors of fear and they will sabotage you.

Now, if you happen to find yourself doing any of these behaviors, you are *not* a rotten person, going off the rails, unable to learn, or any of that silly nonsense.

I still from time to time find myself engaging in some of these fear behaviors. Fortunately, I'm learning to catch myself sooner and correct it before it gets out of hand. Soon you will too if you're not there already. Just give yourself time.

Whenever you *feel* threatened (about to engage in fear behavior) stop for a second and *notice* it without judgment.

Take a deep breath, then reframe the threat as a *challenge.*

When something becomes a *challenge* as opposed to a threat, your mind shifts from fear to curious. Your demeanor changes from aggressive (negative) to energized (positive).

If your automatic mind is programmed for threat and fear (which is most people, by the way) it'll take some time to reprogram it for challenge and curiosity. Eventually, things that used to upset you will become minor inconveniences, then no big deal at all.

For example, if rejection or confrontation is an issue for you (and it is for most people) you may have responded fearfully by becoming defensive or lashing out.

By viewing these situations as a challenge and not a threat, you reduce the fear response and become more *curious.*

Curiosity is energizing and will motivate you to listen more, ask more thoughtful questions, and remain confident in the wonderful and fantastic person you are.

There's another really good reason to reframe threats as challenges and reduce the fear response: you *think* more clearly and rationally. You make much better decisions. The outcomes from those decisions are usually much more favorable. That in itself is worth the effort.

When you're fearful, you don't think clearly or rationally, don't make good decisions, and can't lead well. Again, that does *not* make you a bad person. It just means you put a lid on your potential as a leader for as long as fear governs your thinking.

One way you'll know you're fearful is you'll *stop breathing.*

That's right. Even if you're not demonstrating one of the "fear" behaviors, you'll temporarily stop breathing.

Noticing you've stopped breathing is a signal to take a deep breath and reflect on what's making you fearful or tense. Then reflect on how you can reframe the matter in more positive terms. You may find yourself doing this often, and that's ok You're striving, and that's admirable.

51 LEAD WITH RESULTS AND GRACE

Often people promoted into a new leadership position focus on *problems*. That's understandable because they probably got promoted by being such great problem solvers. They believe it's their *role* as leaders to find and solve problems.

Focusing exclusively on problems is a common mistake many leaders make.

The problem with focusing too much on problems is they get stuck on the problems instead of steering the team toward the outcome desired. They might be solving a lot of problems, but they may not be getting the outcome they want. Or worse, they could be heading the team toward ruin.

It's sort of like the captain of a ship getting caught up in the drama of the galley or engine room, all while the ship steers off course and heads toward an iceberg. The captain may solve a lot of problems in the bowels of the ship, but his ship is not heading toward it's planned destination. Worse, the ship is at risk of crashing and sinking.

Focusing on *outcomes* instead of problems is a different mindset. It's the mindset of being at the helm of the ship, watching the horizon, reading your people, and monitoring your instruments. If you get pulled into a problem, you engage just enough to get it unstuck, let your people finish solving it, and then get back to the helm again, ensuring the ship stays on course and making course corrections as needed. In other words, you stay focused on the End State, monitor the Current Picture, implement your plan, and make corrections to that plan as warranted.

When you focus on the End State, you see things differently. You notice more opportunities and risks that can either help or hinder the outcome you want to achieve. While it's tempting to focus on problems, new leaders need to adjust their focus on outcomes.

Now, that does *not* mean sit back and relax while your people do all the work.

That does *not* mean you focus on what's fun and interesting while delegating everything that's boring.

What that means is you focus on what's important to achieving the outcome desired. If that means getting dirty with your people or helping with the hard or boring stuff, so be it.

Achieving the *End State* consistently is what it means to "Lead with Results."

Now for the "Grace" part.

You want the journey to be fun, energetic, opportunity for growth, and in the end, something you and everyone else can be proud of.

It doesn't matter if you're working on a simple work task or a noble mission. It doesn't matter if it's a personal or professional goal. It doesn't matter if you're raising a family or overcoming setback or obstacles in life. You want your hero's journey to be something you and others can reflect on, learn from, and be proud of.

"Lead with Grace" does *not* mean everything is rosy.

Quite the contrary, chances are the journey will be difficult. There will be stress, negative people, setbacks, and bad luck.

"Lead with Grace" means learning, growing, maintaining your awareness, keeping your cool, and choosing to be happy and grateful even when life throws lemons at you.

It means treating others with dignity and respect, even when they don't reciprocate.

It means emitting a high emotional frequency vibration (love, joy, optimism, curiosity) and avoiding the low, sabotaging vibrations (disdain, anger, pessimism, and fear).

It means being humble and serving others, all while asserting yourself and pursuing your interests in a healthy way.

Finally, it means keeping yourself *healthy* so you have the physical, mental, and spiritual strength to "Lead with Results and Grace."

In fact, your health is so critical to your ability to "Lead with Results and Grace," there's an *entire* series dedicated to SELF-CARE. That series is next, following the summary page.

As we close on the LEADERSHIP series, understand there's a great deal more to the subject of leadership. We've only just viewed the tip of the iceberg. There are follow-up educational materials leveraging the wisdom of numerous thought leaders and my own expertise.

I hope you take advantage of it.

52 SUMMARY OF THE LEADERSHIP SERIES

Congratulations! You've completed the LEADERSHIP Series.
    This is a noteworthy achievement as it was the longest series with the most content. To fully benefit, you had to complete the five series that came before it. There is much to be said for your commitment.

Detailed summaries of each of the GEMS maxims, and the VEGEMS/C were already provided. So we'll keep this summary at a high level, and add detail that was not included in previous summaries.

✓ GEMS
  ☆ Get things done: focus on End State, avoid procrastination.
  ☆ Empower: yourself and others, make others feel relevant.
  ☆ Model: VEGEMS/C, people will do what you do.
  ☆ Stretch: continuous improvement of yourself and others, avoid complacency.

✓ VEGEMS/C
  ☆ Vision: grand and optimistic.
  ☆ Energy: a form of communication, enables Grit.
  ☆ Grit: don't give up just because something is hard.
  ☆ Empathy: for both yourself and others, beware of treating yourself/ others like objects
  ☆ Morality: perfection not required, but you need to strive for better.
  ☆ Self Control: cool cucumber when Hot Buttons pressed.
  ☆ Communication: medium by which VEGEMS is exercised.

✓ Strategy

    ☆ End State: Scope, Cost, Schedule, Quality, Who. Not the same as vision or mission.

    ☆ Current Picture: Status of the five parts in terms of alignment on path to End State.

    ☆ Plan: How you intend to achieve End State. May change often.

✓ Leadership Operating Zones

    ☆ Between rigidity/chaos. Too rigid = inflexible. Too chaotic = can't Get things done.

    ☆ Between simplicity/complexity. Too simple = sacrifice. Too complex = cumbersome.

    ☆ Between doing/being. Exessive doing = burn out. Excessive being = can't Get things done.

    ☆ Leadership can be scary. View as a challenge, not threat.

    ☆ Lead with Results (consistently meet End State) and Grace (enjoy and grow with others).

PART 3
THE SELF-CARE SERIES

GENETICS AND PIANOS

Welcome to the seventh and final series of our program!

You've been exposed to knowledge, tools, and techniques to reset your brain, increase your awareness, improve your communication skills, empower you with neuroscience and wisdom, and develop you into a role model and leader. You may not have known about these things growing up, but knowing them now, no matter your age, will empower you to get promoted at work, find the love of your life (or reignite the love you already have), achieve health and fitness goals, increase your wealth, and accomplish your goals and dreams.

With all that said, your health, particularly your *brain* health, contributes to your ability to learn, and provides the energy you need to pursue your goals or persevere through setbacks. You don't need to be the perfect model of health, unless you want to, but you do want to be healthy enough to pursue what you want out of life.

Perhaps being super healthy and fit is one of your life goals. I personally think it's a great idea and hope you make it a life goal. Maybe you've tried in the past and didn't quite get there. Or maybe you're confused by all the conflicting information on the topic.

The good news is the lessons in this series will help bring some clarity to your journey so you can make better decisions on how to pursue your health goals.

My undergraduate degree is in Nutrition Science. As I completed courses in genetics, biochemistry, endocrinology, and advanced nutrition, it became increasingly obvious to me that "one size" diet and exercise programs do *not* fit all.

I was shocked to learn that medical doctors receive only a few *hours* of nutrition education in medical school, I was, and still am, a firm believer that nutrition, lifestyle, and environment should be the foundation for healing as opposed to pharmaceuticals. Yes, drugs have a role, but they shouldn't be the *foundation* for health and healing like they are today. Now, before going any further, here's the legal disclaimer I must get out of the way first:

> *I'm not a doctor. Do not take anything I communicate as medical advise. Consult with your physician before implementing anything discussed by me, here or anywhere else.*

Now onto the good stuff.

Your health is what it is right now because of two things: environment and genetics.

Your environment is nutrition, physical activity, stress levels, water you drink, air you breath, clothes you wear, your relationships, job, hobbies, and beliefs. Your environment is the totality of all these things working together, and not any one thing in and of itself. With that said, it's possible for just one or a few things to play a strong role, which indeed can matter in a big way.

Your genetics is the DNA you inherited and carry in every cell of your body. Genetics determines things like your sex, eye color, shape of your nose, and such, but they also play an important role in your *health*. For example, if your genetics predispose you to having high or low levels of a certain enzyme, a sensitive immune system, or hormone imbalance, you may experience anything from minor health inconveniences to life threatening diseases.

Your environment plays a huge role in genetic expression. For example, if you're out in the sun a lot, the genes you have for skin pigmentation will be expressed and your outward appearance will be affected. If you have a lot of stress in your life, then the genes you have for cortisol (a hormone) production will be expressed and a whole host of consequences will take place.

Think of your genes as a *piano* where each note represents a set of genes. No two pianos are exactly alike. There are different styles, designs, and sounds. Some pianos may have a few notes a little or a lot out of tune. That's pretty normal. Think of those "out of tune notes" as your less than helpful genes. The rest of the notes (genes) are pretty good.

Your environment is the *player* on the piano. If your piano has a few notes out of tune (a few bad genes) but your player (environment) is really good, than he can skillfully avoid the bad notes and still produce beautiful music (great appearance and health). If you have a magnificent piano (great genetics) but a terrible player (poor environment) then the music will not sound good at all (poor appearance and health).

Even with a few bad genes, if your environment is good, then it's possible to avoid expressing "bad" genes and stay healthier.

The opposite is true in that you can have the best genes in the world, but if your environment is terrible, your health will suffer.

WHAT MUSIC IS YOUR ENVIRONMENT PLAYING?

In the last lesson we equated your genetics to a piano, of which the individual notes on the piano represent genes.

No two pianos are exactly alike. It's not uncommon for a few notes to be slightly (or a lot) out of tune. These "bad" notes represents your genetic imperfections.

We equated your environment to the player of the piano.

If the player is skilled and knowledgeable on your specific piano, then even with some bad notes in the piano, beautiful music is still possible. If the player is unskilled and does not know your specific piano, then even with a magnificent, perfectly tuned, grand piano, the music will be just awful.

We equated the music played on the piano as your appearance and health.

If the music is good, then your health and appearance is good. If the music is bad, then your health and appearance is poor.

The question is, how do we develop a highly skilled and knowledgeable player of *your* piano to make beautiful music even if some of the notes are bad? In other words, how do we create an environment tailored to *your* genetics that will keep you healthy and looking good, even if your genetics have some flaws?

As I mentioned in the last lesson, I don't believe in "one size fits all" nutrition and exercise programs. Your genetics are specific to you. Things that work for someone else may not work for you and vice versa. For example, think of something as simple as your blood type. Different blood types indicate different genetics going on. If you receive an infusion of blood that's not compatible with your blood type, bad things can happen (you could *die*).

Here's another example. Do you know of someone with a severe peanut, gluten, or dairy allergy? Many people are born with these allergies because of genetics. I know people who are deathly allergic to spinach, strawberries, tomatoes, and other seemingly healthy foods. These are just a few of the more visible examples. Many people don't show strong symptoms but instead feel fatigued, foggy brained, unenergetic, or just plain off. They may have skin problems, frequent illnesses, or be prone to injury. Many people diet and exercise and still look and feel unhealthy. They have no idea why this is and sometimes live in this state for decades or even all their lives. This does not bode well for feeling great and being your best self.

Since my years of studying nutrition science, I have always believed that anything going *into* your body (food, air, water, drugs, nutrients, *anything*) and everything you do or is done *to* your body (exercise, cold exposure, sleep, stress, *everything*) interacts with your unique genetics to produce a unique outcome. I didn't know the details of exactly what does what, but sensed this truth would be revealed by smart, scientific people over time. Fortunately others felt the same way and entered medical research fields to find out. For decades I hoped the proof would come, and I'm pleased to see increasing evidence and proof for this truth making it's way into mainstream knowledge. I studied this information for the most relevant content, and synthesized it in a way that's easy to understand and apply. What you'll learn from this series are the many ways you can manage your environment in order to realize better outcomes from your genetics. With that said, let's get started.

There are five areas of your environment that play into your genetic expression. These five areas are not independent of each other. What happens in one area affects the other four areas, creating a complex and dynamic situation. The five areas are:

#1. NUTRITION/WATER

#2. PHYSICAL ACTIVITY

#3. NON FOOD INTAKE (air, drugs, absorption through skin, exposure)

#4. SLEEP/REJUVENATION

#5. MINDSET/THOUGHTS/BELIEFS

These five areas are not listed in order of importance. The first three areas are what most people think of first. The last two areas are less well known but play no less an important role.

I think you'll be surprised in what you learn about these five areas. Some of the information is fairly well understood and accepted by health experts, while other information is less understood and even a little controversial. The resource and reference section lists the sources for this information, and you are encouraged to explore further to better understand the science.

3 ★ NUTRIGENOMICS

I remember studying nutrition science, genetics, food science, physiology, endocrinology, and biochemistry in college during the early 1990s. I saw a clear connection between nutrition and genetic expression, and was shocked and surprised to learn that few others did. I thought, "Am I the only person who sees this connection?" I found it frustrating that medical doctors received only a few *hours* of nutrition education in medical school, so I pursued becoming a medical doctor specializing in nutrition science. I quickly learned there was no such thing as a *medical* doctor of nutrition. Obtaining a doctorates in nutrition got you a job as a research professor at best. I wanted to treat and cure people of their ailments, not teach theory in school. It turned out my grades weren't high enough to get into medical or graduate school anyhow, so my quest to prevent disease through tailored nutritional approaches came to an end. Although I had to take a different course in life, I still cared deeply about this subject.

Over the years, I observed different diets come into fashion: vegetarian, vegan, paleo, South Beach, Lemonade, etc. I had my own professional opinion about the merits of these diets. The one that intrigued me the most was the Blood Type diet by Dr. Peter J. D'Adamo.

The Blood Type diet offers a tailored diet based largely on one's blood type. The differences are interesting. A blood types benefit the most from vegetarian or vegan diets, but such a diet would not be ideal for an O blood type who benefits most from a more "paleo" diet emphasizing red meat and no grains. B blood types benefit from dairy while other blood types should avoid dairy. AB blood types get to enjoy the best of both worlds from A and B. There's much more to the diet than this, but these are the main highlights and it was the first diet I ever saw that was not "one size fits all."

Blood type is a *very* simplistic way of categorizing people by extremely large buckets of genetic coding. A, B, AB, and O blood types (+ and -) have different genetic codes. In fact, they're so different that if you get a blood transfusion from an incompatible blood donor you could die. That's no joke. Animals have different blood types too, but they usually don't die if they receive blood from another animal of the same species. What I saw in this diet was the the first indication of a doctor who saw the connection between *nutrition* and *genetics*. I studied the diet with great interest and told anyone who would listen about the diet. Then a surprising thing happened.

Most of my family and friends rebuked me for believing such "hype," much less were they interested in following such a diet. Some A types would never give up their red meat and the vegetarian O types would never eat the flesh of an animal, *ever*. Yet interestingly, they all had health problems they insisted were unrelated to their diets. To my surprise, the rejection didn't stop there. I was shocked at the strong criticism and outright rejection of Dr. D'Adamo's theories and work by the medical community. It was so widespread I began to suspect some sort of strange political collusion against the idea of linking nutrition to gene expression and health. What else was I supposed to think? To me, the link had been obvious for decades. I didn't need to conduct hundreds of experiments to prove it. A basic, undergraduate level understanding of genetics, nutrition, biochemistry, physiology, and endocrinology would reveal this truth. Why wasn't it obvious to everyone else? I became frustrated and pretty much gave up on the subject for a number of years. Then one day, I was listening to a podcast on nutrition and health and heard a word that got me excited once again.

Nutrigenomics.

Nutrigenomics is the study of the link between nutrition and gene expression—a field of science that's in it's infancy. Apparently, there are now a number of doctors out there who *do* see the connection, are determined to explore it and make it obvious to the naysayers. I suddenly felt as though I had finally found my lost tribe. I felt redeemed and couldn't wait for the revolution in medicine that would surely come. Someday doctors will be able to take your DNA, run it through a machine, and produce a highly-tailored, specialized diet that optimizes your gene expression for ideal health.

The diet will likely include unusual ingredients or foods you're not used to eating, and you'll likely have to give up foods causing adverse gene expression. When medical doctors start doing this, then opportunistic businesses will take these specialized diets and formulate wonderful recipes you can cook at home, or they make for you. When this takes place, the problems of obesity, heart disease, diabetes, cancer, arthritis, dementia, and many other ailments will diminish.

The good news, you don't have to wait for the revolution. More on that in the next lesson.

GOING MAINSTREAM

The science of nutrigenomics is exploding.

Universities are starting to offer courses of study and research opportunities in the subject. Scientific journals focusing on nutrigenomics have emerged. Medical doctor's are paying closer attention and some doctors have fully embraced the science. Except for a few hard sells, no one is scoffing at Dr. D'Adamo anymore. Already there are a number of businesses and medical clinics who offer to test your DNA and produce for you a diet tailored to your unique genetics. A simple web search of "nutrigenomics companies" will turn up numerous results. For a price (somewhat steep, I might add) you can learn about your unique genetics and the diet that works best with it. Some companies are good at explaining things, while others use a lot of scientific jargon and you practically need a medical degree to understand it.

The tests and clinic visits can get quite expensive. It's also important to understand the science is still very new, so the results you get today will not be as precise as in the future. New discoveries are made frequently. The least expensive option right now is probably learning your blood type (it should be in your medical record, or a simple blood test will tell you), and then buying the Blood Type diet book. I'm guessing that will give you about a 50 percent solution, which is not bad. It won't be perfect but it gets you a little closer.

To get more precise from there, you'll need to purchase a DNA testing kit. There are a number of mail-in kits available starting at around $200. Once you receive your DNA results, you can download the "DNA doctor" app by Aaron Krumins, or purchase the SWAMI kit from the Blood Type diet website, and share your DNA information there. You will then receive a detailed diet report for your genetics. In time, well after this book is published, there will likely be many more options available. I don't mean to leave anyone out, it's just that these are the two lesser expensive nutrigenomic systems I know about as of this writing.

If you follow the Blood Type diet and then advance to DNA testing or clinical visits, you'll likely find your food list change, perhaps substantially. Items once forbidden could become "superfoods" and items once permitted may become discouraged. Remember, blood type consists of only eight large buckets of genetics, so a diet based on blood type will only take you so far. There is a tremendous amount of variation *within* each bucket. When you take the DNA test you'll get much more specific within your blood type. That means your diet will become more specific as well.

Other concepts are going mainstream as well. Here's a short list of concepts once considered hype, but are now gaining acceptance thanks to overwhelming evidence coming to light.

Organic Produce. If ordinary food affects your genetic expression, just think about what pesticides do. Organic produce are farmed without pesticides or other harmful chemicals. Farmers use natural means, such as swarms of ladybugs, to control pests.

Hormone/Antibiotic Free Animal Products. Animals are often injected with hormones and antibiotics to make them bigger and more resistant to disease when they're crammed in extremely close quarters. You'll find most hormone/antibiotic free animal products are also "free range" or "grass fed." That's because animals who live more normal lives (not crammed in cages with concrete floors, which is extremely stressful to them) are naturally more healthy and don't need antibiotics to fight off disease. Hormones and antibiotics absolutely affect gene expression in unpredictable ways, so you really want to avoid them whenever possible.

Four Pillars of Food. Dr. Catherine Shanahan explains humans throughout history survived disease and extreme environments when their diet consisted of the following four pillars: bones (meat cooked on bones and bone broth), fermented (yogurt, kimchi, etc.), organ meat (yummy), and raw foods (veggies, fruits, sprouted grains). Human genetics and diets containing the four pillars produce more ideal health outcomes than diets that don't.

Adpatogens. These are special herbs, fungi, tubers, and plants that seem weird and unusual to us today but have actually been used by certain human populations for millennia to promote health. Adaptogens are things like reishi, ginseng, licorice root, ashwaganda, and others. Adaptogens effect gene expression by helping to regulate hormones and help the body adapt to stressful environments, such as disease, climates, and changing situations. We will have a whole lesson on this topic later so don't worry if you've never heard of this before.

In fact, we'll have a number of lessons covering the nutritional concepts above, and more.

Those are coming up next.

WHAT DOES "ORGANIC" MEAN?

"Organic" farming of produce and animals is similar to farming the old fashioned way before we started using chemicals on crops, or feeding chemicals to livestock.

It's also considered to be more ecologically friendly and environmentally sustainable. Organic farming methods are less dependent on chemicals and less damaging to soil and air.

If you know the farmer (maybe it's you), and you know how the crop was grown or the animals raised (without chemicals) then you may consider the food "organic."

However, if you don't know the farmer and you're buying your food at the market, then depending on the country you're buying your food in, you'll want to look for the "organic" label.

A number of countries, in an effort to protect consumers, apply strict standards in order for a farmer to declare his produce "organic" and label it as such. The standards vary in every country, and the label doesn't mean the produce is 100 percent pesticide or chemical free. Some organic products are allowed to use a small amount of pesticides or chemicals, just not as much as conventional growers.

It can be expensive to buy organic, and it may not be in your budget. Due to the growing consumer demand, more farmers are offering organic products so prices are starting to drop.

Nevertheless, organic-labeled produce still costs more. There are some things you can do to reduce your intake of harmful chemicals from produce without always buying organic.

One way is to prioritize purchasing organic produce well known to be high in pesticide residue, such as all berries and grapes, all leafy greens, apples, celery, tomatoes, bell peppers, nectarines, peaches, and cucumbers. The conventional version of these products will expose you to about fourteen pesticides, so it's better to buy organic.

Produce that is usually safe to buy conventionally are avacados, pineapple, cabbage, asparagus, mangos, melons, honeydew, onions, sweet corn, kiwi, bananas, sweet peas, broccoli, eggplant, and cauliflower. These products will expose you to one or two pesticides, which is much better than fourteen.

Also, sometimes frozen organic produce is cheaper than fresh.

Generally, the skin is most exposed to pesticides so if you peel it, you reduce your intake. This is not a perfect solution, but it helps.

Finally, you'll want to wash everything really well, and dry the produce with a towel, or use a spinner. This should help clean off some of the residue on the produce. Again, not a perfect solution, but it's helpful. Now you should wash everything anyway because many hands, dust, dirt, wind, critters, the unwashed sides of trucks and boxes, and dirty floors and streets will leave unhealthy residues on your food. So washing your produce before cooking or eating is a good habit to have anyway. It's a small hassle that will add health benefits over time.

The "organic" label is also applied to meat and dairy products. The label *should* mean that no hormones, chemicals, or antibiotics were used, but in some cases a small amount may be allowed. Organic animal products are still quite expensive, and there are no good alternatives. The best thing you can do, if you're on a budget, is prioritize your purchases. Usually organic eggs and dairy are more affordable so you may want to start there. Organic chicken is next, and finally beef and pork would be last because they're the most expensive.

Conventional farmers inject their animals with hormones to grow them faster to market weight. These hormones stay in the animal and then enter your body. Not good.

Conventional farmers inject animals with antibiotics in order to prevent the spread of disease. Animals are confined to tight spaces and under tremendous stress. This situation creates the perfect environment for disease to spread. Additionally, animals are exposed to harsh chemicals used to clean the cages from dirt and excrement. The antibiotics and chemicals then get passed on to your plate. Again, not good.

Finally, some conventional farmers feed their animals some really strange and awful stuff to save on feed costs (I will spare you the details or you may lose your lunch). Such unnatural foods do not get excreted very well and can end up on your plate. You don't want that.

Remember, every single thing you eat our drink, every morsel and sip, interacts with your unique genetics for better or worse. If you have a "healthy" diet but still struggle to lose weight, sleep, gain strength, or be more energetic, then you'll want to re-examine your diet. If you have a "healthy" diet and still have health problems then you *really* want to re-examine your diet.

The conventional wisdom on what constitutes a "healthy" diet is under increasing challenge. One-size-fits-all diets of the past will soon go the way of the dinosaurs, along with the naysayers who continue to deny the importance of the interaction between food and genetics on health. When that happens, perhaps many drug companies will die off as well.

6 OUR ANCESTORS KNEW HOW TO EAT

D r. Catherine Shanahan is another nutrigenomic pioneer. She studied the diets of humans across cultures, continents, and history. She found that in every case, no matter the culture, geographic location (desert, jungle, arctic), and across time, there were four common denominators in the human diet: bones, organ meat, fermented foods, and raw foods. She calls them the four pillars of the human diet. When these four pillars were in the diet, humans were better able to resist disease, environmental stress, and live longer. When any one of these four pillars were missing, humans didn't do so well.

Meat cooked on the bone and bone broth contain vital nutrients not typically available in meat cooked alone. So when you prepare your holiday prime rib, cook it with the bone in it. Chicken and other poultry are also more nutritious when cooked with the bones. Cooking large bones in stews and soups is an inexpensive way to add nutrition to your meals.

Fermented foods (yogurt, sourkraut, fermented beans) are tremendously helpful to gut health. The beneficial bacteria in fermented foods do a good job of replacing the bad bacteria in your gut. Bad bacteria makes you unhealthy (bloated, constipated, gassy, nauseous, fatigued, etc.), while good bacteria helps you eliminate better and keep your guts in good shape.

Organ meat (liver, heart, brain, intestines, etc.) is a tough one for some westerners because this is *way* outside their normal diet. Many places around the world still eat organ meat, so this isn't a big deal to them. Organ meats provide very dense nutrition and protein that meat alone doesn't provide.

Finally, there's raw foods (fruits, vegetables, and even some raw meats such as fish). The process of cooking tends to destroy nutrients. Raw foods tend to be more nutritious than cooked foods. This is not always the case or even safe, so be sure to check.

If your diet is wholly missing one of these four pillars, then your genetics are having to make do with less quality materials. As Dr. Shanahan puts it, it's like trying to build a house out of packing peanuts instead of bricks. Your genes will still build the house, but you won't like what it looks like and it certainly won't serve you well.

Our ancestors may not have known these four pillars were keeping them healthy, but they did have some good intelligence on specific herbs and fungi. In the past, they may have referred to these special foods as "magical." Today, we refer to them as *adaptogens*.

Adaptogens may seem new to many of us in the modern world, but they've been part of the human diet for thousands, if not tens of thousands of years. You may recognize things like ginseng and licorice root, but you may never have heard of reishi, ashwaganda, and other seemingly strange foods. A simple internet search on "adaptogens" will turn up a lot of information on the subject. Adaptogens interact with DNA in powerful ways to help your body adapt to stress. If you have no stress in your life then maybe you don't need adaptogens. But if you have a stressful life, and most people do, then you're putting a heavy load on your hormone system. When you overload your hormone system, you get out of balance and feel exhausted or unwell. When your system is *really* out of whack, you can end up with diseases such as diabetes, heart disease, or cancer.

Before you blow your paycheck on adaptogen supplements of every sort (they can be expensive), consider these three things:

First, research the right adaptogens that fit with your lifestyle or mode of intake. For example, do you prefer pills or a powder to put in your food or drinks? Also, you don't need to take every adaptogen under the sun. Do your research and take what's best for you.

Second, *cycle* the adaptogen(s). In other words, don't take the same thing every day consistently forever. Take the supplement a few days, then stop taking it a few days, then back on again. The concept of cycling is important in other areas of your health as well, and I'll have a lesson on that later.

Third, simultaneously manage your stress. Adaptogens are helpful, yes, but they will not solve every health problem. They work best in concert with a nutrigenomic diet and with thinking and emoting habits that don't aggravate your hormone imbalance. When you feel or experience "stress" it's usually your thinking and emoting that evokes the hormone imbalance, and not the actual situation itself. Stress can cause enormous health problems, even kill you. Managing stress is so important; we'll have several lessons on it in this series.

THE CONVENTIONAL NUTRITION SCOREBOARD

Conventional nutrition has some things right and some things wrong. The things they have right are in three broad areas.

The first is the requirement for certain vitamins and minerals in the diet. A person with a sustained vitamin or mineral deficiency could develop painful diseases such as beriberi (lack of vitamin B-1), scurvy (lack of vitamin C), or a long list of other diseases pronounceable only by medical professionals. Conventional nutrition advocates recommend taking vitamin and mineral supplements, and I agree that's a good idea.

The second is the absolute requirement for plenty of fresh water. If you're deprived of fresh water, you can suffer from dehydration and die within days or even hours. Conventional nutrition suggests at least eight glasses of water daily. I agree. Sodas, juices, and coffee don't count. Water doesn't just flush you out. It helps you burn more calories too.

The third is that sugar is *evil*. Contemporary nutrition is right about that one with some caveats. Some may argue certain sugars are "healthier" than others. Sugar as syrup, agave, honey, or *any* form is…sugar, so that doesn't mean you can have all you want. Sugar substitutes are controversial and I wouldn't consider them healthy alternatives. Artificial sugars tend to stimulate appetite so you eat more. Some studies suggest a link between artificial sugars and health problems such as hormone imbalances and dementia. My suggestion is to limit artificial sugar intake, or better still, eliminate them entirely.

The things contemporary nutrition has wrong will take more time to explain.

The first is that dietary fat is evil and it's best to keep fat intake to a minimum. This assertion is partly true and partly false. Too much fat of any kind is not good for you, as it contributes to weight problems. However, eliminating fat altogether and/or, not having enough of the "good" fat can be problematic to your health. In some cases, having an extremely low-fat diet can cause you to *gain* weight. That's because people on very low-fat diets can't get satisfied so they overeat.

The fact is humans *need* some fat in their diet, particularly the "good" fats. For example, there are *essential* fats you must have in your diet or else there will be unpleasant health consequences. Essential fats are omega-3 and omega-6. They largely come from fish, nuts, seeds, dairy, eggs, and olive oil.

In another example, fats called "medium chain triglycerides" (or MCTs) are quite good for you. They help you burn calories, balance hormones, and protect your brain. Another nice feature of MCTs is they help you feel full longer so you don't overeat. MCTs are found in coconut oil, full-fat dairy products, and grass-fed cattle (both meat and dairy).

Grass fed cattle and their high MCT content is a perfect example of how an animal's diet affects *your* diet. It takes five times as long to bring grass-fed cattle to market weight as opposed to cramped, grain fed cattle, but then there's up to five times as much MCTs. Yes, grass fed animal products cost more, but you don't need to eat much of it anyway. You don't need gigantic steaks or buckets of butter. A little bit on most days goes a long way.

The second thing conventional nutrition has wrong is vegetarian diets are "healthier." There are loads of problems with this assertion. The primary problem is lack of protein with enough *essential* amino acids. Amino acids are the special building blocks of protein. There are lots of different amino acids, but humans require eight essential amino acids in their diet to be healthy. It's difficult to obtain the essential amino acids in a vegetarian diet without supplementation. Animal products provide a plentiful supply of the essential eight. Plants do not. There are other nutritional deficiencies that can occur in meatless diets, like iron and B-12.

Now, I know vegetarians who are *very* passionate about being vegetarian. That's fine if they're doing it for religious or moral reasons. If they're doing it for "health" reasons, their arguments are not strong, with one exception. Some people have the genetic gift of thriving on a vegetarian or vegan diet. In their case, they are truly healthier on a meatless diet. But that is definitely not everybody because a lot of people actually do *worse* when they have no meat in their diet. Yes, some people do better, but those are fewer.

There's more that conventional nutrition has wrong, so I will cover the rest in the next lesson.

8 THE ARGUMENT OVER ADDITIVES

Conventional nutrition asserts food additives such as artificial flavors, colors, stabilizers, and preservatives are safe to consume.

There's a lot of controversy behind this assertion.

Supporters of this assertion point to the numerous studies showing little to no harm with these additives. While this is true on the surface, the controversy comes in the interpretation.

For example, if a certain food additive was shown to not "cause" cancer in lab rats, does that necessarily mean it's "safe" for humans to consume? There's too much information the studies leave out. What about effects on the endocrine system, neurological system, and others that may not lead to *cancer* but can lead to more minor health consequences like adrenal fatigue, brain fog, or a screwed up metabolism?

Opponents of food additives believe most food additives are so foreign to human genetics that we cannot be sure of the efficacy of these additives no matter how many experiments are done. Opponents also believe such additives are used by big business to gain worldwide market share and crush small, local producers who largely do not use additives. There's some merit in this argument. But in all fairness, our busy lives are just as much to blame. I'll explain in a moment.

First, there are several reasons why large food producers use additives.

The primary reason is to prevent spoilage. When food is shipped far from it's origin (thousands of miles or halfway around the world) then spoilage is a real concern. Additives also extend the shelf life. Have you ever noticed a package that said "good until..." some distant month or *year* in the future? That's a clear sign a lot of preservatives were probably used in the processing of that food product.

The second reason is to give food the appearance of being fresh and appealing (artificial colorings largely do this). Many fruits, vegetables, and meats change color very quickly when exposed to air, so the additives help to maintain their original color.

The third reason is to boost flavor. Artificial sugar, monosodium glutamate (MSG), and artificial flavorings largely do this. We become accustomed to the boosted flavor and soon natural food products without flavor enhancers simply won't do anymore.

We instinctively know "fresh" is always better, but our busy lives and economic situations can sometimes give little room for "fresh." This is where *we* contribute to the problem of additive use. When we're in a hurry, we reach for fast food or microwaveable dinner. We reach for products like these and other processed foods that are loaded with additives. What's worse is they taste so good (thanks to flavor enhancers) they keep us hooked.

We have little time to shop the farmer's market, buy fresh meat from the butcher, or cook. Strike one.

Fresh, organic, produce without additives or preservatives, usually cost more and are hard to find. Strike two.

Finally, fresh and organic food can sometimes taste bland in comparison to processed foods with additives. Strike three.

Soon, we develop a habit of prioritizing our time, money and energy toward other things as opposed to seeking and preparing fresh, quality food without all the weird stuff in it. In fact, it's more than a personal habit; it's a widespread social *culture.*

Fortunately, more companies are turning the corner to offer more fresh, organic, additive-free alternatives. Many larger grocery stores are starting to carry more organic products (make sure you check the label because organic does not mean additive free). Some restaurants are starting to offer healthier choices as well. Still, the challenge of staying clear of pesticides, chemicals, hormones, and food additives is not exactly a small one.

The good news is you don't have to be perfect. If you follow a nutrigenomic diet tailored to your genetics, and you seek fresh, organic, additive free foods about 80 percent of the time, you'll make a significant different in the quality of your health. If you fall off the wagon now and again, or travel and get stuck eating fast food, there's no reason to fret. If you enjoy a delicious desert or forbidden food every now and then, you're not going to suddenly die.

What matters is you don't do that as a matter of habit.

What matters is you quickly return to healthier habits that include prioritizing a little more time, money, and effort toward eating your tailored nutrigenomic diet (to include fresh water and adaptogens), seeking fresh, organic produce, and cooking your own meals.

9 ⭐ LECTINS AND GLUTEN

It may surprise you to learn that most plants do not want to be eaten.

While animals defend themselves from predators with sharp teeth, stingers, and camouflage, plants defend themselves through *chemistry*.

Some plants are straight-up poisonous, while others do their dirty work slowly over time, like death by a thousand cuts. Many of the slow killers do this through special proteins called *lectins*.

Lectins are plant proteins that can cause problems for people. Unlike most animal proteins that break down into individual amino acids during digestion, lectins do not break down like that. They enter the bloodstream from the gut either intact or partially broken down. The immune systems sees these proteins as foreign invaders and develops antibodies to them. These antibodies then start to confuse what's good and what's not, and autoimmune system problems develop. As a result, one can develop allergies to lectins, some mild and some very serious.

Many lectins also damage the gut lining so that it "leaks" things it shouldn't into the bloodstream, thereby triggering additional immune system responses. The immune system is further confused and compromised because it sees everything as a threat. When the immune system becomes this confused, one can experience excezma flair ups, rashes, asthma, arthritis, migraines, lupus, irritable bowel syndrome, Crohn's disease, and a long list of other inconvenient health ailments.

The outer coating of beans and grains are particularly high in lectins. One can reduce the lectin content of some of these foods through sprouting, soaking, fermentation, and high pressure cooking. For this reason, many cultures around the world apply these lengthy processes, to render these and other high lectin foods safer to consume. However, these laborious processes do not remove all lectins and some very sensitives individuals may still react unfavorably to them. The take-

218

away here is to monitor your reaction after consuming *any* grains or beans. If you find indigestion, irritable bowels, heartburn, flatulence, and/or a health ailment flaring up within twenty-four hours after consumption, then you could be sensitive to that item. Sometimes the manner of preparation will make a difference, and sometimes not.

Gluten is a type of lectin found in nearly all wheat products and it is particularly difficult for many people to deal with. It does not break down, it enters the bloodstream, it "sticks" to things, and causes havoc with the immune system. A great many people are starting to realize their health ailments improve when they remove gluten from their diets. There are many "gluten free" products coming out, and not to be a wet blanket, but there are problems with them too.

Many gluten free products are made from non-wheat grains, and chances are, if you're sensitive to gluten, you're sensitive to the lectins from these grains too. You may find that as your body heals from the gluten onslaught of many years, it becomes even more sensitive to the other grains, putting you right back to where you were before. I am one of these people and while my heart broke to give up my wonderful pasta and cookies, my health is better than it has ever been in a very long time. It just might be worth it for you too.

I remember in the 1990s when the nutrition "experts" encouraged everyone to eat "whole wheat" products. Little did they know they were making matters *worse*. A lot of people (including me) consumed "whole wheat" everything. I could not figure out why I was working out for hours almost daily, witholding calories, and still had weight problems. Well it turns out it's hard to lose weight consuming a diet high in whole wheat products. Whole wheat is very high in lectins and contributes to health problems such as obesity, diabetes, and other ailments. So if you're consuming whole wheat products for "health" reasons, you may not be doing much good for yourself.

I realize removing grains and beans from the diet may be too much of a leap for some people. What you'll want to do instead is ensure they are prepared thoroughly and correctly, through soaking, fermentation, and/or high pressure cooking. If you cherish your bread, consider white flour, sourdough bread made from *real* yeast and not from some weird chemical (as many in the United States are.) In other words, bread made the old fashioned way.

Finally, use non-genetically modified organism (GMO) products. The reason is these products were specially bred to resist insects, meaning they make their own pesticide. Remember, plants don't want to be eaten and it's easy to breed them so\their chemical makeup becomes dangerous to potential "predators," including humans. They may look safe, even yummy, but they aren't.

10 ⭐ OXIDATIVE STRESS

There's a kind of stress at the cellular level that you don't feel or notice until it's almost too late.

It's called *oxidative stress*, and it can cause a long list of diseases such as obesity, liver disease, degenerative diseases, diabetes, cardio vascular disease, neurodegeneration, hypertension, alzheimers, autoimmune disorders, and more.

Oxidative stress is when the body can't keep up with the amount of *reactive* oxygen in the body, and the reactive oxygen accumulates causing damage to proteins and DNA. If the damage continues for a long time, it will lead to inflammation, cell death, and disease.

Oxygen molecules come in two forms: the safe form and the reactive form. When the safe form of oxygen is used by a chemical or metabolic process, it produces the reactive form as a *by-product.*

The reactive form of oxygen is often referred to as "free radicals."

Free radicals come from two sources: 1. Icky things in your environment, such as tobacco smoke, pesticides, and chemicals; and, 2. A natural by-product of metabolism.

Your body produces natural agents to neutralize free radicals, and render them safe. These natural agents are called "antioxidants." However, the body can only produce so much by itself. It needs significant help from your diet in order to have enough antioxidants to do the job.

The more free radicals you ingest and make, the more your body needs to ingest antioxidants, otherwise the free radicals accumulate and cause cell damage. Over time, the damage accumulates leading to inflammation, disease, serious disabilities, even death.

Whenever you ingest drugs or harmful foods, you *suppress* your body's natural ability to make it's own antioxidants. Additionally, you *add* more free radicals to your body, so it's a double whammy.

Ingesting food and supplements high in antioxidants and low in free radicals is the best way to defend yourself from oxidative stress.

Foods high in free radicals often include foods cooked with chemical agents (like some BBQ), foods fried in rancid oils, are highly processed, or have antibiotics, additives, preservatives, or pesticide residue. They may taste yummy, but it's a nasty trick. They are *not* good for you.

Foods high in antioxidants include berries, many organic fruits and vegetables, certain adaptogens, and a number of high quality supplements such as vitamin C and grapeseed extract.

What's more is when you ingest food high in antioxidants, you also boost your body's natural ability to make it's own antioxidants, so there's an added bonus.

It's important to obtain your antioxidants from a variety of sources. Chowing down on a gallon of blueberries everyday is nice, but your body needs more variety than that.

I'm not sure it's possible to overdose on antioxidants. I've known many people who gave up junk food, consumed high-antioxidant diets and found more energy, weight loss, fewer joint problems, and feeling better overall.

A high-antioxidant diet with organic fruits and vegetables, and minimal additives and preservatives is more expensive than the conventional diet. Very true. However, think of it this way, if your health declines and you're diagnosed with something like Type II diabetes, you'll end up spending about $10,000 annually to manage it.

Additionally, you'll spend more time and hassle on blood tests, seeing the doctor, and worrying about losing a limb.

You don't need any of that. It's much wiser to invest in healthy nutrition and enjoy your life than to give it to away to a health care system.

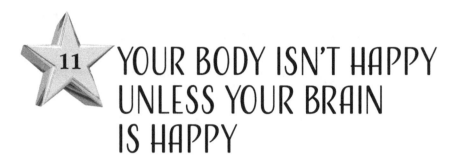

11 YOUR BODY ISN'T HAPPY UNLESS YOUR BRAIN IS HAPPY

In the BRAIN RESET series, we talked about how certain parts of the brain renew themselves.

Neurogenesis (as this is called) happens when you sleep. In fact, sleep is so important to your brain health we'll have a whole lesson dedicated to this topic. For now, its important to understand your brain is always changing. The brain you have today is not the same as ten years ago, last month, or even ten minutes ago.

There's a dynamic interaction between four major areas producing the brain you have right now and the person you are at this moment. These areas are listed below and not in any order of importance or priority. They're all important and affect one another significantly:

Genetics. Genetics program the body for certain hormones, proteins, enzymes, and such that all play a role in health, including brain health. Genetics is the code we're born with, but we are *not* helpless when it comes to gene expression. Remember, your genetics is like a unique piano with a few keys out of tune. A skilled player who knows where the bad keys are can still produce beautiful music. In other words, if you understand your genetics you can consume, avoid, and do the right things to stay healthy, even with a few bad genes.

Nutrition. The brain is so important it has a special gatekeeper called the "blood brain barrier." Certain essential amino acids such as tryptophan, tyrosine, and phenylalanine are allowed to cross the barrier, while others are prohibited from entering. These special amino acids play a role in neurochemistry. Too much or too little of these special amino acids can cause problems, sometimes very serious problems, in the brain *and* the body. Blood sugar (called glucose) is also allowed exclusive entry. Things that aren't supposed to be in the brain, but somehow get past the barrier can cause very serious problems, even kill you. Weird things in our diet, drugs, and toxins we breath or absorb can hurt us because some of them manage to sneak their way past this special barrier.

Activities. Both physical and mental. If you practice yoga everyday, you'll shape and wire your brain differently than if you practice Kung Fu, body building, or play hockey. The same goes for mental activities. If you play chess, you'll shape and wire your brain differently than you will from playing poker, video games, or practicing safe cracking. If you spend a lot of time on social media reading provocative posts, you'll wire your brain differently than if you read uplifting or educational books. If you watch a lot of violent, disturbing movies, you'll wire your brain differently then if you watch movies that uplift you or teach you something valuable.

Thoughts. Dr. Mario Martinez is a pioneer in the science of *biocognition,* the science of how thinking and emoting affects health. Like the concept of food affecting gene expression (nutrigenomics), the concept of *thoughts* affecting gene expression (biocognition) has actually been around a long time. Like nutrigenomics, biocognition was long ignored or discounted by the medical community. Now, scientists are giving serious attention to this concept, and freshening it up with a new science term, "biocognition."

As Dr. Martinez explains it, negative thoughts about yourself, others, the future, and how you might react to things, affects the construct of your brain, neurological and hormonal chemistry, and *gene expression.* Negative thinking such as anger, fear, and frustration causes a tightening of DNA which leads to poor gene expression. Love, joy, happiness, and gratitude opens up DNA leading to healthier gene expression. For example, if you're angry or stressed, then you'll release a hormone called *cortisol* which causes unwanted outcomes such as weight gain. Even your imaginations can affect gene expression. If you imagine yourself in a peaceful tropical paradise with happy thoughts, you'll affect gene expression differently than if you imagine yourself committing some sort of violent act against someone you don't like. Dr. Martinez asserts that most of our physical and mental problems actually stems from our *thinking.*

What happens when your *brain* isn't happy? Your body isn't happy either. This unhappiness can show up in the form of a headache, aching joints, indigestion, and so on. Left unchecked, things like migraines, arthritis, ulcers, heart disease, and cancer can ultimately result.

What happens when your *body* isn't happy? It sends negative feedback to your brain and contributes to it being even *more* unhappy. In other words, we create a vicious feedback loop.

The opposite is also true. When your body is happy, your brain is overjoyed. You're more energized, more motivated, and sending off wonderful vibrations to the world, making you a real pleasure to be around. You become a better version of yourself, role model, and leader.

That is exactly what you want.

12 THE BRAIN IN YOUR GUT

You may be surprised to learn there are more nerve cells and neurochemicals in the gut than in the spinal cord or peripheral nervous system.

Many of the neurochemicals are exactly the same as the ones operating in the brain. When the brain sleeps, so does the gut, and when the brain dreams, the gut "dreams" by moving around.

When you're feeling upset, your gut informs the cells of your body and you'll feel unwell. When you're happy, your gut squirts it's neighboring cells with pleasure chemicals to let them know it's time to celebrate.

This communication between your gut and its surrounding neighbors explains phenomena such as knots in your stomach, butterflies, warm feelings, and tingling. Information flow between the gut and brain tends to be more one-way, from gut to brain. In other words, the gut talks to your brain, and your brain listens. It almost makes you wonder who's really in charge.

The brain in your gut is often called the "second brain" or Enteric Nervous System (ENS). While the brain picks up and processes information from the five senses (sight, sound, touch, smell, and taste) our ENS picks up and processes information from *inside* the body and passes it on to the brain.

Much of this information comes from what you ingest, your microbiome (the bacteria in your gut), physical activities, and sleep. We'll cover these areas in more detail later.

What you ingest. Your gut reads and responds to everthing you swallow. It senses both the physical elements (hard, soft, shape) and chemical elements (sugar, salt, protein, fats, carbohydrates; as well as pesticide residue, drugs, and supplements). The gut has an extremely intimate relationship with the microbiome living within it, which also responds to everything you eat. We'll talk about that next.

Microbiome. These are billions of bacteria in you gut, and they're almost infinitely diverse. There's bad bacteria that makes you unwell (diarrhea, constipation, bloating, nausea, fatigue, etc.) and there's good bacteria that makes you feel wonderful and full of energy. The microbiome is highly sensitive to what you eat. So if you eat a lot of junk food, the bad bacteria will proliferate while the good bacteria struggle to survive. It's like having weeds take over your lovely garden. It won't take long before the garden is destroyed, just as it won't take long for you to feel foggy brained, bloated, and lazy should the bad bacteria take over. If you eat highly nutritious food, then the good bacteria will eventually recolonize your gut and help you feel more energetic and alive. Antibiotics and drugs kill off much of the microbiome, which is why they often cause digestive upsets. The bad bacteria are more resistant, so they'll survive, then take over and cause havoc. It can take a long time for a healthy microbiome to return naturally, so it's a good idea to invest in high quality probiotics. Probiotics re-introduce healthy bacteria into your gut. Along with a healthy diet, probiotics can be a simple and highly effective way of nurturing a healthy and strong microbiome so you feel healthy and strong too. It's like nurturing a garden inside your body. You want to tend to the flowers and not let the weeds grow.

Physical activities. Exercise affects your gut, and it's not just the crunches you do. Studies show low to moderate exercise tends to improve microbiome health. On the other hand, intense and highly rigorous exercise can lead to gut damage, regardless of a person's fitness level. Endurance athletes need to hydrate well, avoid drugs, consume a healthy diet, and take probiotics. Generally, when exercise is enjoyable and not stressful it tends to help gut health. When exercise is not enjoyable and a stressor, it tends to harm gut health.

Sleep. Gut health affects sleep, and sleep affects gut health. The two are mutually supportive when all is well, and mutually harmful when out of whack. The better your gut health, the better your sleep, and vice versa. This is yet another good reason to take a good, quality probiotic regularly. Lovely dreams happen when the garden inside you is blossoming and beautiful.

The brain in your gut doesn't possess consciousness like the brain in your head, but it senses just about everything going on in your body. It responds to the environment, to everything you ingest, to your activities, and even to your very thoughts. If you've ever thought something iliciting a strong emotion, you probably felt it in your gut.

If you're gut is happy, then your body is happy.

If you're body is happy, your brain is happy.

When your brain is happy, you're healthier overall, and have the energy to enjoy your life with more verve and vigor.

Your gut plays a big role in making your brain healthy and happy. In then next lesson, we'll talk about another key player in the health of your brain: *sleep*.

 # 13 SLEEP

Contrary to popular belief, sleep is not a waste of time. In fact, it's a critical part of your physical and mental health.

The brain uses up more energy than any part of the body. Any organ or system using energy creates by-products. The brain is no different, and by-products must be removed for the brain to stay healthy. By-products build up during waking hours, and are cleansed away during sleep.

Think of your brain like a vacuum. All day long it's working hard and doing great things, all while filling it's chamber with gunk. When the chambers get full of gunk, nothing more can be taken in. If you don't turn off the vacuum and clean out the chamber, the vacuum won't work. So if you don't let your brain shut off and clean out it's chambers, it won't work very well.

If that analogy doesn't work, then imagine you're eating and drinking day after day and not going to the bathroom. At some point, there'll be a disaster. So if you don't let your brain cleanse itself regularly, then it's just a matter of time before something bad happens.

Studies show sleep deprivation impairs your driving ability as much as alcohol.

Sleep deprivation impairs reasoning, awareness, problem solving, learning, and emotional intelligence.

Chronic sleep deprivation contributes to health problems, chronic inflammation, poor gut health, weight gain, and dementia. A life of chronic sleep deprivation is about as bad as smoking. It's just bad news.

Temporary deprivation is a normal part of life, but chronic deprivation is not. In fact, if the deprivation is long and severe enough, it can cause death.

I remember in Marine Corps training we were purposely sleep deprived while undergoing rigorous physical and mental endurance tests. We all learned very quickly we were not our normal selves under these conditions. Given that combat operations offer precious little time for quality sleep, it was important for us to learn how we behave when sleep deprived. I learned I was much grouchier, less considerate of others, and tended to make snap decisions favoring convenience over safety and security. After learning this about myself, I paid extra attention to these areas when sleep deprived so I wouldn't say or do something I'd later regret.

The brain's janitor during sleep is the *glymphatic system*. During sleep, the brain will shrink up to 60 percent while the glyphatic system is working. Studies show the glymphyatic system is more efficient when sleeping on your side as opposed to on your belly or back.

You may have noticed during sleep that sometimes you dream, and sometimes you don't, and you're right. The brain cycles back and forth between dreaming and non-dreaming sleep.

During *dreaming* sleep, our judgment center is turned off. The brain paralyzes us to prevent our physical body from flying over canyons, chatting with lions, or swimming underwater for extended periods, lest we not surivive our dreams. The latest thinking on dreaming sleep is that our memories and learning are consolidated during this time.

During *non-dreaming sleep*, our brainwaves slow down to delta, and a host of unique biological processes take place, such as the release of certain hormones that only take place during non-dreaming sleep. There are different phases of non-dreaming sleep, which we'll talk about in the next lesson. Not all non-dreaming sleep is the same and different things happen in the body during different phases of non-dreaming sleep.

It's important to have the right amount of both dreaming and non-dreaming sleep, in the right phases. For example, if you're only getting dreaming sleep, and not enough non-dreaming sleep, you may still wake up tired even after a full eight to nine hours of rest. This can happen when your sleep is interrupted during the night by crying children, a snoring spouse, ringing phones, sirens, or physiological problems.

We typically cycle through the dreaming and non-dreaming phases in ninety-minute intervals. Once an interval is finished, we'll cycle through another ninety-minute interval. If an interval is disrupted, it's almost like it never happened. Humans typically need four to five full intervals of sleep to feel fully rested. So if after eight hours in bed you only got two or three full intervals (the other intervals were disrupted) then you may still feel tired in the morning. On the other hand, if the quality of your sleep is good, and you obtain four to five full intervals, then you can get by on as little as six hours of sleep and still feel fully rested.

In the next lesson, we'll go a little deeper into the cool world of brainwaves.

 # 14 BRAINWAVES—PART TWO

In the NEUROSCIENCE series (volume one), we introduced the five different brainwaves: gamma, beta, alpha, theta, and delta.

Awareness of your brainwave state at any given moment can be useful to your productivity, rejuvenation, and physical and mental health. It's why we revisit brainwaves here in the SELF-CARE series. If any one of these five brainwaves is over or under produced, it can lead to health problems. There's no brainwave that's "better" than another. You need all of them in the right mix.

Gamma waves are the most energetic of the brainwaves with a small amplitude. It's the most mysterious of the brainwaves, showing up alongside alpha, theta, and beta states, and during dreaming sleep. Some scientists believe gamma waves are associated with being "in flow" or "in the zone"—the feeling of high mental productivity. High gamma activity is associated with excellent memory recall, sharper senses, and increased focus. Additionally, high gamma activity is associated with feeling blessed, gratitude, and compassion for others. The pre-frontal cortex is more active while the amygdala is less active. The exact opposite is found when gamma activity is low. Low gamma activity is associated with learning disabilities, depression, low empathy for others, lack of focus, and impulsiveness. The amygdala is more active in people with low gamma activity, meaning one's F3 response is more sensitive. According to experts, the best way to get more gamma in your life is meditation (brain hygiene.)

Beta waves are the second most energetic brainwaves, and are active when you're accomplishing mental tasks such reading, writing, logical reasoning, or socializing. Beta waves give you energy, focus, and are associated with high productivity. There's a dark side to beta and that too much is harmful. Exessive beta can lead to worry, anxiety, tension, and stress, thereby releasing stress hormones which can lead to health problems such as insomnia, high blood pressure, weight problems, and inflammation. Too little beta leads to inability to focus, daydreaming, depression, and poor learning. The right amount of "busy beta" is optimal to life.

Alpha waves are right in the middle between fast brainwaves (gamma and beta) and slow brainwaves (Theta and Delta). Typically when you're relaxed and calm and not thinking deeply, you're in the alpha state. Alpha is often associated with the meditative states, and is sometimes referred to as the link between the conscious (manual) mind and the subconscious (automatic) mind. Alpha helps us to stay calm and in control of ourselves when things get stressful. Too much alpha leads to lack of focus and excessive daydreaming. Insufficient alpha leads to axiety, stress, and in some cases, obsessive compulsive behavior. Alpha is found in the non-dreaming sleep state just as you're nodding off to sleep, before you start dreaming. When something is really boring, your brainwaves will slow down to the alpha state and you may start to nod off.

Theta waves are the second slowest brainwaves. They're associated with the hypnotic state and with dreaming sleep. Theta is seen as a window into the automatic mind. Too little theta leads to poor emotional intelligence, anxiety, stress, and general unhappiness overall. When one has advanced in their meditation abilities, they can enter into theta at will and truly reshape their mind.

Delta waves are the slowest brainwaves and are associated with deep, restorative, non-dreaming sleep. If you don't get enough delta, you'll feel tired. Many hormones, including growth hormone, are released during the delta state. Babies and children need more delta because they're growing very fast. Growth hormone is critical to long bone growth. Often, parents coax their children to eat by explaining how food makes muscles grow. Parents can coax their children to sleep by explaining how sleeping makes bones grow. When you were growing up, did you ever wake up one morning and feel just a tiny bit taller? Delta brainwaves and growth hormone release during a good night's sleep is the reason why.

Remember how we talked about dreaming and non-dreaming sleep, and how it takes place in ninety-minute intervals? Well, here's the full run down:

From your wakeful beta state, you enter into alpha and nod off. From alpha, you enter into theta and start dreaming. After a dream or two, you'll fall further into delta and hang out there for a while. At some point you'll return to theta, and then alpha which is usually when you wake briefly to reposition yourself. Then you'll return to sleep and repeat the cycle.

What about afternoon naps? Naps under an hour can be quite restorative for your brain. Longer than that and you may enter into delta sleep. Too much delta and you may feel groggy. A short nap where you enter into alpha and theta for a few minutes, sets up your "second-beta wind," so to speak. As long as you don't enter into delta, you won't feel as groggy when you wake. So short naps are very good. Just remember, naps are not a replacement for good, quality sleep at night. You need time in delta and several full sleep cycles to feel fully rested.

15 BRAIN HYGIENE, ROUND TWO

I remember entering into a philosophical debate with my twelve-year old niece about the merits of making one's bed every morning. She questioned why bother making the bed when it's only going to get messed up again?

Making your bed is not for the bed, it's for *you*. It's about honoring yourself and giving your day a fresh start. There's a sense of comfort and satisfaction in that.

We mentioned how the brain cleanses itself when you sleep. Sleep provides a fresh start for the brain. We clean our bodies, brush our teeth, and wash our clothes, each time honoring ourselves and providing a fresh start. These habits are a valuable use of our time and energy because they strengthen us. When we practice good hygiene and habits, we are happier and healthier.

Brain hygiene (meditation) is another excellent habit that *strengthens* you. It's a way of honoring yourself and giving yourself a fresh start. Everything could go wrong with your day, but with brain hygiene, you're still in your right mind. There's a sense of comfort and satisfaction in that.

Just as sleep cleanses the brain of chemical by-products of wakefulness, brain hygiene cleanses the mind of *thought* and *emotional* by-products of life. If you don't clean, then these thought and emotional by-products build up and cause problems for you such as: worry, anxiety, anger, depression, stress, poor awareness, scattered thoughts, insomnia, impulsiveness, poor judgment, toxic communication, procrastination, defensiveness, impatience, poor empathy, and self-sabotaging behavior.

I like the term "brain hygiene" because it better explains what's happening. It also includes other forms of being "present" such as mindfulness, yoga, and tai chi. "Meditation" sounds and feels too much like I'm just sitting there like a monk, and I have no interest in that. I *do* have an interest in cleaning my brain from thought and emotional by-products so "brain hygiene" works for me, even though it *is* largely meditation. That is why you'll often see the term "meditation" next to "brain hygiene" in my work.

Your awareness, emotional intelligence, judgment, productivity, focus, health, and sleep improves when you practice good brain hygiene.

Brain hygiene not only helps to clear out toxic thoughts and emotions, it strengthens your mind so you can manage the conversation in your head. For example, when Inner Critic starts piping up, you'll more quickly recognize it and tune it out. When an ugly lie deposit starts piping up, you'll more quickly correct it. When Toddler gets upset, you'll more quickly sooth and settle him or her.

Brain hygiene also strengthens your awareness abilities. You'll better notice and recognize what's happening in social situations and relationships so you can respond as opposed to react.

A few minutes a day is better than zero. Working your way up to twenty minutes on most days is a good goal.

I use a guided meditation app on my phone, which I've found tremendously helpful. At first, I struggled to do something as simple as focus on my breath, sit still, and not engage my mind on every random thought. I found it difficult to be "present" and not think about changing the oil in my car, an upcoming meeting, or feeding the dog. Additionally, I do a few minutes of yoga on most days, and practice mindfulness several times a day, even if it's just for few seconds. Mindfulness is the practice of Being, and we'll have a lesson on that soon.

As Marines, we used to ridicule people who meditated as "unwarrior-like." Only hippies and monks meditate. I had no idea what meditation really was, much less that it helps make you *more* of a warrior, not less. I wish I had understood this sooner in my military career as I could have been a better leader to my people, and handled the stress of high tempo operations in arduous conditions with a little more grace. You may not have issues with meditation, but if you do, then let me serve as an example. If a Marine can do it (and trust me, we ridiculed people who meditated) I think it's possible anyone can do it too.

As you practice brain hygiene, especially meditation, you'll notice you're better able to identify what brainwave state you're in—gamma, alpha, beta, theta, or delta. To me, it's fun to recognize my own brainwave state. I've also learned to better manage my brainwave states, and to optimize the advantages of each. This is possible for you too, as you advance in your brain hygiene practice.

16 EXERCISE

Attempts to save time by chronically sacrificing good nutrition, sleep, and brain hygiene, will backfire by impairing your productivity and sabotaging your health. At the risk of adding more to your daily calendar, you can add exercise to the list.

Contrary to popular belief, good health doesn't require lengthy exercise sessions. In fact, too lengthy and too strenuous can be detrimental.

For athletes seeking improved performance, a series of stretch goals (strength and endurance) over time is better than trying to accomplish too much, too soon and injuring yourself. You'll end up further behind instead. You can't lay off exercise for a long spell and expect to do what you did before. You need a consistent training schedule. If you don't train for a long time, then you'll need to start at a lower level and carefully build back up again. You almost need to treat it like a part time job. I know this from thirty years in the Marine Corps where organizational fitness standards require a high level of athleticism. For me, exercise was truly a part-time job.

For everyone else, exercise doesn't need to be a part-time job, but rather a consistently fun and enjoyable part of your life. After retiring from the Marine Corps, I wanted to stay healthy without committing so much time and energy to fitness. I researched the matter and learned three important things about exercise and health for non-athletes.

The first is: *Short, strenuous bouts give you bang for the buck.* For example, twenty seconds of push-ups, burpees, or jumping jacks followed by forty seconds of rest, then repeat. In as little as three minutes a day, consistently, you can make a big difference in your health. What's beautiful about this fact is time and equipment are no longer barriers. Short, daily bouts of body weight exercises are very effective, and efficient. You can do more than three minutes if you like, but consider giving yourself a limit as opposed to a minimum. For example, if you do three minutes one day, then five the next, then ten the third day, you may feel obligated to keep going, or to do at least ten minutes. This sets you up to eventually quit altogether. Instead, consider giving yourself a *limit* of five minutes by saying to yourself, "I only get to do five minutes so I better make the best of it," as opposed to telling yourself "I *must* do ten minutes," a demotivating statement inclining you to quit. Of course, a limit of three minutes is just fine too. To make it fun, consider playing some motivating music. You'll be done before one song is over.

The second is: *Make exercise fun and enjoyable*. It's human nature, if you don't like what you're doing, you'll eventually stop doing it. You'll want to find an active hobby, and it doesn't need to be strenuous unless you truly enjoy the challenge. For example, golfing with friends, fun sunrise swims, hiking the hills with your dog, dancing with your spouse, just to name a few. I like to surf and hike nature trails on weekends and holidays. It's an important part of my weekly activities. Having an active hobby truly does make a difference in your health.

The third is: *Take one, short, gentle walk daily*. This is *not* a power walk. It should be easy, without many stairs or steep hills, for about ten to twenty minutes, ideally after meals. If it's strenuous, you defeat the purpose. The purpose of the walk is to stimulate the lymphatic system, hydrate the spinal discs, and soothe the second brain in your gut (enteric nervous system, or ENS).

Gentle walking does this, while strenuous exercise can *aggravate* all these areas. If you're not able to walk, then sitting on one of those large exercise balls, and very gently bouncing up and down, is a great alternative. You may even consider replacing your office chair with one of these large balls. It'll doubly serve to improve your posture and spinal health. Stimulating the lymphatic system through gentle movement helps remove metabolic by-products. The discs in the spine hydrate best with gentle, bouncing movement. The ENS is usually soothed by gentle walking, which aids digestion, and makes the microbiome happy (the flower garden in your gut.) Even if you're highly athletic, a short, gentle walk every day will do you much good. A heavy exercise regime cannot take the place of this.

Exercise, when it's fun and done right, is a *good* form of stress. We've mentioned in previous lesson how too much stress, the bad kind, can be harmful to your health, but good stress contributes to vitality, health, and richness of life. We'll talk about good stress in an upcoming lesson. For now, we'll begin our discussion on what stress is, and what it does to the body.

That lesson is next.

WHAT IS STRESS?

Stress is any condition in which your fight, flight, or freeze (F3) response is triggered in some way.

In the NEURO-SCIENCE series (volume one) we mentioned the parts of the brain, and how the amygdala is part of the automatic (subconscious) mind. Our little amygdala, no larger than an almond, is the center of the F3 universe. It's the grand wizard of stress.

In the AWARENESS series (volume one) we talked about Hot Buttons (U-HIDE-CUPID). Every single one of these Hot Buttons is an F3 trigger.

In the NEURO-SCIENCE series we talked about Dr. David Rock's five hard-wired elements of the automatic mind: Status, Certainty, Autonomy, Relatedness, and Fairness (SCARF). Whenever you perceive a threat to any one of these elements, it'll trigger an F3 response.

During an F3 response, ugly-lie deposits can present themselves. Inner Critic can start piping up, and Toddler can enter tantrum mode. That's when the self-sabotage happens.

As you can see, the amygdala can quickly become overwhelmed with perceived stressors, triggering the F3 response at every turn.

Just about anything can ilicit an F3 response ranging from very mild to very strong.

Minor triggers can include driving in traffic, being wrong about something, or spilling your chardonnay. You may be annoyed, defensive, or frustrated.

Major triggers can include a car accident, going to jail, or spilling twenty million gallons of oil into the ocean. You may become irate, belligerent, or even suicidal.

During an F3 response, even mild ones, the body responds in a cascade of different ways. Stress hormones and neuro-chemicals like cortisol, adrenaline, and norepinephren flood the bloodstream. Your muscles tense up, blood pressure rises, and eyes dilate. Your breathing will become faster and shallower. Your memory center and judgment will be somewhat impaired. Even a minor F3 response can trigger this cascade of physical and mental responses, just on a lower scale.

Now imagine this low scale F3 response continuing throughout your day, every day, for weeks, months, years. Everyday events such as the alarm going off in the morning, getting an email from the boss, being late to work, dealing with traffic, having a disagreement with a co-worker, forgetting to bring your lunch, dropping and cracking your phone, working on a project that's overdue, a call from the school about your misbehaving child, coming home to the dog having chewed up your passport (which has happened to me), can provoke a chronic F3 response throughout the day. On top of that, when you can't sleep at night, the fatigue only aggravates the F3 response to a larger scale. You're basically a walking time bomb and at any moment could have a meltdown at the slightest provocation. This is just one example of what chronic stress looks like. It could be worse. Everyone's daily stress load is different.

The impact of chronic stress on the body, brain, and overall health are significant. High blood pressure, autoimmune disorders, learning disabilities, memory problems, heart disease, arthritis, heartburn, obesity, diabetes, depression, dementia, and many other diseases have a strong link to chronic stress. Children experiencing chronic stress may develop health problems and struggle with their emotions as adults. Adults experiencing chronic stress may struggle with their relationships, and develop life-threatening illnesses. None of this bodes well for living one's full potential. That is why it's critical to manage stress, and our perception of stress.

As you can see, our little grand wizard of the F3 universe, the amygdala, once critical to human survival, is now something of an impediment.

There are three things that influence the strength and longevity of one's F3 response in life:

The first is *genetics*. While some people may have stronger F3 tendencies, genetics is not destiny as you'll soon see.

The second is *environment*. This is everything happening to and around you. Just like genetics, environment is not destiny. Even if you're truly a victim of your environment, holding on to a victim mindset and laying blame will keep you prisoner there. You can influence your environment in strong ways through your attitude, communication, perception, and behavior.

The third is *mindset*. Mindset trumps genetics and environment, but it's not easy. It takes real, dedicated work to strengthen your mindset and overcome genetics and environment. This is entirely within your control. That's why resetting your brain, building your awareness, improving your communication, and strengthening your manual (conscious) mind was the focus in volume one. It's truly an area where everyone can use lifelong support and mentoring.

18 EVERYONE HAS THEIR STRESS LIMIT

While deployed to combat zones in Iraq and Afghanistan, I underwent exactly the same combat experiences as my close military cohorts.

Some of my brethren emerged with post traumatic stress disorder (PTSD), which disrupted their lives, while others were not impacted at all. In non-combat related situations, there were moral and ethical wrongs, or having to do some very distasteful tasks. Some brushed these matters off with no ill effect, while others became depressed, angry, or vengeful to the point of either shutting down or lashing out.

Everybody copes with stress differently. Some cope in a healthy way, such as seeking counseling, talking to friends and family, exercise, and taking on a beneficial hobby. Others cope by drinking, drug use, gambling, or other unhealthy ways that only aggravate their situation.

One thing I learned from these experiences is everyone has their limit. As a leader, I recognized when the stress load was too much for some people, and took measures to assist each individual according to his or her need.

Genetics, environment, and mindset affect stress tolerances and how much of a load one can bear. Each element contributes to one's stress load in some way.

Genetics plays a role in how reactive the amygdala is to the environment. Some people are a little more reactive than others, and it's not a problem as long as they're aware and learn to manage it. I personally have a slight predisposition, and while it was problematic in my early life, once I learned to manage it, the difference in my relationships and in my personal growth was significant. This personal experience allowed me to recognize it in others, have empathy, and provide individualized encouragement and mentoring.

Environment presents loads from many sources: health and physical discomfort, work and career, finances, relationships, social norms, and more. A health problem will present a certain stress load. A relationship problem will present a certain stress load. If the problems are mild, then both together may not be an issue. However, if the problems are severe, say someone is dealing with cancer while undergoing a divorce, that would be a very serious stress load for most people. Indeed, just one of those problems could present a serious stress load for just about anyone. Even the strongest people can break under a severe, environmental stress load. For example, being deployed to a combat environment is very stressful for most people.

So when someone under my care began to experience serious health, financial, or relationship problems with their spouse back at home, I took these matters seriously. I understood everyone was already carrying a heavy, environmental stress load just by being deployed into a warzone. Additional heavy stressors could potentially become a breaking point for someone.

Mindset plays a huge role in one's stress tolerances. A victim, awfulizing, or self-pity mindset will increase one's stress load. Chronic anger, depression, worry, or anxiety will increase one's stress load, and mindset plays a huge role in the manifestation of these feelings. A victor, reframing, gritty mindset is a release valve on one's stress load. Consequently, happiness, optimism, and confidence help reduce the perception of stress.

At the end of the day, stress is a matter of *perception*. One person may view buying a house as exciting, despite daunting paperwork. Another may view it at terrifying and the paperwork as overwhelming. The difference here is entirely perception.

There's a famous quote from Colonel "Chesty" Puller, USMC, when informed by his men they were utterly surrounded by enemy troops during the Korean War, "Well that simplifies our problem. Now we can shoot in every direction." Facing imminent death in a hostile, freezing environment, thousands of miles away from family is no doubt stressful. Instead, Colonel Puller viewed the situation as "simplifying the problem" so he could win the battle, and eventually return home. Colonel Puller's gritty perspective was contagious and his unit prevailed in the ensuing battle. If he held a defeatist perspective, his men probably would have surrendered and died.

Yes, everyone has their limits, but perception can greatly extend those limits. Cracking jokes, seeing the opportunities, and staying positive helps lesson the stress load on yourself and others. By understanding this concept, you can better manage your own stress. As a leader, by understanding that *your* perception is contagious, and by communicating a confident, calm, and determined perspective, you can ease the stress load on your followers and achieve the impossible.

As an individual, stress management is critical to your health, relationships, and personal success in life.

As the leader of an organization, you must understand your actions and words either aggravate or lighten the stress load on your people.

19 GOOD STRESS VS. BAD STRESS

Two people prepare to jump out of an airplane.

The amygdala is firing up the F3 response in each of their brains. The first person is scared, but thrilled and eager. The second is terrified, feeling sick to his stomach, and thinking of a way to back out. Both are undergoing exactly the same event, but their perception of the stress is very different. This difference in perception slightly alters the cascade of events emanating from the F3 response. This ever so slight difference in the cascade has a profoundly different impact on the mind and body.

In the first person, the stress experience is actually *good* (beneficial to the mind and body.) The person is feeling energized and motivated, even though he's scared.

In the second person, the stress experience is bad (harmful to the mind and body.) The person is feeling terrible, and doesn't want to jump out of the plane.

Good stress enhances cognitive abilities, learning, and memory. It can also help build your mental and physical tolerance for stress.

For example, a child who enjoys school is excited about a difficult, upcoming exam. She passes the exam with ease which qualifies her for the next, more challenging course – a course she's eager to take. When she takes the more challenging course, although it's stressful, she continues to perform very well.

Bad stress impairs cognitive abilities, learning, and memory. It also adds to your stress load such that you're even *less* tolerant of stress.

For example, a child who hates school is dreading a difficult, upcoming exam. She barely passes the exam, which qualifies her for the next, more challenging course, a course she doesn't look forward to at all. When she takes the more challenging course, the stress is simply too much for her and she drops out.

Stress can be good and beneficial when it's perceived as a *challenge*.

Stress is bad and harmful when it's perceived as a *threat*.

People generally *enjoy* challenges, even if the challenge is daunting, dangerous, scary, or burdensome. The F3 response is still happening, but in a different way.

People nearly always *fear* threats, especially if they're daunting, dangerous, scary, or burdensome. The F3 response is doing it's normal, icky thing.

Stress is a part of life. The alarm clock will go off. The kids will get sick. Your back will hurt. The boss will be a grouch. The stock market will crash. Your new dream car will roll off the end of the pier, into the ocean, and become inundated with starfish and inking squid.

There are two options for responding to stressful events.

Your first option is to dread, lament, or awfulize these events. This will trigger the F3 response down its normal path, resulting in bad stress. You'll be less smart, more unhealthy, and less tolerant to future stress. You're more likely to engage in unhealthy behavior, such as eating too much, drinking, or using drugs because the stress will have depleted your willpower. The unhealthy behavior will only serve to make matters worse.

Your second option is to view such events as challenges that can help you learn something new or present interesting opportunities. This will send the F3 response down a more beneficial path, resulting in good stress. You'll be smarter, healthier, and more tolerant to future stress. You're more likely to engage in healthy behavior such as exercising, laughing with friends, or writing in your journal. The healthy behavior will serve to further reduce your stress load.

The good news is the choice is entirely up to you. Genetics and environment have nothing to do with the choice you ultimately make. You have complete control. With that said...

Many people go through life not realizing there's a choice. Perhaps their parents or other role model viewed stress as threats and responded in unhealthy ways. Because they had few, if any, models for viewing stress as a challenge and responding in healthy ways, they get trapped in a negative mindset. They don't know there's another way.

If you think you may fall in this category, consider actively looking for people who manage their stress well. Then watch, listen, and emulate their thinking and habits. It's one thing to say "view stress as a challenge instead of a threat." It's quite another to actually *live* it. It helps to know what it looks like from someone else who's good at it. Having a mentor also helps.

If you're a parent or lead others in any capacity, they'll cue off you. If you view stress as a threat, so will they. If you view it as a challenge, they will too.

⭐ 20 DEPRESSION

Persistent feelings of helplessness is a form of bad stress.

Some people feel helpless in their lives because of perceptions about their upbringing, resources, environment, health, or relationships.

Unmanaged, chronic, bad stress leads to depression.

Depression is a feeling of profound sadness that won't go away. A depressed person may have little interest in fun or joyful activities, seek to be alone, and struggle with ordinary life.

I'm not talking about temporary sadness over the loss of a loved one, learning bad news, or major hormone fluctuations. Temporary depression happens to everybody. In time, we move on and become our happy selves again. The kind of depression I'm talking about is the kind that moves in and stays as an unwelcomed guest for a long time.

People who feel helpless in their life circumstances, are under a heavy load of chronic stress, or have a major chemical imbalance in the brain, are prone to depression.

Depression is a widespread problem, impacting the lives of millions of people.

There are many theories on why this is. I personally believe culture, media, and social media contribute to this problem. Allow me to unpack this.

Our modern culture prizes multi-tasking and feverish productivity. There's a constant tension in our lives to "keep up," to get a thousand things done in a day, to sleep less, and to acquire more stuff. We're pushed to constantly think about the future, with little time or patience to enjoy the present. In the lesson on Doing vs. Being, we'll speak more about this tension. For now, it's sufficient to say that people addicted to Doing can perceive themselves as never being good enough, and impose a tremendous load of chronic stress on themselves.

Rarely do we see good news in the news. Although we're living in the best time in human history, with the best education, medical care, housing, opportunities, arts, technology, and creature comforts ever known on planet earth, you would think by watching the news that we're in constant peril and suffering. Yes, there are problems around the world, and their suffering is very real. The good news is there are more activists and people who care than ever before as well. News media outlets know negativity sells, so that's what they focus on and deliver. When all you get is bad news, it can become challenging to perceive your environment in a positive way. A constant drip of bad news is stressful and contributes to feelings of helplessness.

Finally, there's social media. Once again, humans naturally focus more on the negative than the positive. When the seeming perfect lives of others show on social media, we compare ourselves and think we have it bad. When negative news spreads on social media, is can be further fueled by toxic comments, and then spun into something worse than ever before. Too many people mistakenly believe they're being helpful by expressing their opinion in a toxic, mean spirited way. This could not be further from the truth as it serves to poison our perception of how amazing our world truly is. Sadly, this behavior is contagious and contributes to our collective unhappiness.

Recovering from depression takes time and a multi-pronged approach. Medications, affirmation audios, counselors, supplements, and therapists can help for a time, but will ultimately fail without two key components in place: a sincere desire to overcome the condition and a willingness to change one's thinking and lifestyle in drastic ways. As strange as this may sound, some people are more comfortable being miserable than they are in changing themselves. There's nothing that can be done for them, but for everyone else, there's high potential for success.

Chronic stress and depression can disrupt brain chemistry leading to a condition in which negative thinking becomes pervasive, even if you're trying really hard to change. In these situations, supplements such as St. John's Wort or 5HTP are known to help people get out of the rut so they can reprogram themselves. In some cases, a prescribed anti-depressant may be necessary. It's best not to stay on them forever, just long enough to get the boost needed so reprogramming can take place. Reprogramming includes learning to think more rationally, perceiving stress as a challenge as opposed to threat, learning to forgive, practicing Ground Control, building self-awareness, applying good communication skills, using the manual (conscious) mind to reset the programming in the automatic (subconscious) mind, and practicing brain hygiene, good nutrition, sound sleep habits, and exercise habits. Over time, once you've conditioned your mind, body, and spirit to your new thinking, emoting, and behaving habits, your chronic stress will ease, your depression will lift, and you can wean off the supplements or meds.

As you can see, there's much time, effort and work involved to overcome depression, but it's totally worth it.

21 IMMUNE HEALTH

Chronic stress is bad news for the mind, body, and spirit.

In addition to impairing cognitive abilities and causing depression, chronic stress can impair the immune system, sometimes to the point of causing serious health problems.

The immune system is the body's defense mechanism against infection and disease. When the immune system is impaired, inflammation in tissues, organs, joints, digestive track, skin, and other areas result. Over time, chronic and severe inflammation can lead to serious conditions such as heart disease, irritable bowel syndrome, arthritis, autoimmune disorders, diabetes, and alzheimers. Additionally, the body is less resistant to pathogenic bacteria and viruses, meaning you'll catch the cold or flu more often, or worse, contract a serious infection or disease.

Inflammation and disease add even more stress to a chronic stress condition. Should the stress and disease continue to worsen, one can become gravely ill and die.

Everyone's physical response to chronic stress is different. Some may develop arthritis. Others, heartburn. Others still, skin problems. Some may develop a number of problems at once. Genetics and environment play a role, sometimes significant. However, minimizing chronic stress through management techniques can go a long way toward easing some of our ailments.

Isolation and lonliness, poor emotional regulation, and strained relationships significantly contribute to chronic stress, depression, and impaired immune function. One cannot live their greatest potential under these conditions. Fortunately, much of this is within our control so long as we know what to do. When given the right education, tools, and mentoring, we can apply what we learn and change this situation completely. It requires perseverance, a willingness to change, and embrace an entirely new (healthy) identity.

Good friends who are positive influences, healthy emoting habits, and loving relationships strengthen one's stress tolerance, mental abilities, and immune function. In this environment, you not only live fully, you're an inspiration and role model for others. Your positive energy and enthusiasm are contagious. You help make others feel good, thereby helping to ease their stress and improve their health. Their happier outlook feeds back to you, and you feel happier and healthier as well.

Reducing chronic stress will go a long way toward improving immune health, and easing afflictions related to inflammation or disease, but it takes time—sometimes a long time, especially if there's a great deal of emotional baggage to deal with.

In the meantime, if you have a health issue, especially a serious one, it's a good idea to seek treatment with a medical doctor. Reprogramming your mind and practicing healthy habits should be used in addition to sound medical care. It should not replace sound medical care.

Keeping all this in mind, drugs present a two-edged sword. On one hand, they're great for easing pain, targeting symptoms, or even curing some diseases. On the other hand, drugs can confuse your immune system, and sometimes impair it in significant ways.

For example, if you're taking a drug for one problem, that problem may resolve so long as you're taking the drug, but then your immune system becomes further impaired and another problem emerges. Now you're on two medications. The immune system becomes further impaired, a third problem emerges, and now you're on three medications. Over time, the body becomes tolerant to the first drug, which no longer works for the problem. Now you're on a new drug for *that* problem, further compromising your immune system. Your system can become so compromised that catching a flu can become life threatening for you.

Aging has less to do with your body falling apart than the cumulation of chronic stress. If any doctor tells you you're just getting old and gives you a pill to take for the rest of your life, that's code for "chronic stress has caught up with you and if you don't change your thinking, emoting, lifestyle habits quickly and permanently, then it's all downhill for you from now on." The reason most doctors won't come out and say that is because most people would never listen to such a diagnosis. They don't want to change. They just want a pill to fix the problem, even if it's just a temporary fix.

You may not even realize you're under chronic stress until you start developing ailments. When an ailment crops up, that may be a good time to re-assess your stress meter and habits. With meaningful adjustments to your personality and lifestyle, it's possible to reverse the problem. If you do not pay attention and do nothing about it other than take a pill, it will only get worse from there.

In the next lesson, we'll discuss a significant lifestyle shift to consider for better health.

22 DOING VS. BEING

In the LEADERSHIP series, we talked about the three Leadership Operating Zones. The continuum between Doing and Being is one of those zones. This zone is not only important in leadership, it's a critical component of your self care.

Doing vs. Being is sometimes referred to as "work-life balance," but it's much more than that. It's about allocating time to deal with stressful things, and time to decompress. Stressful things include anything large or small that contributes to chronic stress. Anytime you're dealing with something stressful, you're Doing.

Time for Being does not necessarily mean taking long vacations or going to the day spa every month, although there's nothing wrong with that. Time for Being can take place in micro-moments while you're Doing. This is especially important to do when your really can't stop long from your work, much less take a vacation.

For example, when I was deployed to Iraq in the winter of 2004, we camped in a desolate place where the dirt was flat and bare as far as the eye could see. Then in the spring came some rain and a wild weed started growing in the middle of the camp. It grew quickly and soon a large, hot-pink flower bloomed. Everyone gingerly walked around the flower, stopping to gaze at it from time to time.

In the backdrop of this desert flower, the evenings presented beautiful sunsets. People would sit and watch the sunsets, then gaze at the stars at night. In the hustle and bustle of wartime operations, people made their micro-moments of Being, by focusing on what was beautiful, and finding some measure of decompresive relief through them. It made all the difference in the world.

Doing is about giving your time and energy to others, whether its work, family, or some cause you support. You may actualy really enjoy what you're Doing, and that's great. You still need time for Being because that is where you recharge yourself, physically, hormonally, mentally, and systemically throughout your body. It gives your mind and body a break from the bath of stress chemicals circulating your bloodstream. If you don't give your mind and body this break from the stress chemicals often enough, health consequences will eventually result.

Being is about honoring yourself with quiet, reflective time, and being in the present moment. The focus is on yourself, not others; and on the present moment, not the future. It's not selfish at all. It's necessary.

Being is hard for many people, while others still have no idea how to do it. They just drive on and on, focusing on work, their family, and everyone else but themselves. I've known people like this who seemed healthy, and then dropped dead from a sudden heart attack. I've known people who could never slow down for themselves, grew obese and unhealthy, and then could no longer serve their work or family because they had become so ill. I'm sure you know plenty of people like this too. It's such a tragedy.

You cannot make a difference in this world if you're not in it. You won't be in the world for long if you allow Doing to consume your life and hijack your health.

A few tools to help you with Being are: gratitude, noticing beautiful things, taking deep breaths, brain hygiene, gentle exercise you enjoy, reading something inspirational, watching nature, getting a massage, or just sitting and people watching. This is not an exhaustive list. What's important is you're not enduring stress during the time you are committed to Being. You're truly in the present moment.

Quality, balanced time in Being will not only help make you a healthier person, it will make you a better role model and leader. People are watching you, and a great many of them will do what you do.

23 ★ LEADERSHIP AND HEALTH

Your ability to lead yourself and others is exponentially enhanced by great health. Sometimes we focus on health to look or feel good, and there's nothing wrong with that.

However, the higher purpose of good health is to be more influential in making your impact.

What are you denying yourself and the world because of your health setbacks?

The purpose of the SELF-CARE series was to introduce you to some of the latest, cutting edge information about health, and spark a serious interest on your part to pursue better health. The reason?

You're more likely to achieve better results and stick to your goals in life when you're eating food that works with your genetics, energizes you, repairs you, and keeps you strong.

You'll strengthen your awareness and communication abilities when you get enough quality sleep.

You're more likely to stay out of the badlands of self-doubt, Inner Critic, and negativity when you brain health supports you and is not weighed down by stress and depression.

You'll get much more done when you're feeling great than when bogged down down by health ailments.

One way you lead others is by being a role model. When others see how vibrant, strong, and articulate you are, they're going to ask how you do it. That's when you influence and make an impact. You could change, even save someone's life, by telling your story on how you maintain great health.

If that is not your goal with others, then if you have kids, think of the impact you'll have on them. They will do exactly what you do.

252

In the reference section you'll find my sources, and I encourage you to learn more from these experts, especially if you're skeptical about anything I presented.

If you're experiencing a troubling health problem, I hope this series inspires you and gives you hope that you can heal yourself.

Remember, the healthcare system, writ large, largely profits off sick people. There's no money to be made off healthy people. Many doctors and specialists (not all), who should know better, are addicted to the money they make every time they prescribe a drug or procedure. Yes, there are individual exceptions; people who help you heal without drugs or procedures (I have encountered them.) But the system is set up against them because they are not making profits for the corporation.

A few medical doctors listed in the reference section of this book were once part of the conventional health care system. They share the same reason on why they're no longer a part of that: they're tired of the cover up, want to reveal the truth about how to become and stay healthy, and sincerely want to heal people. I hope you'll look into them further, get the full details from the experts, and empower yourself with the gift of health.

You will certainly find doctors and organizations who continue to "dubunk" the science herein presented, and the science presented by the doctors listed in the reference section. I urge you to look at their funding sources. They may try to keep this secret, but many of their big donors are giant food companies, big pharma, and healthcare companies who stand to gain big by keeping you confused and encouraging you to "trust" them for your nutrition and health information. The doctors I reference are not funded by these conglomerates. I will leave it up to you on who you wish to trust. I prefer to trust people not supported by big business.

The proof will be in your results. If you're healthier on the conventional western diet, then there's no need to change. If you have health problems, are fatigued, foggy brained, and struggle to be your best self, then maybe the conventional diet is not working for you. It can be difficult to change because the conventional diet is loaded with things to hook you, so don't beat yourself up if you find it difficult to adapt to a nutrigenomic, low-grain, organic, low-lectin, high-antioxidant diet. The commercial food industry puts out slick commercials to keep you hooked on their products and build it into the fabric of life. So yes, it will be hard to change, but remember, just because something is hard doesn't mean it's not worth doing.

Health is something I care about deeply, and while I could say much more about this topic, I prefer to focus on my area of expertise which is leadership. So I will say little more on this subject and defer to the experts from here on.

SUMMARY OF THE SELF-CARE SERIES

Congratulations! You've completed the SELF-CARE Series.

True, authentic leadership requires a strong foundation of self awareness, confidence, vision, communication skills, understanding of human behavior, strategic planning, organization, and *health*. You don't just read a book and "arrive" at being a leader. It takes years of cultivation and work, self education, humility, open mindedness, and growth. Growing as a leader requires a willingness to change, even if others around you are not willing to change. A significant, and arguably most difficult part of change is changing your attitude and habits about nutrition, sleep, exercise, and stress management. Why?

Survival and competition is deeply embedded in our automatic programming. We are programmed to consume what is yummy (and lots of it), conserve energy, and continuously look for danger in order to compete and survive. Of course, this programming is sabotaging us today, so we want to change this. The habits that help us overcome this self-sabotaging programming and lead a healthier life translate directly into everything else you do in life: commiting to priorities, goal setting, organization, managing relationships, communication, awareness, overcoming fear, openness to change, continuous learning, and taking real action.

Below is a summary of the SELF-CARE Series. You might want to print or copy this summary section as a handy reference.

☆ Health and appearance = dynamic between genetics and environment.

☆ Environment: food, air, water, exercise, thoughts, relationships, skin contact, smells, heat, cold, disease, stress, anything that can influence the cells of your body.

☆ Genetics: DNA, what genes are expressed/not expressed, damaged, or repaired.

☆ Nutrigenomics: the science of how food interacts with your unique genetics.

☆ Nutrigenomic tests and labs can identify a diet ideal for your genetics.

☆ Organic: low or no pesticide products.

☆ Non GMO: not genetically modified.

☆ Grass fed/pasture raised: not corn fed, raised the traditional way in pastures of grass.

☆ MCT: medium chain triglycerides, critical brain food.

☆ Four pillars (Dr. Shanahan): organ meat, bones, fermented, raw.

☆ Adaptogens: help your DNA adapt to stress.

☆ Conventional nutrition is right about: need for supplementation, drink lots of water, avoid sugar.

☆ Conventional nutrition is wrong about: restricting fat (need to consume essential fats), additives and preservatives are safe (no they are not), pesticides and antibiotics are safe (no they are not), eat lots of whole wheat (best to avoid), eat lots of grains (best to minimize).

☆ What to eat: fresh & local, organic, antiobotic free, GMO free, MSG free, vegetables (crucifereous, green leafy, and roots), fish (wild caught, smaller fish), beef (grass fed), chicken and eggs (pasture raised), fruits (mostly safe, berries are best).

☆ Lectins to avoid: all grains, legumes (beans and peanuts), all squash, nightshades (eggplant, peppers, tomotoes). Exceptions can be made if prepared properly (ferment, soak, pressure cook).

☆ Oxidative stess: reactive oxygen (free radicals) damage proteins and DNA

☆ Antioxidants: render free radicals safe, make some naturally, but need a lot of help from diet, get from organic fruits and veggies, adaptogens, and supplements (like vitamin C, grapeseed extract, and turmeric).

☆ Diabetes diagnosis will cost about $10,000 a year plus much inconvenience. Cheaper to spend money on healthy foods and supplements to avoid.

☆ Brain health = foundation to overall health: genetics, activities, nutrition, thoughts, sleep.

☆ ENS: Enteric Nervous System = second brain. Senses inner world, micobiome communication.

☆ Sleep cleans brain and allows specific hormone release. Need four to five cycles (ninety minutes each)

1. Gamma: fastest/creativity/ah ha moment.
2. Beta: fast/working/thinking.
3. Alpha: medium/relaxed/ present.
4. Theta: slow/hypnosis/re-programming.
5. Delta: slowest/deep sleep/rejuvenation.

☆ Brain Hygiene: meditation/yoga/tai chi/alpha and theta states/being present/no stress/not judging.

☆ Exercise takeaways:

1. Short strenuous bouts give biggest bang for the buck.
2. Have a fun active hobby.
3. Short, gentle walk daily, especially after meals.

☆ Stress = F3 trigger ranging from mild to severe, perceived through thoughts, triggers DNA tightening and stress hormone release.

☆ F3 influences: genetics, environment, and mindfulness. Everyone has different limits.

☆ Good Stress = challenge, exciting, lean into it. Bad Stress = depression, anger, anxiety, fear.

☆ Depression: a form of bad stress, avoid ugly news and social media, watch thoughts and perceptions, must want to change oneself, can be addictive because it's "safe" there.

☆ Doing vs. Being balance is crucial. Higher purpose of health is to make a positive difference.

JOIN OUR MISSION

As we close on volume two, remember this is certainly not the end of your growth journey. There is much more to learn and enjoy. You have dreams and goals for yourself, and Teeming With Talent can help you achieve them.

You're invited to join the Teeming With Talent Mission. Members commit themselves to personal growth, authentic leadership, being role models, and mentoring other members in their growth journey.

We stand out. People around the world desperately yearn for authentic leaders and they are drawn to our members. Corporations, government, and non-profit organizations are always looking for true leaders to hire, promote, and take their organization to the next level. It may as well be you.

There are books, online courses, webinars, workshops, live events, mentorship groups, and individual coaching products and services available. There are opportunities to become certified as a Teeming With Talent Instructor and Coach. Become a member and join our small our talented group of influencers, highly admirable people, and authentic leaders.

www.berubeteam.com

Other works and content available:

☆ Online courses, webinars, live workshops, speaking engagements, group mentoring, and corporate consulting available at www.berubeteam.com

☆ Follow me on Face Book at Valerie L. Berube

☆ Follow me on Twitter @ValerieLBerube

☆ Follow me on LinkedIn at linkedin.com/in/Valerie-berube-b835b871

☆ Follow me on Instagram at teemingwithtalent

☆ Follow me on Tumblr at vberube

ACKNOWLEDGEMENTS

I am deeply appreciative to my editor, Anna Floit, whose patience and expertise polished this work beyond my expectations; to Terry Whalin, who encouraged and mentored me during my journey as a first-time author; and, to the Morgan James Publishing team, whose faith and support earned my admiration and gratitude. Most important of all, my deepest appreciation goes to my husband, Brian, who sacrificed several years of evenings with me as I poured myself into this work. His love and support made this book possible, and his fun and playfulness made this journey a joy.

ABOUT THE AUTHOR

Valerie was born in California in 1968 to teenage parents. After graduating high school in 1987 she enlisted in the USMC Reserves and attended college. She took on odd jobs to pay for her education and noted significant differences between civilian and military philosophies on leadership and workforce development.

After graduating college, she entered the USMC full time and was commissioned an officer in 1996. She led thousands of diverse people in arduous conditions around the world, and advanced her leadership knowledge through senior military schools, a master's degree program in leadership, and a substantial amount of self-study. After retiring as a lieutenant colonel in 2017, she re-entered the civilian world full time and once again noted the stark philosophical differences in leadership and workforce development. Most notably, she noticed that most junior and mid-level employees were not set up for success in their careers or personal lives by their employers or schools. She saw an opportunity to make a difference and endeavored to write books, develop courses, and offer workshops to fill this critical gap.

In 2017, Valerie started Teeming with Talent, LLC., to serve both individuals and businesses in their quest for individual and organizational excellence. Valerie and her husband Brian live in Phoenix, Arizona.

REFERENCES AND RESOURCES

Melissa Ambrosini

Melissa Ambrosini is the bestselling author of *Mastering Your Mean Girl*, host of 'The Melissa Ambrosini Show' podcast, and motivational speaker. *www. melissaambrosini.com*

Dr. Daniel G. Amen

Psychiatrist, neuroscientist, professor, and brain health expert. Author of several best-selling books and has appeared on many popular television shows. *www. danielamenmd.com*

The Arbinger Institue

A leadership training and consulting organization founded by Dr. Terry C. Warner in 1979. Author of *Leadership and Self Deception. www.arbingerinstitute.com*

Dr. Elizabeth Blackburn and Dr. Elissa Epel

Dr. Elizabeth Blackburn is a biological researcher, Nobel laureate, and president of the Salk Institute for Biological Studies. Dr. Elissa Epel is a psychologist who studies the interface between psychology and physiology, and the effects of chronic stress. Co-authors of the best-selling book, *The Telomere Effect: A Revolutionary Approach to Living Younger, Healthier, Longer.*

www.telemereeffect.com

Dr Ken Blanchard and Dr. Spencer Johnson

Management experts, speakers consultants, and co-authors of *The One Minute Manager*, an international best seller. Both are also authors of numerous books under their own name. Dr. Blanchard founded The Ken Blanchard Companies, a leadership development and training firm. www.kenblanchard.com

Dr. Peter J. D'Adamo

Naturopathic doctor, creator of the "Blood Type Diet," and early pioneer of of the science of nutrigenomics. World-renowned best selling author. *www.dadamo.com*

Dale Carnegie

Lived from 1888 to 1955 and was an early pioneer of the modern self-improvement industry. His most famous book *How to Win Friends and Influence People* was a national best-seller in 1936 and is still highly relevant today. *www.dalecarnegie.com*

Dr. Angela Duckworth

Psychologist, CEO of the Character Lab, and best-selling author of *Grit*. Studies focus on why some people work harder or have better self-control than others. *www.angeladuckworth.com*

Dr. William Davis

Cardiologist and "health crusader" who exposes dangerous health advice given by health agencies and big business. Best-selling author of numerous books, including *Wheat Belly* and *Undoctored: Why Health Care Has Failed You and How You Can Become Smarter Than Your Doctor.*

www.wheatbellyblog.com

Dr. Carol Dweck

Psychologist specialized in human motivation, particularly in children. Authored several best-selling books; one of the leading experts on mindset. Creator of the "Fixed" versus "Growth" theory of mind. *www.mindsetonline.com*

Dr. Albert Ellis

Psychologist; creator or Rational Emotive Behavior Therapy (REBT); considered one of the most influential psychotherapists in history. Author of several books and founder of the Albert Ellis Institute. *www.albertellis.org*

Dr. Daniel Goleman

Psychologist and science journalist who popularized the term "Emotional Intelligence." Author of several best-selling books; co-director of the Consortium for Research on Emotional Intelligence (*www.eiconsortium.org*); co-founder of the Collaborative for Academic, Social, and Emotional Learning (*www.casel.org*). *www.danielgoleman.info*

Dr. John Gray

World renown relationship expert and best-selling author of numerous books, including *Men Are From Mars, Women Are From Venus.* Leader in personal and brain health. *www.marsvenus.com*

Dr. Steven R. Gundry

Cardiologist who now devotes his life to helping people stay out of the operating room through sound nutrition. Best selling author of several books. *www.drgundry.com*

James Kouzes and Barry Posner

Authors of *The Leadership Challenge* and developers of The Five Practices of Examplary Leadership ® based on decades of research on leadership. *www.leadershipchallenge.com*

Dr. Bruce Lipton

Developmental biologist, author, and producer of several books and films. Pioneer in science of epigenetics (how thoughts affect genes/DNA). *www.bruceliption.com*

John C. Maxwell

World renown leadership expert, speaker, and author, and founder of the John Maxwell Team, an international leadership development organization. *www.johnmaxwell.com*

Lisa Nichols

World famous motivational speaker and "Breakthrough Specialist" known for helping others to overcome their difficulties. *www.motivatingthemasses.com*

Christopher Peterson, Steven F. Maier, & Martin E. P. Seligman

Psychologists and authors of *Learned Helplessness: A Theory for the Age of Personal Control.*

Bob Proctor

World renowned author and motivational speaker whose work largely focuses on the mindset of prosperity. He popularized his long-held instincts on the power of the subconscious mind, much of which is now supported by modern science. *www.proctorgallagherinstitute.com*

Dr. David Rock

Social neuroscientist and best-selling author focused on the neuroscience of leadership. Coined the word *neuroleadership*; created the SCARF® model; CEO and co-founder of the NeuroLeadership Institute. *www.neuroleadership.com*

Dr. John E. Sarno

Professor at New York University, author of several books, and leading expert on pain management and the mind-body connection. *www.johnesarnomd.com*

Edgar H. Schein

Former professor at the MIT Sloan School of Management and creator of the "Schein Model" of organizational culture. Author of *Organizational Culture and Leadership.*

Dr. Catherine Shanahan

Medical doctor, nutrigenomic pioneer, and best-selling author of several books, including *Deep Nutrition: Why Your Genes Need Traditional Food. www. drcate.com*

Shawn Stevenson

Health expert, creator of *The Model Health Show*, and founder of Advanced Integrative Health Alliance. Best-selling author of *Sleep Smarter. www.theshawn stevensonmodel.com*

Liz Wiseman

Author of *Multipliers* and founder of the The Wiseman Group, a leadership research and development company. *www.thewisemangroup.com*

Morgan James
Speakers Group

↗ www.TheMorganJamesSpeakersGroup.com

We connect Morgan James published authors with live and online events and audiences who will benefit from their expertise.

Morgan James makes all of our titles available through the Library for All Charity Organization.

www.LibraryForAll.org

Printed in the USA
CPSIA information can be obtained
at www.ICGtesting.com
JSHW022214140824
68134JS00018B/1057